Christianity and the Religions

*Number 2 in the
Evangelical Missiological Society Series*

Evangelical Missiological Society Series

1
SCRIPTURE AND STRATEGY
The Use of the Bible in Postmodern Church and Mission
by David Hesselgrave

2
CHRISTIANITY AND THE RELIGIONS
A Biblical Theology of World Religions
Edward Rommen and Harold Netland, Editors

These books are available fromthe publisher:
William Carey Library
PO Box 40129
Pasadena, California 91104
800-647-7466

Christianity and the Religions
A Biblical Theology of World Religions

Edward Rommen
and
Harold Netland
Editors

Number 2
Evangelical Missiological Society Series

William Carey Library
Pasadena, California

Copyright 1995 by Evangelical Missiological Society
All Rights Reserved

No part of this publication may be reproduced, stored in a
retrieval system, or transmitted in any form or by any means—
electronic, mechanical, photocopy, recording, or any other—
except for brief quotations embodied in critical articles or printed
reviews, without prior permission of the publisher.

Published by William Carey Library
P.O. Box 40129
Pasadena, California 91114
(818) 798-0819

Library of Congress Cataloging-in-Publication Data

Christianity and the religions : a biblical theology of world
    religions / edited by Edward Rommen and Harold Netland.
        p. cm.
    Includes bibliographical references.
    ISBN 0-87808-376-6
    1. Christianity and other religions. 2. Bible--Theology.
I. Rommen, Edward, 1947-   II. Netland, Harold A., 1955-
BR127.C47423   1995   95-36773
261.2--dc20   CIP

PRINTED IN THE UNITED STATES OF AMERICA

CONTENTS

INTRODUCTION
  Harold Netland   3

PART I: BIBLICAL PERSPECTIVES

1. Religions and the Bible: An Agenda for Evangelicals
     Gordon T. Smith   9

2. Yahweh and the Gods: A Theology of World
   Religions from the Pentateuch
     Ed Mathew   30

3. Selected Perspectives on World Religions
   from Wisdom Literature
     Michael Pocock   45

4. "To whom shall you compare me?": Yahweh's
   Polemic against Baal and the Babylonian Idol
   Gods in Prophetic Literature
     Robert B. Chisholm, Jr.   56

5. The Contribution of the Gospels and Acts to a
   Biblical Theology of Religions
     William J. Larkin, Jr.   72

6. The Apostle Paul and First Century Religious
   Pluralism
     Don N. Howell, Jr.   92

7. The Contribution of the General Epistles and
   Revelation to a Biblical Theology of Religions
     Andreas Köstenberger   113

PART II: HISTORICAL AND DOCTRINAL PERSPECTIVES

8. Christianity and the Religions in the History of the Church
   James F. Lewis — 145

9. Religious Borrowing as a Two-Way Street: An Introduction to Animistic Tendencies in the Euro-North American Context
   A. Scott Moreau — 166

10. The Uniqueness of Christ in Mission Theology
    Charles VanEngen — 183

11. Christianity as a Minority Religion
    Larry Poston — 217

PART III: SYNTHESIS

12. Synthesis
    Edward Rommen — 241

13. Application
    Harold Netland — 254

CONCLUSIONS

14. Conclusion
    David J. Hesselgrave — 273

INTRODUCTION

Harold Netland

As the Christian Church approaches the twenty-first century it faces both unprecedented opportunities and challenges in missions. On the one hand, the fall of communism, advances in communications technology, and the remarkable rise of the non-Western missionary force all indicate opportunities for world evangelization undreamed of just fifty years ago. However, the tragic irony is that at this time of great opportunity the church finds itself increasingly troubled by internal and external pressures resulting in a deep sense of insecurity about its mission in the world.

The modern missionary movement was inspired and sustained largely by firm theological convictions concerning the nature of God, Jesus Christ and humankind. While the significance of social and historical factors in the rise of modern missions cannot be discounted, it was primarily belief in the holiness and righteousness of God, the sinfulness of human beings, and the necessity of repentance and faith in God through Jesus Christ for salvation that motivated the earlier missionaries to carry the gospel to peoples in Asia, Africa, and Latin America.

However, whatever consensus there might have been in the past is currently being eroded by pressures from both inside and outside the Christian community. Missions theory and practice have always been influenced by trends in the broader theological community, and the present is no exception. Traditionally, a focus upon the priority of evangelism has been at the heart of missions. Yet today evangelism, with the explicit intention of eliciting conversion, is increasingly seen as theologically and morally unjustified (Marty and Greenspahn 1988).

Perhaps no other issue illustrates current theological and missiological ferment as clearly as the question of the relation between Christian faith and other religious traditions. The past

4 Christianity and the Religions

several decades have produced an enormous body of literature dealing with the subject. The implications of this debate for missions are clear and highly significant. If Jesus Christ is not the unique Lord and Savior for all peoples in all cultures, and if it is not the case that people can be reconciled to God only through the person and work of Jesus, then the traditional missionary movement has been seriously off track. Christian mission—if we are to think in these terms at all—will need to be radically redefined. Not surprisingly, then, missiologist Gerald Anderson says, "No issue in missiology is more important, more difficult, more controversial, or more divisive for the days ahead than the theology of religions... This is *the* theological issue for mission in the 1990s and into the twenty-first century" (Anderson 1993:200-201).

Religious pluralism raises several distinct sets of issues which demand careful consideration. One cluster of issues concerns the fact of non-Christian religions: Why are there other religious traditions? How should we as Christians think of them? Are they to be dismissed as nothing but satanic deception and falsehood, with no redeeming features whatsoever? Or are they merely sincere but somewhat misguided human attempts to reach God? Do they reflect any genuine knowledge of God? Can they be regarded in any sense as "fore-runners" or "precursors" of Christian faith, so that Christianity is somehow the "fulfillment" of other religions? How should we even try to answer these questions?

Given the centrality of Jesus Christ to Christian faith it is not surprising that questions of Christology and soteriology are at the center of discussions over pluralism: Just who is Jesus Christ? In what sense is he unique and different from other religious leaders? Is he the only Savior for all persons in all cultures, or is he merely one among many alternative saviors? What is the relation between the universality of God's concern and work in human history and the particularity of God's self-disclosure in the Incarnation in Jesus? Must one hear about the gospel of Jesus Christ and respond explicitly to Jesus in order to be saved, or is it possible in principle for people who never hear the gospel of Jesus to be saved? If the latter, can we hope that many are saved apart from explicit knowledge of the gospel or just a few? And so on.

It would be a mistake to suppose that these are merely theoretical questions of interest to theologians. Anyone with experience in ministry in pluralistic contexts will recognize that such questions have profound implications for the praxis of missions: To what extent, if any, can one build upon beliefs, practices, and values of other religions in attempting to communicate the message of Scripture to a particular people? How are such decisions to be made? Just what is the biblical understanding of idolatry, and how should current religious practices (ancestor veneration and funeral rites, for example) be evaluated? Is there room for interreligious dialogue in Christian mission, and if so what form should it take? What should be its objectives?

Today there is need for careful and responsible treatment of these questions from a solidly evangelical perspective. This book is an effort in that direction. The first step in formulating an evangelical theology of religions must be a deliberate and comprehensive examination of the biblical data as they relate to these issues. For questions about other religions must always be considered from within the context of God's self-revelation in the Scriptures. Certainly any adequate theology of religions must be fair and accurate phenomenologically in its depiction of the various traditions. But ultimately a sound understanding of other religions must be shaped and disciplined by what God has revealed in the inspired Scriptures.

The essays that follow attempt to address the contemporary questions raised by religious pluralism by looking again in a fresh manner at the biblical data. It is sometimes assumed today that the world of the biblical writers was so different from our pluralistic world that we cannot expect Scripture to provide reliable guidance for the issues of today (Knitter 1985:182f). In fact, nothing could be further from the truth. The worlds of the Old and New Testaments were characterized by considerable religious diversity. And it is within this syncretistic and pluralistic context that we find God calling his people to worship and acknowledge him alone as God. Thus, the essays in Part One consider the Old and New Testament writings in an effort to see what light they shed upon contemporary questions of pluralism.

Christian doctrine and practice do not emerge in a social or historical vacuum. Although the current debates over pluralism are unique in some respects, the fundamental issues are not new. Much can be learned through a careful examination of the encounter of Christian faith with other religious traditions throughout history. Essays in Part Two take a fresh look at some historical perspectives on the encounter with other traditions, as well

6   Christianity and the Religions

as an examination of some of the dynamics unique to the current situation.

The two essays in Part Three attempt to provide a theological and missiological synthesis in the form of an evangelical theology of religions which is both biblically faithful and relevant to current concerns. Some of the practical implications of this for Christian missions in our pluralistic world are suggested.

As might be expected with an issue as controversial as this one, not all contributors agree with each other on every point. All, however, share a common commitment to the inspiration and authority of God's Word and are convinced that the resources of Scripture are fully adequate for enabling us to come to a proper understanding of the relation between Christian faith and other religions. While not every question one might raise today will be addressed explicitly in Scripture, there is sufficient clarity on the fundamental issues so that a broad framework for understanding is possible.

Our prayer is that greater understanding of these issues will result in increased confidence in the majesty and greatness of the one true God, and in greater commitment to carrying out the tasks of world missions—"that your ways may be known on earth, your salvation among all nations" (Psalm 67:2).

PART I
BIBLICAL PERSPECTIVES

1

RELIGIONS AND THE BIBLE: AN AGENDA FOR EVANGELICALS

Gordon T. Smith

The current discussion on the Christian attitude towards non-Christian religions is one of the most critical theological debates of our day, particularly when it includes the question of the uniqueness of Christ. While the identity and the saving significance of Christ have always been a central question in the history of the church, it has come again to the foreground of theological debate around two themes: the status of non-Christian religions and the destiny of the unevangelized. This study focuses on the Christian view of non-Christian religions and takes as a given the uniqueness of Christ.

I was raised within a community that had a very clear and undebatable attitude towards non-Christian religions: they were viewed as false, destructive forms of intellectual, emotional and spiritual bondage. The only hope for humanity was a radical conversion to the Christian religion. The issues were black and white, simple and clear. There was no need for debate or even discussion.

Though this attitude still prevails within my tradition, there is a growing awareness within conservative, evangelical Christianity of the need for critical reflection on these questions from new perspectives, and of the need to do this without being defensive or negative.

Also, it is important that we develop an understanding of non-Christian religions that is accessible to lay Christians within our churches. The reality of non-Christian religions is not something they see on television or read of in the *National Geographic*. They live and work with men and women from all the major religious traditions. They have Hindus as their neighbors, their children go to school with Muslims. Religious pluralism is a fact of their lives, and these people seem to be decent, ordinary people who wrestle with the same problems and concerns that face any Christian.

The Challenge to Evangelical Exclusivism

On the whole, the last decade (and more) has seen the general acceptance of a threefold classification of Christian attitudes towards non-Christian religions: exclusivist, inclusivist and pluralist.

Pluralism, espoused by Paul Knitter and others, affirms the validity of all religious traditions. Knitter's relativism leads him to view all religions as equally valid answers to the human predicament.

Inclusivists tend to agree that Jesus Christ is the unique provision of God but they also affirm that God works through other religious traditions and thus that in some form or another, there is saving grace outside of the Christian religious tradition. Karl Rahner was a noteworthy exponent of this position, which has become a dominant view within contemporary Roman Catholicism. Though this perspective has come under severe challenge, it has found a noteworthy spokesperson in the writings of Gavin D'Costa, an Indian Roman Catholic, who has provided able responses to the standard critique of this view.

The exclusivist position has been the dominant view in the history of the church and on the whole is still that held by conservative evangelicalism in North America.

Those who affirm an explicitly exclusivist position hold to the view that the Scriptures are unique, authoritative and true. Further, it is affirmed that Jesus Christ is the unique manifestation of the God who created the universe, and as such is the one through whom humankind knows the saving grace of God (Jesus Christ alone can be termed "Savior"). As such, other faiths are false, at least where they differ with the Scriptures.

Generally speaking, those who espouse this position have also concluded that the only hope for humanity is a personal encounter with the gospel. There is no salvation apart from knowing Christ as preached by the Christian community. That is, this position generally is exclusivist with respect to both those who have the opportunity to hear the gospel and those who do not: both are in a similar predicament if they do not respond positively to this Gospel.

This position has been affirmed by Lausanne and more recently in the Lausanne II Manila Manifesto. The first conference rejected any notion that "Christ speaks equally through all religions or ideologies," as well as any sense that salvation would be known through other religions. The second reinforced this with the statement: "We affirm that other religions and ideologies are not alternative paths to God, and that human spirituality, if unredeemed by Christ, leads not to God but to judgment, for Christ is the only way."

This argument has been viewed by many as the single most compelling basis for Christian missions and evangelism.

The Challenge of Evangelical Inclusivism

But, there has been a recent challenge to the assumptions inherent in the exclusivist position from the evangelical camp—most notably in the writings of Clark Pinnock.

Pinnock approaches the question with the affirmation of a high Christology on the one hand and what he calls a basic optimism on the other--an optimism about the will and power of God and thus the possibilities of divine grace.

Pinnock is not naive about false religion. Rather, he notes that Canaanite religion was so false it deserved nothing but destruction. But, he also reminds us that the religion of Israel was not flawless; it too came under divine judgment—as evident when Jesus himself condemns the religious leaders of his day.

But Pinnock's point is that this is not the whole of the picture. There is within Scripture another dimension, no less significant, he says. Pinnock draws the attention of his readers to what he calls "pagan saints"—Enoch, Noah, Job, Ruth, Naaman, Cornelius and others. Pinnock speaks of these who enjoyed a relationship with God on the basis of the Noahic covenant (92).

Noting these individuals, Pinnock asks the question: "Is there evidence in the Bible for seeing *any* positive features in the religious aspects of cultures due to God working in this sphere?" (emphasis his). His assumption behind this statement, of course, is that there is a close interconnection between religion and culture. In response, he notes the following three basic factors that support his case (93ff).

First, he reminds us that Israelite religion was not entirely original; its religious institutions came about through ex-tensive borrowing from the religions of Mesopotamia and Egypt.

Second, he notes that there was authentic religious expression outside of the confines of the covenant with Israel. Pinnock identifies several of these, all of which anticipate what he calls the most significant or influential story of this kind in Scripture —Peter's encounter with Cornelius—"one of those men of faith outside the covenant communities of Judaism and Christianity ... God was present with him in the religious sphere of his pagan life" (95). It is not clear what Pinnock means by saying that God was present with him, but it would seem evident that this has some redemptive significance.

He goes on to discuss what he calls the crowning verse in the account, which seems to be a kind of Pinnock theme verse, Acts 10:34-35: "I now realize how true it is that God does not show favoritism but accepts men from every nation who fear him and do what is right." Pinnock then concludes that the criteria for authentic faith is not so much that an individual names the name of Jesus as the twofold criteria which he gleans from this text: does an individual fear God and seek to do what is right?

Thirdly, Pinnock notes that Paul acknowledged the God of the Athenians as the Creator God, while still indicating that they did not know whom they worshipped, and that further Paul quotes from their philosophers.

Pinnock thus joins others, such as William J. Abraham, in concluding that it is possible to maintain a high Christology but yet affirm that "people may genuinely encounter God outside the Christian church without explicitly knowing about Jesus of Nazareth" (Abraham 1989219). Acts 10:34 is very significant for these authors. It is a critical vantage point from which they affirm that God is generous towards others in other traditions, such as Cornelius, and this generosity is viewed as compatible with a high Christology.

For Pinnock, this basic generosity is found throughout the Scriptures. The affirmation of Pinnock is that persons can relate to God through the cosmic covenant established by Noah. What matters to God is faith rather than the content of theology; God himself is generous. Pinnock's overall conclusion, then, is that "it is not necessary to approach the faith of other persons negatively"

(108). He rejects the naiveté of contemporary Roman Catholic scholars in the tradition of Karl Rahner, but he does call for a more positive appreciation of the hand of God at work in other religious traditions, believing that one can be positive without being naive, that one can be generous but at the same time discerning—alert to both the good in other religions as well as that which is evil.

The Challenge from Evangelicals within Mainline Protestantism

Evangelicals need to come to terms with the issues that Pinnock and others have raised. But there is another perspective that needs to be considered as well—that of a group of scholars who are unquestionably evangelical but who come to this and other questions through different lenses. I am thinking here of individuals like Lesslie Newbigin of the United Kingdom, and David Bosch of South Africa. Stephen Neill would also have a similar perspective.

Paul Knitter classifies these thinkers as a subset of the "Mainline Protestant Model" (1985:108), rather than what he calls the "Conservative Evangelical Model." But a significant number of evangelicals are growing in their appreciation of the perspective that Newbigin, Neill and Bosch bring to this kind of discussion. Their value lies, in part, in the very fact that they have not been part of the orbit of North American evangelicalism. It seems that this different context to their life and work enables them to come to the text of Scripture with a different set of questions.

To take Leslie Newbigin's and David Bosch's writings in particular, they are emphatic in their affirmation of the uniqueness of Christ and speak of the scandal of particularity that inevitably confronts all religious traditions, including Christianity.

But they are also emphatic in the affirmation that we cannot speak of a total discontinuity between the gospel and non-Christian religions. This is evident in missionary practice, where concepts and words are borrowed to express the gospel and where the religious experience of the hearers is the starting point for conversation and the presentation of the gospel.

Further, Newbigin and Bosch challenge us with regard to the questions that shape our conversation and thus our conclusions. Newbigin notes that:

> The quest for truth always requires that we ask the right questions. If we ask the wrong questions we shall get only silence or confusion. In the debate about Christianity and the world's religions it is fair to say that there has been an almost unquestioned assumption that the only question is, 'what happens to the non-Christian after death?' . . . this is the wrong question (1989:176-7).

Rather, he suggests that:

> to understand the word [salvation] we must begin from its eschatological sense, from the end to which it all looks. Salvation in this sense is the completion of God's whole work in creation and redemption, the summing up of all things with Christ as head (Eph. 1:10) . . . (178).

He speaks of the reconciliation of all things to Christ and the subjugation of all things to his lordship and thus concludes that we cannot view the salvation of the human soul apart from the work of God in human history (179). We must begin with God and his glory and not with the individual. For Newbigin, our perspective must be the work of God in history rather than the salvation of the individual human soul. The implications for the present discussion are that we are drawn to think not merely in terms of the individual and the individual's eternal fate, but rather to consider that God's work is more comprehensive and all-encompassing.

David Bosch comes at this differently, but still challenges us with regard to the questions we ask (1991:485f). He questions whether the debate about non-Christian religions should, as it often does, revolve around the question of personal, post-death salvation. This leads to the assumption that if Christianity expands, more people are saved. But, is this what religion is all about? Should our understanding of salvation be limited to a post-death state? Where and how does this shape our understanding of God's redemptive work in our history, in our time, in our world? And Bosch further urges us to avoid thinking of conversion as the act of joining a particular religious group in order to gain salvation.

The perspectives of Newbigin and Bosch on the one hand, and the writings of Clark Pinnock on the other, are unavoidable. Evangelicalism must come to terms with the issues Pinnock is raising and the questions he is posing; and, further, we are well advised to at least listen to Newbigin and Bosch. Pinnock himself puts it well when he simply notes that:

> The reader will have to decide who is right, and who is listening to the Bible most carefully. Let us heed Paul's advice in 1 Thessalonians 5:21-22: "Test everything. Hold on to the good. Avoid every kind of evil" (1992:84).

And in posing the question in this way, Pinnock is focusing our attention where it rightly belongs, on Scripture. Pinnock will have achieved his own purposes and will have been a servant to evangelical Christianity if he serves as a catalyst for the examination of Scripture. Newbigin and Bosch may have their greatest significance for us in the way they challenge us to consider the questions we ask as we approach Scripture.

We are called to fresh discernment; we must listen carefully and respond with a clear sense of what the Scriptures *do* and *do not* affirm. What follows is not the examination of Scripture itself but a suggested agenda for evangelicals. As we wrestle with this pivotal issue, what are the kinds of questions that we need to ask so that we can hear the Scriptures clearly and respond effectively to the perspectives of evangelical inclusivists and of those from within mainline Protestantism.

Re-examining the Scriptures

We need a model that can enable Christians to effectively encounter men and women of other religious traditions—whether as missionaries/evangelists, or as people who meet their neighbors over their back fence.

David Bosch puts it bluntly when he states: "We need a theology of religions characterized by creative tension, which reaches beyond the sterile alternative between a comfortable claim to absoluteness and arbitrary pluralism" (1991:483). As Bosch notes, we simply cannot reduce this question to simple, neat answers and categories. We cannot rationalize paradox out of the equation; we need to be willing to embrace mystery.

But to achieve this requires a frontal examination of the Scriptures. I am convinced that the creative tension that Bosch calls us to will only be found in letting the authoritative Scriptures speak for themselves.

That may be easier said than done. We always approach Scripture with certain theological categories. Often, the theological categories that serve as our lenses to Scripture are inadequate. They fail us by blocking our vision, limiting the scope of our perception and failing to provide us with the insight we need. It may be that we do not have the theological categories we need to ably respond to the challenge of religious plurality. We need new language, new categories, so that we can read Scripture effectively and be able to simultaneously hold the uniqueness of Christ together with the reality of truth within non-Christian religions. What follows is an examination of some of these categories.

The Categories of Exclusivism and Inclusivism

First, perhaps we need to question the very categories that tend to shape the discussion. One wonders if they do not create an artificial polarity. It would seem within the present discussion that we are forced to choose between inclusivism and exclusivism. But in our study of the Scriptures we need to carefully examine whether the text itself falls neatly within either of these two categories.

On the one hand the text of Scripture is unapologetically exclusivist, particularly when it comes to the uniqueness of the work of Christ and the human predicament apart from Christ. But, we need to also acknowledge that there is evidence of divine work outside of the confines of the covenant people of Israel. It often seems as though the neat categories of inclusivist or exclusivist are less than helpful at this point.

General Revelation and the Immanence of God

It has become commonplace in conservative theology to make a distinction between general and special revelation. While this is helpful to a point, the claim for a narrow exclusivism is perhaps based on an artificial construct. We need to ask ourselves: Is there such a sharp distinction between general and special revelation as we often think?

On the one hand, the premise of general revelation is that some knowledge of God can be found without the specific revelation and work of Jesus Christ. Other religious traditions, by this account, may then have some measure of truth. Romans 1:16-17, 20 and 2:10-15 are basic texts that are understood as supporting the notion of general revelation. The universality of the human predicament is spoken of in Romans 1-3, and also the fact that God is revealed in the created order and human conscience. Though corrupted by the Fall, it is evident that there is some knowledge of the nature, will and character of God. In some sense, God is knowable and it is for this reason that all of humanity is accountable for its actions.

Though the faith of Israel stands alone, at the same time we have within the Old Testament the clear affirmation that the Lord is the lord not only of Israel but of the nations as a whole— whether or not they are conscious of this (he uses the Chaldeans in battle against the people and in judgment against the people of Israel—Hab). Amos 9:7 makes the compelling and explicit statement that the Cushites, the Philistines and the Arameans belong to God.

Further, within the Old Testament there is virtually no discussion of whether or not Yahweh can actually be known outside of the covenant with Israel. We have no discussion, but we have plenty of examples of individuals who certainly knew Yahweh but were not part of the covenant people. Melchizedek is a prime example, as are Job and Enoch. Then in the prophets, Jonah alone is portrayed as worshipping Yahweh, but when the sailors on the ship cry out, they are heard. It is Yahweh who responds.

Others have noted that the wisdom literature shows extensive dependence on the insights of other cultures—including the affirmation of human life. John Eaton suggests that the wisdom tradition could be a starting point for interreligious dialogue in a pluralistic society and provides a model for how this might be done (1989: 1ff).

Finally, at the consummation of history, the assurance of Revelation 22:24-26 is that the glory and honor of the nations will be brought into the new city, the city in which God himself dwells with his people. God affirms the work of the nations.

The unavoidable conclusion is this: Though the religion of Israel is unique, reflecting in some special way the self-revelation of God, God is nevertheless at work in the history, culture *and* the religion of other peoples. He does not leave himself without a witness. While this witness may not be salvific, in the narrow sense of the word, it cannot be discounted as being of no value.

All of this raises the question whether or not the category of general, in contrast to special, revelation can be maintained in sharp distinction. Are there really two distinct categories with regard to the content of revelation? Can we really think of one category as being the means of redemption while the other is but a means of judgment? Is there such a sharp discontinuity between the two modes of revelation?

Bruce Demarest provides a critique of Pinnock that concludes that Pinnock and others overstate the significance of general revelation, noting that though there is grace outside of Israel, "providential care," it is not saving grace (1992:202-203). Again one must ask if this too is an artificial construct—a category that arises in an effort to formulate our faith, but that may not be entirely appropriate when we are listening to the Bible.

Demarest may be right in suggesting that Pinnock overstates the possibility of salvation outside of special revelation. But, Demarest bases this on an assumption that all religion that arises in response to general revelation is by definition an act of rebellion. He gives no credence to the possibility that this religious expression may in some measure at least be the expression of an honest seeker after God (1992:200-205). All religion, it would seem more accurate to believe, reflects both an authentic search for God as well as human pride and rebellion. As such, then, we need to come to terms with the honest seeker after God whose only avenue of expression is the religious environment in which he lives. It seems rather preemptive to simply call this rebellion. It may be rebellion, but it could also be viewed positively as an authentic and sincere quest that is distorted by human fallenness.

Consequently, our challenge as we read the Scriptures is to clarify what the Bible does and does not say with regard to God's self-revelation outside of his unique intervention in the history of the people of God and apart from the Scriptures.

Further, if we are going to develop a theology of religions that accurately reflects the Scriptures we will need to come to terms with how God's self-revelation outside of the history of Israel—through creation—is and has been significant in the shaping of the religions of the world. In what sense are these religions flawed attempts to know the Creator? And what is the significance of these attempts when it comes to what is valid and true within these traditions and what is clearly a perversion, nothing more than rebellion.

In so doing we will develop the ability to do *three* things in response to the religions of the world. The first is the gracious acceptance of the reality of religious plurality and the end of Christendom. As David Bosch notes (1991:483), we will not be effective agents of Christ in a pluralistic context if we resent the presence of other faiths or the views held by others. He calls us to accept with grace and patience the presence of different faiths and to accept this as part of daily life, for we do not live in segregated communities.

The second is the affirmation of the good. We must celebrate all that is good, wise and noble. We cannot call good evil. We can and must welcome and celebrate all signs of the grace of God in the lives of others. The affirmation of the good must be complemented by an alertness to all that is oppressive and a perversion or enemy of the good. Evil comes in many forms and disguises. Discernment means that we have learned to test everything in light of the Scriptures and in light of the ultimate work of God. We have learned to avoid hasty judgments, appreciating what is different and good and valuable, but also alert to that which will ultimately undermine the kingdom work of God.

Third, our understanding of religion as the response to general revelation will affect what it means to have dialogue with those of other religious traditions. Much has been discussed about the actual nature or extent of authentic dialogue. Harold Netland (1991: 283ff), for example, has an excellent discussion of the place of dialogue from the perspective of the exclusivist position. He and others have ably shown that witness and dialogue are not mutually incompatible.

I would just add the following. First, dialogue means that we take the other person seriously. This of necessity means that we take beliefs, worldview, convictions and values seriously. We may differ with an individual; we may have major problems with the religious perspectives of another. But if we enter into dialogue, we are simply acknowledging that these are important to the other person and that they hold these things with greater or lesser degrees of personal conviction. And, we take another person seriously, first and foremost, by listening well. Dialogue must mean that we learn to listen and that we listen before we speak.

But further, there is no authentic dialogue unless there is the possibility of learning. Dialogue must not be just a subtle form of pre-evangelism. It may in the end be a form of evangelism. But to be authentic, it also needs to include the possibility of learning. We only enter into dialogue if we come to the encounter looking for the signs of the wisdom and grace of God, willing to learn and respond to God as we are taught by another of a distinct religious tradition.

Further, dialogue can also include debate, when this is understood in the broad sense of gracious, reasoned contention—conversation that enables people to understand, to think clearly, and to wrestle with the human predicament.

The Cross

A critical theological category or concept is the question of the cross. What role or place does the cross and our understanding of the cross play in our development of an attitude towards non-Christian religions?

The cross of Christ defines the nature, character and meaning of Christian faith more than any other event or symbol. As such the cross defines the Christian attitude towards non-Christian religions.

Several perspectives are simultaneously affirmed by the cross. The first is that the cross is an inevitable stumbling block, an offense to human reason—the scandal of particularity. But second, the cross is also the massive declaration of love and vulnerability. While it calls humanity to account—humbling each individual on account of our sin—it also is a majestic manifestation of God's vulnerability, his love towards humanity.

Is not, then, the cross the vantage point from which we of necessity meet those of other religious faiths? On the one hand we witness to an event that will, inevitably, raise an obstacle. We have no apology for this; we know that life comes through the cross. But at the same time, our own lives and our own witness is such that we display an uncanny humility, vulnerability and love towards others in our witness to the cross. If there is an obstacle to the gospel, it is the cross itself and not our triumphalism, or our proud isolationism, that offends. Humility does not mean that we depreciate our own values or that we lack conviction. It merely means that we realize that we are fellow seekers, fellow pilgrims and that we approach another not as those who have and know everything, but as those who are open and vulnerable. We recognize our own limitations.

Third, the cross is a reminder that our witness for the gospel is and must be a witness in both word as well as deed. Our witness will be marked less by triumph and more by suffering. Christ's encounter with the religion of his day was one of sacrificial service.

In our examination of the Scriptures, we can and must continue to note the defining place of the cross within the Bible and thus within our theology.

Conversion

For evangelical Christians, conversion is an important theological category in any discussion about religion and religious encounter. Our understanding of conversion can have a formative influence on our reading of Scripture and our understanding of religion and religious encounter.

It is normally assumed that we would first develop a theology of non-Christian religions and then from this perspective shape and determine our understanding of conversion. It is worth considering these in reverse, asking the question: How can an understanding of conversion enable us as we develop a biblical perspective on non-Christian religions?

First, we must be alert to the danger of associating conversion with a change of religious affiliation, or the idea that if one becomes a part of a particular religious group one has a secure salvation. Conversion is fundamentally a matter of allegiance to God and his kingdom. Though we need to affirm that there is no complete conversion without identification with the people of God, the point here is that the heart of conversion is this change of allegiance.

Second, we must beware of the individualistic notions of conversion that have often blinded us to the eschatological vision of the work of God in history, in the church and in the world.

Third, it is also helpful to remember that in a religious conversion there is never a complete discontinuity with one's past. In a conversion many elements of one's life could remain intact and indeed should remain in place insofar as they do not undermine one's loyalty to Christ Jesus.

Further, this would be a means of affirming that there is no wasted time with God. With a change of allegiance, there is a gradual redemption of the whole of one's life including one's past. All that we are and all that we have been is brought into perspective by our change in allegiance. There is discontinuity; there must be. But the point of discontinuity is at the point of fundamental allegiance. This is the issue.

Fourth, our understanding of religion and religious encounter will include what we understand to be the nature and character of saving faith. Clark Pinnock suggests that one finds salvation through faith, that it is faith that saves, quite apart from whether one names the name of Jesus and personally knows Jesus.

But this hardly seems to reflect the biblical evidence. Faith has a certain primacy—as is evident in the experience of all who respond to God, beginning with Abraham. But it of necessity must be a faith that comes in response to the self-revelation of God. It is not faith as an end in itself.

As such, there is no avoiding both the person of Christ as well as the cross and the need for radical submission to the crucified one. Because the cross shapes our vision of reality and thus of religion, we make no apology for the crisis of the cross or the inevitable obstacle it brings to those of any religious background.

But we can still ask, even though we might differ with Pinnock, what does it mean to have faith in God and what is the significance of the quest for God of those who as yet have not found God? What is the relationship between their quest, their sincere search for God and the faith that is an actual response to God when he is found?

Fifth and finally, it is becoming increasingly clear that we need to question the traditional notion of conversion which associates salvation with a specific decision or prayer at a particular time and place. Conversion, we are seeing, is quite complex. And though we can and must be able to distinguish between those who know Christ and those who do not, in actual fact many are on the road, many are coming to faith, many are in a process of conversion that cannot be pinned down to a specific time or place. It will be a series of events wherein they choose in smaller steps to respond to the Gospel and become part of the covenant people of God. To create an artificial crisis construct into our understanding of conversion blinds us from the reality that there is an experiential continuum in virtually every believer's response to the grace of God. It is helpful to keep a clear distinction between regeneration, which is God's unique supernatural act, and conversion, the human response which is often an experiential process.

In this regard, it is helpful to add another question. There are many reservations that an evangelical would have with recent Roman Catholic thought with regard to non-Christian religions. But there is at least one aspect of this perspective that may be very helpful for evangelicals. The attempt has been to reflect on non-Christian religions from the center of Christian faith and theology rather than from certain boundaries or fringes. By this perspective, what it means to be a Christian is as much a matter of orientation as of where one stands on the religious spectrum. Many people are seeking God and on the way to a knowledge of God in response to the revelation they have received. They are not baptized believers as yet, but their focus and direction is right.

In the same way, it may be that we have baptized believers in our churches who have long ago stopped seeking the Lord. It may be that we need to define our mission from the center, not from the fringes, the boundaries. We may need to think of people not according to where they stand in terms of the religious fence but rather in terms of the direction and sincerity of their search.

The example of Cornelius is an important one in this discussion; his conversion is used by groups from several perspectives to buttress their case. Pinnock and others, as noted above, see Cornelius as an example of an individual who knew the saving grace of God prior to an encounter with Christ. For those from an exclusivist position, such as Adjith Fernando (1987:133), Cornelius does not have saving knowledge of God until Peter arrives and preaches to him. He suggests that the reference in Acts 11:14 affirms this, indicating that Cornelius knew salvation through the message of Peter. Fernando echoes the standard observations of the exclusivist position in concluding, then, that God will reveal the gospel even if this requires a miracle, if there is a sincere seeker after God (such as Cornelius).

Part of our response to this must be to ask what is it that amazed Peter when he made this statement? Does the text affirm the sincerity of Cornelius and his search, or does the statement of Peter affirm the availability of the gospel for all of humanity, both Jew and Gentile? It is hard to avoid the conclusion that the reference is to the availability of the gospel to all peoples. Pinnock and other evangelical inclusivists miss the point of the text. Peter is affirming that the gospel is gospel to all peoples; he is not affirming the validity of all religious quests.

Cornelius experienced the saving grace of the Lord Jesus Christ when he responded to the message of Peter. But his conversion, understood in its fullest sense, was not merely a single action or decision he made in the presence of Peter. He had been on the road to this moment for a significant amount of time. He was a sincere seeker and in his case we know the whole story; we know of his encounter with the gospel and of his reception of the gift of the Holy Spirit. But what of those who seek, and who though sincere in their search do not have the opportunity to hear? Does the Bible make a definitive statement or conclusion in this regard?

God's Work in Human History

In considering the overall agenda of God in the history of human affairs, evangelical exclusivists have on the whole tended to emphasize the tasks of mission and evangelism. This focus is appropriate, but one wonders if this is the whole story. God's kingdom work is pervasive. God is present within every sphere and sector of culture and society, amongst all peoples. He is working, despite the presence of sin and rebellion, in and through each culture (which inevitably includes religion). In ways we cannot detect, God is working through the arts, the sciences, philosophical endeavor and even in the commercial enterprises of humanity.

God is establishing a kingdom of truth and light. This kingdom will find consummation in the return of Christ, but even then this work will continue until all things are brought into submission to the lordship of Jesus Christ. Surely our reflection on Scripture must be guided by this eschatological vision, this kind of all-encompassing view of the kingdom work of God.

The Need to Answer all the Questions

Evangelical theology is often characterized by a resolve to have answers to all the questions; it has been normative to assume that we can and must have a clear outline of what God is doing and not doing.

One example of this would be that noted earlier: the assumption that if there are sincere people in other religious traditions, then God will send them a messenger of the gospel, and that if they were truly sincere, this preacher would arrive before they died.

On the one hand, this stretches the biblical evidence; we have little basis on which to hold this conclusion. As noted, the Bible is not explicit on what happens to one who has never heard or had the opportunity to hear specifically of Jesus.

Also, I wonder if this assertion is but a subtle attempt to answer all the questions, leave no stone unturned, to be sure that we "know" how God will act in all situations. Perhaps we need to hear Newbigin and Bosch at this point. Maybe we need to allow for some space in our theology for the unknown. Maybe we can tell our children, our teens, our congregations: we must witness and preach, we must declare the glory of Christ . . . and we can leave to God and his mercy those who do not have the opportunity to hear and know. God has not answered all our questions.

Job, Melchizedek and others described in the Old Testament all represent, in different ways, matters in God's mind that are not accessible to us. These are mysterious individuals, and it may be that we are not privy to all that God is doing in the world. It is not for us to know.

Clark Pinnock uses the category of "pagan saint" to refer to those outside of the covenant who seem to know Yahweh. While the evidence is scanty on which to make this conclusion, the evidence is also scanty on which to refute it. We are responding to a significant unknown. We are called to glorify Christ and call people to respond to the Gospel of Jesus Christ. As we review the Scriptures, can we really make definitive conclusions about the destiny of those who do not have the opportunity to hear? Or is this something that we will have to leave to the knowledge and wisdom of God?

In this regard reference is often made to the rationale or the motive for Christian mission. Amongst evangelicals this motivation has usually been the human predicament—that apart from Christ humanity is lost. We often speak of the need to preach quickly and urgently lest another soul be lost.

But should not the motive be the glory of God and the saving power of Jesus Christ? The former motive leads to both guilt and presumption. There is the inevitable guilt, since we never preach as much as we should, or witness as frequently as we could. But also there is the overstatement of our significance, the significance of our work, our mission, our strategies, so much so that we sometimes speak as though the coming of the kingdom is actually dependent on our work.

Jesus was clearly motivated by a passion to glorify the Father. This assuredly meant that he was concerned for Israel and he also had a love for the world that led him to sacrificial service. But the central motive was the glorification of the Father.

What would it mean to have the church of one age or generation live and breath and serve out of a desire to glorify Christ? And how the passion to glorify Christ be exemplified in our lives? In part, it will free us from guilt—for Christ himself emphasizes that he had done the work that the Father had given him to do—and from presumption, for we will find that in part the work of Christ is accomplished through the manifestation of his glory.

Having raised these questions, it is helpful to distinguish between the main plot and the subplot of the story. The main plot running through Scripture is surely that God is at work through Christ and in his church. Even if there were pagan saints, faithful outside of the covenant who are recognized by God, this would at most be a subplot. The central theme is that we are to proclaim the gospel and invite people into the kingdom that is embodied in the community of God's people.

We are called to the glorification of Christ in word and deed and it is clear that how women and men respond to the preaching of the gospel has eternal consequences for them, for both life and judgment are found in Christ. This is the central theme of Scripture.

Conclusion

I have outlined some of the issues facing Christians we develop a theology of religion and religious encounter. I have raised questions and indicated how we might begin to respond. Most of all I have sought to stress that we need to examine the Scriptures.

Leslie Newbigin has ably noted that the development of the Christian faith and doctrine happens not simply through theological reflection but necessarily through the missionary commission as well (Newbigin 1988:310). The preeminent biblical example of this is the conversion of Cornelius—a conversion for Cornelius, certainly, but also for Peter and the whole early church. The church came into a greater understanding of her mission and of God's work in the world through the encounter with this Gentile.

It is no surprise then, that the religious plurality of our generation is forcing the church to ask tough questions about the nature and character of our attitude towards non-Christian religions. Peter was threatened by what he at first was hesitant to accept. It did not fit his categories. But his own vulnerability and willingness to look, listen and learn are a model for us in our day. With an affirmation of the uniqueness of Christ and a commitment to be his witnesses in the world, we can and must as yet be willing to look, listen and learn.

Reference List

Abraham, William J.
    1989   *The Logic of Evangelism*. Grand Rapids, MI: Eerdmans.
Bosch, David J.
    1991   *Transforming Mission: Paradigm Shifts in Theology of Mission*. Maryknoll, NY: Orbis.
D'Costa, Gavin
    1986   *Theology and Religious Pluralism: The Challenge of Other Religions*. Worcester: Billing and Sons.

Demarest, Bruce
    1992   "General and Special Revelation: Epistemological Foundations of Religious Pluralism." In *One God, One Lord: Christianity in a World of Religious Pluralism*. Andrew D. Clarke and Bruce W. Winter, eds. Pp. 189-206. Grand Rapids, MI: Eerdmans.

Eaton, John
    1989   *The Contemplative Face of Old Testament Wisdom, in the Context of World Religions*. London: SCM.

Fernando, Adjith
    1987   *The Christian's Attitude Toward World Religions*. Wheaton, IL: Tyndale.

Foster, Durwood
    1990   "Christian Motives for Interfaith Dialogue." In *Christianity and the Wider Ecumenism*. Peter C. Phan, ed. Pp. 21-23. New York: Paragon.

Goldingay, John E., and Christopher J. H. Wright
    1992   "Yahweh Our God Yahweh One: The Oneness of God in the Old Testament." In *One God, One Lord: Christianity in a World of Religious Pluralism*. Andrew D. Clarke and Bruce W. Winter, eds.. Pp. 43-62. Grand Rapids, MI: Paternoster.

Goldsmith, Martin
    1989   *What About Other Faiths?* Reading Berks: Cos and Wyman.

Knitter, Paul F.
    1985   *No Other Name? A Critical Survey of Christian Attitudes Toward the World Religions*. Maryknoll, NY: Orbis.

Neill, Stephen
    1961   *Christian Faith and Other Faiths: The Christian Dialogue with Other Religions*. London: Oxford.

Netland, Harold A.
    1991   *Dissonant Voices: Religious Pluralism and the Quest of Truth*. Grand Rapids, MI: Eerdmans.

Newbigin, Lesslie
    1988   "The Christian Faith and the World Religions." In *Keeping the Faith*. B. Wainwright, ed. Pp. 310-340. Philadelphia: Fortress.
    1989   *The Gospel in a Pluralist Society*. Grand Rapids, MI: Eerdmans.

Pinnock, Clark H.
   1992   *Wideness in God's Mercy: The Finality of Jesus Christ in a World of Religions.* Grand Rapids, MI: Zondervan.
   1990   "Toward an Evangelical Theology of Religions." *Journal of the Evangelical Theological Society* 33(3):359-368.

Thomsen, Mark
   1990   "Confessing Jesus Christ within the World of Religious Pluralism." *International Bulletin of Missionary Research* 14(3):115-118.

Walton, John W.
   1989   *Ancient Israelite Literature in its Cultural Context.* Grand Rapids, MI: Regency/Zondervan.

Wright, David
   1992   "The Watershed of Vatican II." In *One God, One Lord: Christianity in a World of Religious Pluralism..* Andrew D. Clarke and Bruce W. Winter, eds. Pp. 207-226. Grand Rapids, MI: Paternoster.

2

YAHWEH AND THE GODS: A THEOLOGY OF WORLD RELIGIONS FROM THE PENTATEUCH

Ed Mathews

Pluralism is a major challenge confronting contemporary religions. The challenge is a serious one. For, in the past, when various religions encountered each other, new insights and expressions of faith developed.[1] These developments resulted in either different religious formulations or fresh spiritual growth.

Christians are reexamining the foundations of their faith, especially their understanding of God. Who is he? Did the Israelites borrow their understanding of God from their pagan neighbors? How should a Christian respond to the claims of religious pluralism? These questions are the focus of the ensuing examination of the Pentateuch.

Yahweh in the Pentateuch

God revealed himself in the history and culture of ancient Israel. This disclosure occurred among societies that believed in a pantheon of gods. The similarities between Yahweh and the gods are interesting; the differences are convicting. What the Lord did in Israel "simply never happened elsewhere" (Noth 1958:2,3). The central elements of biblical faith are unique in that they could not have emerged by any natural evolutionary process from the pagan world in which they originated (Wright 1968:7; cf. Richardson 1961:71,72). The Hebrews realized their religion was different from other religions because their God was different from other gods.

"There is no one like the Lord" (Ex 8:10)

Yahweh was without equal. None of the pagan gods was like him. He was incomparable (Durham 1987:128). In the Old Testament, several phrases expressed this uniqueness: "there is none, there is nothing, there is no . . . as, like, compared to, on a level with, equal to . . . . " For instance, in comparing himself to other gods, Yahweh said, "There is no one like me in all the earth" (Ex 9:14). While blessing Israel just before his death, Moses said, "There is no one like the God of Jeshurun, who rides on the heavens to help you . . . " (Dt 33:26). As expressions of uniqueness, one-of-a kindness, or singularity, these comparative phrases also described the plagues of hail and locust (Ex 9:18,24; 10:14); the despairing cry of the Egyptians (Ex 11:6); and the leadership of Moses (Dt 34:10). It is obvious that, as a particular linguistic form, these comparisons were part of everyday conversation. They had their origin in the idiom of the people (Labuschagne 1966:15). Only later did Israel apply them to the incomparability of Yahweh.

"Who among the gods is like you, O Lord?" (Ex 15:11)

Besides comparative statements, the Israelites employed rhetorical questions to express uniqueness and singularity. For example, Moses asked, "What god is there in heaven or on earth who can do the deeds and mighty works you do?" (Dt 3:24). Again, Moses inquired, "Has any god ever tried to take for himself one nation out of another nation, by testing, by miraculous signs and wonders, by war, or by great and awesome deeds, like all the things the Lord your God did for you in Egypt before your very eyes?" (Dt 4:34). Yahweh was beyond comparison among all divine beings. "There is simply none like him, none even approaching an equality with him" (Durham 1987:207). He was magnificent in holiness, awesome in splendor, and extraordinary in accomplishment. Moses also used rhetorical questions to describe the uniqueness of Israel, i.e., without equal among the nations (because her God was without equal among the gods: Dt 4:7; 5:26; 33:29). It is clear, then, that a rhetorical question was a communication device for expressing a deep conviction (Kessler

1982:8). The anticipated answer to these "who is like" questions was always "none." When they referred to the Lord, the expected reply was "none but Yahweh" or "Yahweh alone."

"The Lord is one" (Dt 6:4)

The escape from Egypt and passage through the wil-derness shaped the identity of Israel, an identity clarified by the demand to "love Yahweh with all your heart and with all your soul and with all your strength" (Dt 6:5). The force of this demand rested on the profound realization and repeated mention in the Pentateuch that "Yahweh is your God." The Shema goes a step further in affirming that "Yahweh is one" or "Yahweh alone" is the God of Israel. Though the Hebrew text is ambiguous at this point, "monotheism is implicit" in both versions of that grand creedal statement (Christensen 1991:145). If the ambiguity is irresolvable, as some argue (Miller 1990:99), then, the task of interpretation calls for grappling with the sense of both translations.[2]

Undivided loyalty of Israel. The translation "Yahweh is our God, Yahweh alone" anticipates the command to love God with undivided devotion. It describes the appropriate commitment of Israel. Its concern is her loyalty to the God of the covenant, a refusal to permit her to direct only part of her love to God (Wyschogrod 1984:25). Therefore the Shema, according to this rendering, is a radical confession that the loyalty of Israel is one, a loyalty to worship "no other gods" except Yahweh, to have "no other gods" except him (Ex 20:3).

Undivided nature of God. The alternative translation "Yahweh our God, Yahweh is one" speaks of the integrity and the unity of his purpose, thus emphasizing his oneness (Moberly 1990:211-215). The Lord was known as "the one who brought Israel out of the land of Egypt" (Dt 5:6). When his people made a golden calf, God was ready to destroy them (Dt 9:12-14). This threatened destruction made him appear fickle and inconsistent (Dt 9:28,29). In the end, the integrity of God prevailed because he kept his covenant with Israel (Dt 7:8,9).[3] The Shema demanded the same integrity (or undivided commitment) of Israel toward God (Janzen 1987:291-295). To confess that "Yahweh is one" was to claim that he was faithful and consistent in purpose and being, undivided in heart and mind and will.

Yahweh and the Gods

Yahweh was unique and incomparable, whole and undivided, a covenant God of impeccable integrity. Where did these ascriptions originate? Did Israel borrow them from local pagan religions and apply them to their God? The evidence does not warrant that conclusion. Instead, Yahweh was both greater than and distinct from the gods of Babylon, Egypt, and Canaan.

Distinct from the Gods

The Israelites lived in a world shaped by polytheism, by a supposed cosmic struggle between gods and goddesses (Glasser 1989:37). The faith of Israel resulted from "the direct activity of God" (Wright 1968:15), not from a religious developmentalism that evolved out of polytheism into henotheism or out of henotheism into monotheism (Rowley 1950:333-338). Though the Pentateuch reflects some borrowing from local sources, the elements of paganism are so radically reconceptualized that the faith of Israel stood in sharp contrast to the polytheistic environ-ment in which it emerged.

El. The father and omnipotent ruler of the Canaanite gods was El.[4] He was older than the sub-deities. Thus, in age and power, he surpassed them all. After leaving behind the gods of Ur (Jos 24:14) and entering Canaan, Abraham worshipped El, who was also the God of Melchizedek and Abimelech (Ge 14:18-20; 20:1-17; 21:22-24). Likewise, Jacob built an altar and called it "El, the God of Israel" (Ge 33:19,20).[5] About the time Abraham moved to Canaan, the Ugaritic texts were written. They told the myth of Ba'al driving El from the kingship over the Canaanite gods, a myth that began in the north and swept steadily south through Palestine (Kapelrud 1963:40-42). This religious revolution was the result of the coming of the Amorites who brought their god Ba'al with them (cf. Ge 15:16 and Am 2:9,10; Oldenburg 1969: 151-163). The myth reflected in religion what took place in politics—the Amorite conquest of Canaan. Ba'al, as an agricultural fertility god, did not penetrate the desert regions of Midian in the far south, where Abraham migrated at the beginning of the Amorite occupation and where Moses, six centuries later, worshipped El (Ex 2:15-31). While in Midian, Moses came face to face with El, "the God of Abraham, Isaac, and Jacob," at the burning bush (Ex 3:6). There the Lord, who was similar to El, revealed himself as distinct from El.[6] He said his name was Yahweh: "I am who I am" (Ex 3:14).[7] Moses, who had worshipped El, was given a new understanding—an insight into the distinctiveness of Yahweh—to prepare him for confrontations with Ba'al.

Ba'al. When Israel crossed the Jordan and moved into Canaan, defeating the people and taking over the land, the Hebrews became bitter enemies of the Canaanites, and Yahweh became the fierce adversary of Ba'al. In spite of dire warnings (Dt 4:5-20; 7:1-6; 8:19,20; 17:1-3; 18:9-13; 30:17,18), some Israelites abandoned Yahweh (Jdg 2:10; 6:7-10; 10:6,7a). Leaders in ancient Israel adopted Ba'al cult practices (cf. 2Ki 23:4-9 and Jer 32:30-35; Greenfield 1987:546). Deliverers drove out the enemy, abolished the cults, and brought the people back to Yahweh. The rivalry between Yahweh and Ba'al persisted throughout the history of Israel and Judah. The Israelites misunderstood the distinctiveness of Yahweh, the only God who asked his people to love him as he had already loved them (Ex 34:10-14; Christensen 1991:15).

Greater than the Gods

Whenever the Pentateuch mentioned other gods, it assumed the gods were real to the pagans. Yet, when comparing Yahweh with the gods, it portrayed Yahweh not only as distinct from the gods but also greater than the gods. The prohibitions against idolatry and the expressions of exaltation reflect this greaness.

Prohibitions against idolatry. Idols were not to be made or worshipped by the Israelites (Ex 20:4,5; 34:17; Lev 19:4; 20:1; Dt 29:16-18). They were merely man-made pieces of detestable, useless, ineffective, dead wood and stone (Dt 27:15; 29:17; 32:21). Images could not see, hear, eat or smell (Dt 4:28). They disappointed and embarrassed those who trusted in them. Why, then, did Yahweh prohibit idolatry? The Pentateuch does not give a precise answer.[8] In contrast to the gods of Canaan—that were known through idols—Yahweh made himself known entirely apart from images (Dt 4:12-18). The prohibition against idolatry, therefore, set Israel apart from her pagan neighbors (Curtis 1985:285). It distinguished Israel from her contemporaries and

Yahweh from their gods. As the sovereign Lord, he had the authority to impose the ban against idols, Deuteronomy 4:1,2. He was the God of gods, the God not formed or controlled by human hands.[9]

Expressions of exaltation. Some scholars suggest that Israel adopted her forms of exaltation of Yahweh from her pagan neighbors (Wright 1951:4). Since Babylon, Egypt, and Israel employed similar statements of uniqueness for their deities, the question of borrowing must be taken seriously. Considering the evidence, however, "it cannot be proved on sufficient grounds that Israel borrowed the concept" (Labuschagne 1966:129). It seems more plausible to believe that the Israelites formed expressions of exaltation independently from the rich resources of her language. Although the Hebrews probably knew the local idioms of incomparability, the idea developed in the experience of Israel with Yahweh as a distinct, unique God, remarkably different from pagan deities.[10] From the very beginning, Israel linked the uniqueness of Yahweh with her salvation from Egypt (Ex 20:2). The concept was not borrowed from pagan minds but began as a creedal confession—based on the activities of God—that Yahweh was one, entirely different God beyond comparison or imitation. There was none greater. There was none other (Dt 4:39).

Yahweh and Religious Pluralism

The contrast between Yahweh and the gods contributes to an understanding and appreciation of the Lord. It demonstrates the qualitative difference between God and the gods, draws atten-tion to his singular uniqueness, sets the parameters for religious pluralism, and provides a basis for responding to the contemporary voices of religious tolerance. In view of the various world religions with their divergent beliefs and practices, what relationship does Yahweh have with their gods?[11] Three possibilities will be discussed: "One reflected in the many, One reached by the many, and One instead of the many."[12]

One Reflected in the Many

This position assumes that there is a reality at the center of all religions. The different perceptions of that reality in the various religions are true to the people holding them but, as the pluralists argue, they cannot be imposed upon those of other religions (Hick 1977; Smith 1981). Therefore, Yahweh cannot be normative (and no god or ideology can be the standard for all religions). Instead, pluralists say, all talk of Yahweh is "mythological speech about the Real" (Hick 1989:248). This severs any connection between human language and divine reality (D'Costa 1991:67). Pluralism provides no way for people to speak about God and, should they attempt to do so, no way of knowing if they are speaking about the same God (McGrath 1994:463). Therefore, in accommodating all religions, pluralism accommodates none. Truth is relativized. The "One reflected in the many" approach creates an impossible dilemma.

One Reached by the Many

This understanding advocates a utilitarian function for every religion. It assumes all religions are ladders to help their devotees reach the One. The various religions are "traditions of instrumentality" (Coward 1985:96), all supposedly leading to the same God or, at least, the same destiny. Some inclusivists believe that the faithful adherent of a non-Christian religion is an "anonymous Christian" (Rahner 1974:73), that God will ultimately sum up all things in the Messiah, and that, therefore, by whatever way people come to God, they will be saved (Knitter 1985:143). This is problematic. People would receive salvation who do not desire it. They would acquire grace from a God they do not know, acknowledge, or worship.

One Instead of the Many

The exclusivist view says there is only one God and only one way to be reconciled to him. Though people of other religions may live sincere and faithful lives, they cannot be saved by their religions that, at best, are human attempts to reach God—attempts, perverted by rebellion, to find him (Kraemer 1938). The claims of exclusivism are logically possible but present a painful question: Can a merciful God deny salvation to those who have never heard of him (Klootwijk 1993:458)? The answer to that question depends on understanding the God of the Pentateuch.[13]

Yahweh was greater than the gods. He was incomparable, singularly unique. There was no other god like him (Ex 9:14; 15:11; Dt 3:24; 33:26). These ascriptions were not philosophical deductions or cultural adaptations. Israel developed them out of her experience with Yahweh. He intervened in her history with *redemptive power* (Ex 20:2; Dt 4:34; 33:29a). His mighty deliverance was his way of showing the pagans that he was Yahweh (Ex 7:5,17; 8:10), of telling Israel that it was Yahweh who rescued her (Ex 6:7; 10:2; 16:6,12).[14] These are not self-evident truths or humanly devised myths. They are clues to the concern and compassion of God, to his nature and mission in the world.

The *covenant love* of Yahweh also clarifies his incomparability (Dt 7:9; cf. Ex 34:6,7). His nearness to Israel manifested that love (Dt 4:7), a love no one could question, a nearness no god could equal. Yahweh heard the cry of his people, he saw their misery, he agonized over their suffering (Ex 3:7,9). He promised to be with them (Ex 3:12), to be their Immanuel. And he was.

Because of the experiences of Israel, Moses declared, in speaking of Yahweh, that there was no god besides him (Dt 32:39). He was not like a pagan god, namely, a false "rock," a god who disappeared in times of crisis, a "no-god" image, worthless idol (Dt 32:21,31,37). There simply was no other God (Dt 4:35,39). If Israel took the reality of her monotheism seriously, she had an authentic witness within pagan polytheism. If she kept at bay the voices of religious tolerance, the temptations of religious pluralism, she had an incredible purpose, a marvelous privilege—for, like Pharaoh, she was the means of proclaiming his name "in all the earth" (cf. Ex 9:16 and 1Ki 8:56-60). Is that not also our calling, our purpose, our privilege?

Notes

[1] The world religions emerged in and were shaped in reaction to pluralistic environments. In every case, the existing religions were made to question their beliefs and practices (Coward 1985:94,95. See also D'Costa 1986 and Martinson 1987).

[2] Canonical support for the legitimacy of both translations of the Shema is found in Mark 12:32: "You are right in saying that God is one and there is no other but him." This statement points

to both the undivided nature of Yahweh and the undivided loyalty of Israel.

³ A similar scenario is recorded in Numbers 14:11-16.

⁴ Some will argue that "El is rarely if ever used in the Bible as the proper name of a non-Israelite Canaanite deity . . . " (Cross 1974:44). Though that may be true, the Ugaritic texts are the exception to that rule. El is depicted not as a generic name but a specific deity. "El is a word common to all Semitic languages. It occurs as a common noun (the god, god) and also as the proper name for a particular god. This is clearly demonstrated in the texts from Ugaritic in North Syria (fourteenth century B.C.)" (Schneider 1986:67. See also Manley 1962:478).

⁵ Genesis depicts no antagonism between the religious practices of the patriarchs and the inhabitants of Canaan, an antagonism strongly evident elsewhere in the Pentateuch (Ex 23:23-25a; Dt 11:8-17; Moberly 1992:91). Many misread this lack of antagonism as an original polytheism which later gave way to monotheism. Cf. Rowley 1967:14, 15, and Smith 1987.

⁶El and Yahweh were both called "the creator," "the God of mercy," and "the Holy One." They were both authors of social order, teachers of righteousness, and champions of widows and orphans. Among the Canaanite gods, none were like El and Yahweh. Nevertheless, unlike El, the Lord did not rule over a pantheon of gods. He allowed Israel to worship no other god except (or besides) him (Ex 20:3; Clifford 1973:15. See also Wessels 1989:49-51).

⁷ The meaning of the divine name is unclear. Many possibilities are suggested (Gianotti 1985:40-46). "I am who I am" may mean "I am the God who is active in whatever situation you are called to face" (cf. Dt 29:1-6; Davidson 1964:27. See also Kim 1989:108-117).

⁸ Several possibilities have been suggested: (a) An image of Yahweh would not be Yahweh; consequently, any worship of such an image would (by definition) be idolatry (Kaufmann 1960:18). (b) An image of Yahweh would make the assimilation of Canaanite fertility cult practices easier (Childs 1974:485,486. See also Milgran 1985:48-55; Ratner and Zuckermann 1986:15-60). And (c) an image allowed humans to control their god; thus prohibiting the use of idols meant Yahweh did not submit to the

whims of human control (Albright 1968:171, 172; Miller and Roberts 1977:9-17).

[9] Textual and archaeological evidence support the conclusion that from the beginning of the occupation of Canaan the prohibition against idolatry was for the most part kept by Israel. "Figurines of the mother goddess, to be sure, are regularly found in Israelite towns . . . but . . . excavations have thus far brought to light not a single image of Yahweh" (Bright 1981:60). Hebrew polytheism was not existent to a significant degree in Israel until the early monarchy. The exile came as a direct result of such disregard for Yahweh (Tigay 1986:37-41. Cf. Taylor 1988:557-566).

[10] It was Israel who experienced Yahweh as a God of integrity, a holy God, a God of justice, a God of mercy toward the helpless, who gave commandments, who spoke to his people in passionate language, and who demanded complete commitment and undivided loyalty. It was Israel who saw the uniqueness of Yahweh in the plagues, the exodus, and the wilderness journey (Ex 8:6; 9:14). It was Israel who experienced the difference between Yahweh and the gods (Ex 15:11). It was out of the richness of these experiences that Israel knew Yahweh. There was no need for her to imitate, adopt, or borrow from her pagan neighbors. The polemic throughout the Pentateuch (and the Old Testament prophets) is persuasive evidence for an exclusivistic understanding of Yahweh in a pluralistic environment, i.e., Yahweh, instead of the pagan gods, is the sovereign Creator who controls nature, brings fertitlity, and subdues nations.

[11] The author is aware that some religions are nontheistic. In such cases, the question should be reworded: What is the relationship between Yahweh and their "ultimate concern" (Tillich 1957:106), Yahweh and "the holy" (Otto 1958:12-19), or the "Real"? Each religion—whether theistic or nontheistic—is an attempt to seek and respond to that which is considered the One.

[12] These three possibilities are frequently employed as a framework for discussing a theology of world religions, i.e., pluralism, inclusivism, and exclusivism respectively (cf. Race 1982; D'Costa 1986; McGrath 1994).

[13] What ultimately will happen to those who do not know Yahweh can be left in the hands of a just, compassionate, forgiving, holy God. Their destiny, like the rescue of Israel, will be

grounded in his concern for everyone (Thomsen 1990). Our concern should not be THEIR judgment but OUR faithfulness to his missionary call.

[14] The Red Sea event had the same two purposes (Ex 14:4, 18,31).

Reference List

Albright, William Foxwell
    1968   *Yahweh and the Gods of Canaan: A Historical Analysis of Two Contrasting Faiths.* Garden City, NY: Doubleday.

Bright, John
    1981   *A History of Israel.* Philadelphia: Westminster.

Childs, Brevard
    1974   *The Book of Exodus, A Critical, Theological Commentary.* Philadelphia: Westminster.

Christensen, Duane
    1991   *Deuteronomy 1-11.* Word Biblical Commentary. Waco, TX: Word.

Clifford, Richard
    1973   "The Word of God in the Ugaritic Epics and in the Patriarchal Narratives," *The Word in the World.* Richard Clifford and George MacRae, eds. Cambridge, MA: Weston College.

Cross, Frank
    1974   *Canaanite Myth and Hebrew Epic.* Cambridge, MA: Harvard.

Coward, Harold
    1985   *Pluralism: Challenge to World Religions.* Maryknoll, NY: Orbis.

Curtis, Edward M.
    1985   "The Theological Basis for the Prohibition of Images in the Old Testament," *Journal of the Evangelical Theological Society* 28(3):277-287.

Davidson, Robert
    1964   *The Old Testament.* Philadelphia: J. B. Lippincott.

D'Costa, Gavin
    1986   *Theology and Religious Pluralism: The Challenge of Other Religions.* Oxford: Basil Blackwell.
    1991   "The New Missionary: John Hicks and Religious Plurality," *International Bulletin of Missionary Research* 15(2):66-69.

Durham, John
    1987   *Exodus.* Word Biblical Commentary. Waco, TX: Word.

Gianotti, Charles
    1985   "The Meaning of the Divine Name," *Bibliotheca Sacra*, January-March, 38-51.

Glasser, Arthur
    1989   "Old Testament Contextualization: Revelation and Its Environment," *The Word Among Us*, edited by Dean Gilliland. Dallas, TX: Word.

Greenfield, Jonas
    1987   "The Hebrew Bible and Canaanite Literature," *The Literary Guide to the Bible*, edited by Robert Alter and Rank Kermode. Cambridge, MA: Harvard.

Hick, John
    1977   *God and the Universe of Faiths.* London: Fount.
    1989   *An Interpretation of Religion.* London: Macmillan.

Janzen, J. Gerald
    1987   "On the Most Important Word in the Shema," *Vestus Testamentum* 37(3):280-300.

Kapelrud, Arvid
    1963   *The Ras Shamra Discoveries and the Old Testament.* G. W. Anderson, trans. Norman, OK: University of Oklahoma.

Kaufmann, Yehezkel
    1960   *The Religion of Israel: From Its Beginning to the Babylonian Exile.* Moshe Greenberg, trans. Chicago: University of Chicago.

Kessler, Martin
    1982   "A Methodological Setting for Rhetorical Criticism," *Art and Meaning: Rhetoric in Biblical Literature.* David Clines, David Gunn, and Alan Hauser, eds. Sheffield, England: JSOT.

Kim, Ee Kon
    1989   "Who is Yahweh?" *Asia Journal of Theology* 3(1):108-117.
Klootwijk, Eeuwout
    1993   "Christian Approaches to Religious Pluralism: Diverging Models and Patterns," *Missiology: An International Review* 21(4):455-468.
Knitter, Paul
    1985   *No Other Name? A Critical Survey of Christain Attitudes Toward the World Religions.* Maryknoll, NY: Orbis.
Kraemer, Hendrik
    1938   *The Christian Message in a Non-Christian World.* New York: Harper and Row.
Labuschagne, C. J.
    1966   *The Incomparability of Yahweh in the Old Testament.* Leiden: E. J. Brill.
Manley, G. T.
    1962   "Names of God." In *The New Bible Dictionary.* J.D. Douglas, ed. Grand Rapids, MI: Eerdmans.
Martinson, Paul
    1987   *A Theology of World Religions: Interpreting God, Self, and* World *in Semitic, India, and Chinese Thought.* Minneapolis: Augsburg.
Mcgrath, Allister
    1994   *Christian Theology: An Introduction.* Cambridge, MA: Blackwell.
Milgran, Jacob
    1985   "You Shall not Boil a Kid in its Mother's Milk," *Bible Review* 1(3):48-55.
Miller, Patrick
    1990   *Deuteronomy. Interpretation: A Bible Commentary for Teaching and Preaching.* Louisville, KY: John Knox.
Miller, P. D. and Roberts, J. J. M.
    1977   *The Hand of the Lord.* Baltimore: Johns Hopkins.
Moberly, R. W. L.
    1990   "Yahweh is One: The Translation of the Shema," *Studies in the Pentateuch.* J. A. Emerton, ed. Leiden: E. J. Brill.

1992 *The Old Testament of the Old Testament: Patriarchal Narratives and Mosaic Yahwism.* Minneapolis: Fortress.

Noth, Martin
   1958 *The History of Israel.* Stanley Godman, ed. New York: Harper and Row.

Oldenburg, Ulf
   1969 *The Conflict Between El and Ba`al in Canaanite Religion.* Leiden: E. J. Brill.

Otto, Rudolf
   1958 *The Idea of the Holy.* John W. Harvey, trans. New York: Oxford.

Race, Alan
   1982 *Christians and Religious Pluralism.* Maryknoll, NY: Orbis.

Rahner, Karl
   1974 *Theological Investigations.* David Bourke, trans. Vol. 5. London: Darton, Longman, and Todd.

Ratner, Robert and Zuckermann, Bruce
   1986 "A Kid in Milk?: New Photographs of KTU 1:23, Line 14." *Hebrew Union College Annual* 57:15-60.

Richardson, Alan
   1961 *The Bible in the Age of Science.* London: SCM.

Rowley, Harold H.
   1950 "The Antiquity of Israelite Monotheism," *The Expository Times* 61:333-338.
   1967 *Worship in Ancient Israel: Its Form and Meaning.* London: SPCK.

Schneider, J.
   1986 "God, Gods, Emmanuel." In *The New International Dictionary of New Testament Theology.* Vol 2. Colin Brown, ed. Grand Rapids, MI: Zondervan.

Smith, Mark S.
   1987 *The Early History of God: Yahweh and Other Deities in Ancient Israel.* San Francisco: Harper and Row.

Smith, Wilfred Cantwell
   1981 *Towards a World Theology.* Philadelphia: Westminster.

Taylor, J. Glen
    1988   "The Two Earliest Known Representations of Yahweh." In *Ascribe to the Lord: Biblical and Other Studies in Memory of Peter C. Craige*. Lyle Eslinger and Glen Taylor, ed. Sheffield, England: JSOT.

Thomsen, Mark
    1990   "Confessing Jesus Christ Within a World of Religious Pluralism." *International Bulletin of Missionary Research* 14(3):115-118.

Tigay, Jeffery H.
    1986   *You Shall Have No Other Gods: Israelite Religion in the Light of Hebrew Inscriptions*. Atlanta, GA: Scholars.

Tillich, Paul
    1957   *Dynamics of Faith*. New York: Harper and Row.

Wessels, Anton
    1989   "Biblical Presuppositions For and Against Syncretism." In *Dialogue and Syncretism*. Jerald Gort, et. al., eds. Grand Rapids, MI: Eerdmans.

Wright, G. Ernest
    1968   *The Old Testament Against Its Environment*. London: SCM.

Wyschogrod, Michael
    1984   "The Shema Israel in Judaism and the New Testament." In *The Roots of Our Common Faith*. Hans Georg Link, ed. Geneva: World Council of Churches.

3

SELECTED PERSPECTIVES ON WORLD RELIGIONS FROM WISDOM LITERATURE

Michael Pocock

Wisdom literature is a subset of the Poetic literature of the Old Testament. About one-third of the Old Testament is poetic in form. All of it is edifying, but some is more specifically instructional. The instructional works considered to be Wisdom literature are Job, Proverbs, Song of Songs, and Ecclesiastes. Many include Sirach. There are portions of Wisdom literature both poetic and instructional in character found in Psalms (1; 37; 49; 112) and also in the prophets (Isa 40:12-17, 21-26; Am 3:10; 5:4,6,14) (Hill and Walton 1991:248).

Originally, this chapter was to include perspectives from the Psalms, but I have decided not to cover material from Psalms, except for occasional mention relative to our theme, because it is extensive and requires separate treatment.

In this chapter we wish to shed light first on the relationship that existed between the people of God in the Old Testament and the religio-cultural systems that surrounded them. Hopefully, this will guide us regarding possibilities today. In particular, we ask whether there is evidence in the Wisdom literature that Israel recognized either the voice of God or correct (dependable) observations relative to human conduct and obligations sourced in writers outside the covenant people of God. If the answer is positive, we may ask whether insights about God, humanity, and nature gathered by non-covenant peoples are generally dependable, or dependable only insofar as they receive biblical endorsement. Clearly, this bears on the issue of whether God speaks in non-covenant and non-Christian contexts. Have tribal peoples in Africa, sages in ancient China, religionists in whatever cultural context correctly captured, addressed, or received reliable information about God and humanity that deserves to be considered on a par with Scripture?

Holy Scripture is the product of divine inspiration. It constitutes an harmonious and consistent, though not systematic, whole. As such, material from one portion of the Holy Scripture can and should be compared with any other portion. Let Scripture comment on Scripture; but the first step must always be to see what a particular portion says and means within the context, culture, and literary form in which it appears. We hope to do this first while noting observations from outside Wisdom literature as they may apply.

We shall discover that the literary *forms* of biblical wisdom are common to the Ancient Near East and, to a certain extent, the *issues* about which the sages were concerned. The content has some overlap in areas of human relationships and understandings, but many clear distinctives relative to *cosmology* and *theology* emerge. Biblical sages will emerge as more exclusive in their claims than their counterparts in other cultures. The lesson for relationsips between the people of God and other cults and cultures will be that the use of communicational *forms* common to both is acceptable and advisable, while the biblical distinctives of worldview and theology must be maintained.

Although biblical sages consider that they have a proper understanding of God, there is still no comprehensive picture of God and his purposes that emerges in Wisdom literature. God defies total comprehension by humans for the exact reason that he is so radically distinct. This is the message of Job par excellence. No one can say, "I have captured the essence of God and existence perfectly." But the evidence pointing to his nature and the meaning of existence are sufficient to produce *trust* and *hope* in meaning and significance for humanity. The key, repeated time and again, is to begin with fear of the Lord.

Only this realization—that he is the sovereign Lord of our existence Who can do as he wishes, tempered by his lovingkindness, can serve as a reliable foundation for understanding ourselves and our relationship to the world around us. "The fear of the Lord is the beginning of wisdom" (Pr 1:7).

The Nature of Biblical Wisdom Literature

James Crenshaw argues that biblical wisdom is a marriage of form and content. It is not one or the other. Felicitous, memorable form conveys particular content.

> ...formally, wisdom consists of proverbial sentence or instruction, debate, intellectual reflection; thematically wisdom comprises self-evident intuitions about mastering life for human betterment, gropings after life's secrets with regard to innocent suffering, grappling with finitude, and a quest for truth concealed in the created order and manifested in Dame wisdom. When a marriage between form and content exists, there is Wisdom literature (Crenshaw 1981:19).

Scholars like Crenshaw cited above have isolated numerous subtypes of Wisdom literature. But for more popular purposes, wisdom can be said to exist in two major categories. Zuck designates these two kinds as proverbial and reflective. Neither is designed to state or teach guaranteed cause-effect relationships. Proverbial literature constitutes "guidelines, not guarantees; precepts, not premises" (Zuck 1991:132). The reflective material discusses and probes the mysteries of life—as in Job and Ecclesiastes (Zuck 1991:132).

As pedagogical material designed chiefly for royal families and the governing class, Wisdom literature is a very creative approach that invites—and incites—interaction. Perhaps we can say that wisdom, or the final insight the authors wish the students to achieve, is not simply *in* the literature but is a product of contemplation *about* it.

Again and again, we shall return to similarities, particularly in form, between biblical wisdom and that of surrounding nations. "Biblical Wisdom literature, like Hebrew poetry, must be understood in an international context" (Hill and Walton 1991:250). Not only can many parallels in style be noted between Hebrew, Egyptian, and Mesopotamian writers, the Hebrew sages themselves indicate knowledge of other wisdom traditions (Hill and Walton 1991:248-49). There are many startling similarities in the subject matter and content between Hebrew and non-

Hebrew wisdom. More will be said of this later, but the explanation in brief is that humans everywhere must grapple with similar problems of their existence. Hill and Walton do not feel we need to assume borrowing to explain the similarities.

> ...the resemblances are as much the product of the universal nature of attempts to cope with the problems associated with human existence as they are a result of any cultural or literary borrowing (Hill and Walton 1991:252).

Still, if the similarities are there in both form and content and if we believe all Scripture to be inspired by God (2Ti 3:16), we have to ask how the non-Hebrew sages obtained their insights. Shall we conclude that the human mind is universally capable of reliable or true insights within certain limits, but that only those contained in Scripture have the imprimatur of God upon them? We will return to a consideration of "intercultural" relatedness later.

What really constitutes the root concern of Wisdom literature? Some have stressed anthropology—the idea that reflection on the experience of humankind is at the root of wisdom. Others stress that cosmology or world order is the fundamental concern. Still others stress that theodicy—the establishment of God's justice—is the key. This latter certainly has merit based on extensive sections of Job and Ecclesiastes. But over all, each of these may be considered to be rooted in creation according to Perdue (Perdue 1991:12). Unfortunately, while grasping this key fact, Perdue apparently is convinced that the biblical creation account is mythic. He categorizes his approach as "metaphorical theology" (Perdue 1991:22). Although for him the creation account is a myth, it is clearly the main metaphor giving order and purpose in life. This, after all, is the central task not only of wisdom but of religion itself.

While accepting Perdue's conclusion that creation is the central "explanation generating" element of wisdom, it would be sad to stop short at creation, as Paul in Romans 1:18-32 indicates so many have done. Why not find the locus and generating force of wisdom in the Creator himself and conclude as Hill and Walton, "The basic goal of Hebrew wisdom was a proper relationship to Yahweh, the very God of wisdom" (Hill and Walton 1991:259).

The Forms of Biblical Wisdom Literature

The similarity of biblical Wisdom literature to that of other cultures in the ancient Near East is recognized by many. Crenshaw notes that allusions to the wisdom of surrounding nations are scattered throughout the Hebrew Bible. These allusions "have assumed greater force again and again as literature from Egypt and Mesopotamia has come to light. Similarities between Israelite wisdom and that of her powerful neighbors to the south and east abound, but decisive differences also exist" (Crenshaw 1981:212).

The writer of 1 Kings 4:29-34 indicates that a category of wise men or sages existed in the surrounding nations, and apparently some of these were well-known, yet none surpassed Solomon.

Solomon's wisdom was greater than the wisdom of all the men of the East, and greater than all the wisdom of Egypt. He was wiser than any other man, including Ethan the Ezrahite—wiser than Heman, Calcol and Darda, the sons of Mahol. And his fame spread to all the surrounding nations.

References to the wisdom of other nations are scattered throughout the Old Testament, including that of the Edomites and Arabians (Jer 49:7 and Ob 8), the Babylonians (Isa 47:10 and Da 4:4), and, of course, the Egyptians (Ex 7:11). While these citations recognize the existence of sages and wisdom outside Israel, they are frequently critical in tone. The Exodus 7:11 passage indicates that the Egyptian sages are ranked alongside sorcerers and magicians—something quite distinct from the Hebrews. Solomon, who is said to be encyclopedic in his knowledge (1Ki 4:29-34), is never said to be nor shown to be involved with occult arts.

While many similarities in the forms and issues of Wisdom literature can be noted, some experts have flatly concluded that the Hebrew concept of wisdom *(hokmah)* is not strictly parallel to the idea of wisdom in Egypt or Babylonia. Babylonian wisdom means skill in cult and magic lore (Lambert 1967). As we have already seen, this pertained to Egyptian sages also.

The Old Testament Wisdom literature includes the contributions of certain non-Hebrew sages. Agur and Lemuel, writers of Proverbs 30 and 31, respectively, are from Massa. They were from the northern Arabian tribe of Massa, a son of Ishmael noted in Genesis 25:14. Eliphaz the Temanite in Job is from Edom (Job 2:11). In fact, Uz, the home of Job, was apparently in Edom (La 4:21), and Job's name is a shortened form of Jobab, an Edomite king mentioned in Genesis 36:34 who is nevertheless not to be identified with Job himself (Hill and Walton 1991:251). The point that Job may not have been Hebrew is perhaps insignificant, since the general setting of the book seems to antedate the existence of the Hebrews as a people. Job, like the progenitor of the Hebrew people, Abraham of Ur, simply illustrates that God was working more broadly in the ancient Near East than after the "concentration" of the chosen people, the sons of Abraham in Canaan as the Hebrew people, after they were called to be a separate, holy nation (Ge 12:1-3).

In summary, the similarity of forms and subject matter in Hebrew and non-Hebrew wisdom is striking. One has only to read from the *Egyptian Instructions: The Instruction of the Vizier Ptah-hotep* (Pritchard 1969:412-14) to see the resemblance of the vizier's description of old age to that of Ecclesiastes 12. His description of women who lead one astray compares with that of Proverbs 5:3-15, and his instructions for eating with royalty are similar to the instructions in Proverbs 23:1-4. Judging from the amount of movement around the ancient Near East testified to in 1 Kings 4 and observed earlier in the origins of Abraham and Job, it is only natural to see parallels in thought forms and issues and literary styles. Is there a message in these similarities for the Christian movement and, in particular, the Christian missionary?

There is no doubt that the Old Testament writers hoped that their wisdom and the knowledge of Yahweh would spread to all the world. Solomon clearly shows this in his dedication of the temple in 1 Kings 8:41-43. The Hebrew writers were concerned that all the world know of the acts of Yahweh and his wisdom. What better way to communicate in a manner understandable to the nations? How much thought have we given to expressing Christian truth today in forms agreeable to non-Christian hearers? The Catholic De Nobili tried among Brahmin-class Hindus, and William Carey made significant contributions to Indian literature apart from his translation of the Scriptures. We need to use less of the literary or communicational forms familiar in our own cultures and more of those found in non-Christian cultures.

Indigenous theologies and indigenous church movements have multipied in this century. The African Independent Church

Movement has been well-documented by David Barrett (Barrett 1968). Latin American and Asian theologians have produced their own contextualized theologies. There have been evangelical attempts to produce more indigenous theologies, but what is at the root of this effort? Gailyn Van Rheenan, following Timothy Warner, has observed that all religions syncretize to some extent (Van Rheenen 1991:95-96). There seems to be an insuppressible urge to make our own contribution, which probably has a lot to do with establishing a sense of our own significance in the world. One legitimate way to recognize this may be to recognize the truths already found in the wisdom of diverse cultures, insofar as it squares with biblical norms. Another is to encourage both national and expatriate Christian workers to use indigenous literary forms to express Christian truths.

The Content of Wisdom Literature

Wisdom literature differs from the other major bodies of the canonical books of the Old Testament. The Historical books, the Prophets—major and minor and the Poetry of the Psalms abound with instructions about or condemnations of any other worship than that of Yahweh. It seems amazing that in a body of pedagogy as rich as the Hebrew Wisdom literature more would not be said regarding other religions and cultures. For example, Wisdom literature abounds in advice against adultery (Pr 6:20-7:27; Ecc 7:26-28; Job 31:1-12); but Wisdom literature never uses adultery as an analogy for consorting with other cults or cultures. On the other hand, among the Prophets, adultery and fornication routinely constitute the analogies for any relationship between Israel and the worship of foreign gods. Isaiah scorns those who commit adultery: "Among the oaks and under every spreading tree: you sacrifice your children in the ravines...you made your bed on a high and lofty hill; there you went to offer your sacrifices" (57:3-8).

In the same way, Jeremiah uses adultery as the despicable figure for serving other gods (3:8; 23:13-14), as well as a literal sin of the unfaithful prophets. Hosea, likewise (2:2), in the lengthiest living analogy of all, fulminates against the adultery of Israel with foreign gods.

Strangely, though, there is little reference to the evils of other religious cults in Wisdom literature. Once Job refers in 12:6

to the "tents of marauders (who) are undisturbed and those who provoke God are secure—those who carry their god in their hands." In Job 36:13-14, the godless are said to "harbor resentment...they die in their youth among male prostitutes of the shrines." But in forty-two chapters these are the only references—albeit depreciative—to other religious cults.

Proverbs, likewise, contains hardly any reference to other cults or cultures. Certainly, we learn that "Yahweh detests the sacrifice of the wicked, but the prayer of the upright pleases Him" (15:8-9). He sees everything "keeping watch on the wicked and the good" (15:3). These references certainly relate to the wicked and good of Israel and logically extend beyond Israel, but other foreign (or indigenous) cults are not specifically named.

Song of Songs makes extensive reference to the Shulamite maiden who in all probability is or represents someone from within Israel. Solomon had many foreign wives, but it is very possible this woman is from Shunem or that her name simply means "perfect one" from the same Hebrew root *(slm)*. There is also the possibility that her name relates to the goddess Sala or Sulmanitu, equivalents to Ishtar. There are proponents of the theory that Song of Songs represents a sacred marriage; if so, we have serious difficulties in terms of squaring the teaching of the book with other biblical literature. The Ishtar interpretation is not, however, deemed creditable by most (Huwiler 1992:1227).

So, apart from references to rivers flowing from Lebanon (4:15), the Shulamite likened to one of Pharoah's chariot fillies (1:9), and Solomon having a vineyard in Baal Haman (8:11), we see little reference to foreign cultures or religious practices.

The same applies to Ecclesiastes. Yahweh is seen as Creator and Center of Hebrew cosmology (3:11; 11:5); but no other cults receive mention in the book. However, the question remains as to why in a library of Hebrew pedagogy there would not be more instruction on the relation of rulers, nobles, or even common people to the cults and cultures surrounding Israel.

Perdue has commented extensively on this phenomenon in his W*isdom and Cult* (Perdue 1977). He notes that many scholars (among them Paul Humbert, Duesberg and Fransen, McKane, and Von Rad) have observed this lack of interest in cults among the sages. The theory was that the sages saw themselves as distinct from the priestly class and more concerned about the relationships or obligations of humans in society (Perdue 1977:5-6).

Perdue himself takes a differing stance. He believes, as does this writer, that it would be strange for a sage to be unconcerned with cultic matters. The central task of the wise man is to understand himself and find a place for himself (and all who share his wisdom) in the midst of an apparently unstable world. He desires to understand things in such a way that he will never be shaken off balance by events. Achieving this goal demands an understanding of one's relationship to the supernatural and the manner in which it is approached (Perdue 1977:12). The sages may have seen themselves in another "union" distinct from the priests and the prophets whose task more closely related to cults; but they could not and did not either depreciate or separate themselves from it.

Despite the special thematic and literary relationship that may be demonstrated between ancient Near Eastern and Hebrew wisdom, one fundamental difference remains. Unlike the other ancients who paid homage to assorted pantheons of deities, the Israelite wisdom of the Old Testament acknowledged only one God, Yahweh (Pr 22:17-19). Thus, the Hebrews denied materialism (since matter was created by God), pantheism (because Yahweh as Creator was above all creation), and dualism (since creation was originally made "good" by God). Ideologically, this meant that the Hebrews owed allegiance to Yahweh alone and had neither room nor time for these false deities and competing religious systems. Practically speaking, however, the facts of Hebrew history indicate that this was not always the case (Hill and Walton 1991:252).

The relative lack of condemnation of other cults in Hebrew wisdom, together with the paucity of instruction about cults in Israel, should not, then, be taken as openness to the practices of other religions and cultures. We may assume the Hebrew sages (except Job) were fully aware of the Law and the Prophets. They could settle on their task as one complementary to that of the priests and prophets. But their testimony to Yahweh as the unique fountain of wisdom is uniform.

Job tells us that in Yahweh's hands "...is the life of every creature and the breath of all mankind" (12:10). Proverbs claims at the outset that the fear of the Lord is the beginning of wisdom (1:7) and concludes with Lemuel calling that same fear the fundamental characteristic of the perfect woman (31:30). Agur also agreed that "every word of God is flawless" (30:5). Ecclesiastes concludes after all its dark forbodings, "Fear God and keep His commandments, for in this is the whole duty of man" (12:13).

In the content of Hebrew wisdom we see a single arrow pointing to one North Pole. Biblical wisdom is a compass for Israel and all humankind. Yahweh is the One to whom we must turn in reverent submission for the wisdom by which to conduct our lives. As we live among and relate to all the peoples of the earth, we cannot do less than give them the compass imparted to us by these sages and the rest of Scripture writers. Anything else leads to a detour or a deadend—all else constitutes a dangerous trail leading to the precipice of pluralism and the maelstrom of modern confusion.

Reference List

Crenshaw, James L.
    1981   *Old Testament Wisdom, An Introduction.* Atlanta: John Knox.

Hill, Andrew E. and John H. Walton.
    1991   *A Survey of the Old Testament.* Grand Rapids, MI: Zondervan.

Huwiler, Elizabeth.
    1992   "Shulamite." In *Anchor Bible Dictionary.* Vol. 5. P. 1227. New York: Doubleday.

Lambert, W. G.
    1967   *Babylonian Wisdom Literature.* Oxford: Clarendon.

Larkin, William J. Jr.
    1988   *Culture and Biblical Hermeneutics.* Grand Rapids: Baker.

Parsons, Greg W.
    1993   "Guidelines for Understanding and Proclaiming the Book of Proverbs." *Bibliotheca Sacra* 150(598):151-70.

Perdue, Leo G.
   1977   *Wisdom and Cult: A Critical Analysis of the Views of Cult in the Wisdom Literature of Israel and the Ancient Near East.* Missoula, MT: Scholars.
   1991   *Wisdom in Revolt: Metaphorical Theology in the Book of Job.* Decatur, GA: Almond.

Pritchard, James B.
   1969   *Ancient Near Eastern Texts Relating to the Old Testament.* 3rd edition. Princeton, NJ: Princeton University.

Terrien, Samuel.
   1952   *The Psalms and Their Meaning for Today.* New York: The Bobbs-Merrill.

Waltke, Bruce K.
   1979   "The Book of Proverbs and Old Testament Theology." *Bibliotheca Sacra.* 136:302-17.

Zuck, Roy B.
   1978   *Job.* Chicago: Moody Press.
   1991   *Basic Bible Interpretation.* Wheaton, IL: Victor.

4

"TO WHOM SHALL YOU COMPARE ME?" YAHWEH'S POLEMIC AGAINST BAAL AND THE BABYLONIAN IDOL-GODS IN PROPHETIC LITERATURE

Robert B. Chisholm, Jr.

Yahweh, the sovereign creator of the universe and the covenant God of Israel, jealously defends his honor and tolerates no rivals. Throughout the Old Testament we see him attacking the so-called gods of the nations through word and deed. In the days of Moses he emasculated Pharaoh and the gods of Egypt through his destructive judgments, culminating in the death of Egypt's firstborn. Later, as his people faced the temptations of Canaanite religion, he affirmed and demonstrated his superiority to Baal and the gods of Canaan. Still later, while his people languished in exile as a result of their sin, he taunted and then humiliated the gods of the neo-Babylonian empire.

This paper will focus on the second and third phases of Yahweh's ongoing war with the pagan gods, especially as it finds expression in the Former and Latter Prophets of the Hebrew canon. We will first look at Yahweh's polemic against Baalism in Israel's early history and literature, including the Former Prophets (Jos-Ki). We will then look at Isaiah's polemic against the Babylonian gods in Isaiah 40-55. Along the way we will take note of Yahweh's strategy in combating the pagan gods. Hopefully this survey will have some implications for modern Christians as they confront pagan "gods" in their culture and in the context of missionary endeavor.

The Polemic against Baal[1]

Baal was the most important of the Canaanite gods. As a fertility deity and the lord of the storm, Baal promised his devotees children and agricultural prosperity, both of which were highly prized in ancient Canaan.

The Ugaritic myths picture Baal as a powerful warrior king who controls the elements of the storm. Many of his names and titles reflect this role, including "mightiest Baal" (*aliyn b'l*), "mightiest of warriors" (*aliy qrdm*), "Haddu, lord of the storm-cloud" (*hd d'nn*), and "rider of the clouds" (*rkb 'rpt*). According to the myths, Baal appoints a time "for the sounding of his voice in the clouds, for him to release (his) lightnings on the earth" (*CTA* 4 v 70-71; *CML*, 60-61).[2] He hurls "seven lightning bolts . . . eight magazines of thunder," while brandishing "a spear of lightning" (Pope and Tigay 1971:118; Cross 1973:147-48).

As the lord of the storm, Baal was the source of agricultural blessing. He provided rain and food for all:

> A source (of blessing) to the earth was the rain of Baal and to the field(s) the rain of the Most High; a delight to the earth was the rain of Baal and to the field(s) the rain of the Most High, a delight to the wheat in the furrow, (to) the spelt in the tilth. . . . The ploughmen did lift up (their) head(s), they that prepared the corn (did lift up their heads) on high; for the bread had failed (in) their bins, the wine had failed in their skins, the oil had failed in their (cruses) (*CTA* 16 iii 4-16; *CML*, 98).

Baal "fattens gods and men" and "satisfies the multitudes of the earth" (*CTA* 4 vii 50-52; *CML*, 66). When he is dead, the "furrows in the fields are cracked" (*CTA* 6 iv 25-29; *CML*, 78), "but when he lives the heavens rain down oil and the ravines flow with honey" (*CTA* 6 iii 6-8; *CML*, 77).

Baal's quest for kingship is the main theme of the myths. Baal defeats his rival Yam, the god of the sea. Following his victory, the goddess Anat calls him "our king, mightiest Baal, our judge, over whom there is none" (*CTA* 3 E 40-41; *CML*, 54). Baal himself boasts, "I alone am he that is king over the gods" (*CTA* 4 vii 49-50; *CML*, 66). With Anat's assistance Baal persuades the high god El to authorize the building of a royal palace. Baal celebrates with a feast, a victorious military campaign, and an awesome theophanic display. Unimpressed by this show of strength, Mot, the god of the underworld, challenges Baal's authority and defeats him. After mourning Baal's death, warlike Anat seeks vengeance. She grabs Mot, kills him, grinds him to dust, and scatters his remains to the wind. Baal returns from his imprisonment in the underworld and once again occupies his throne. Seven years later Mot reappears and again fights Baal. This time Baal wins and Mot reluctantly acknowledges his king-ship.[3]

It is against this background that one must interpret Yahweh's polemic against Baal in the Old Testament. Throughout her history Israel was vulnerable to the allurements of Baalism (cf. Jdg 2:11, 13; 3:7; 6:25-32; 8:33; 10:6, 10; 1Sa 7:4; 12:10; etc.). Yahweh, through his mighty acts and the inspired poetic words they prompted, demonstrated and affirmed his superiority to Baal in an effort to win the allegiance of his fickle covenant people.

As part of his strategy Yahweh contextualized his self-revelation. Several passages in the Old Testament describe Yahweh and his exploits in Baal-like terms. Many of Yahweh's deeds, especially his victories over kings who challenged his sovereignty, parallel Baal's alleged accomplishments and demonstrate that he, not Baal, controls the elements of the storm and possesses authority over the forces of chaos and death. Several of Israel's early poems, many of which were inspired by Yahweh's salvific intervention in the nation's experience, assert that Yahweh is the incomparable king who, like Baal, reveals himself in the storm and subdues all challenges to his rule.

However, there was no danger that Yahweh would be confused with Baal, for Yahweh's self-revelation is solidly rooted in his claim for exclusive worship. Yahweh's self-revelation in the storm often supports his claim for allegiance and affirmations of Yahweh's incomparability often accompany descriptions of his exploits.[4]

This polemical strategy began while Israel was in Egypt and gained momentum in the judges and early monarchical periods, reaching its culmination at Mt. Carmel. Later prophets, especially Hosea, followed up on Yahweh's victory at Carmel by continuing the attack against Baalism.

The Baal Polemic in the Days of Moses

As early as the time of Moses, Yahweh revealed himself as an incomparable warrior-king who, like Baal, controls the elements of the storm and suppresses all challenges to his rule. Yahweh demonstrated his sovereignty over the storm while Israel was still enslaved in the land of Egypt. In conjunction with the seventh plague, he sent thunder, hail, and lightning against Egypt's crops (Ex 9:23-24), proving his incomparability to Pharaoh, who claimed to be Israel's master and refused to acknowledge Yahweh's authority. Before unleashing this destructive storm Yahweh warned Pharaoh: "Let my people go, so that they may worship me, or this time I will send the full force of my plagues against you and against your officials and your people, so you may know that there is no one like me in all the earth" (9:13-14; cf. 8:10).

The revelation of Yahweh's power reached its climax at the Red Sea, where he used the waters to annihilate Pharoah's army. This revelation of Yahweh's awesome military strength prompted Moses to ask: "Who is like you among the gods, O Yahweh? Who is like you—majestic in holiness, awesome in praiseworthy acts, a performer of wonders?" (Ex 15:11). Moses concluded his song with the affirmation that Yahweh "will reign for ever and ever" (v. 18).

In defeating Pharaoh at the Red Sea, Yahweh exhibited his authority over the sea and the underworld, the opponents of Baal in Canaanite myth. Rather than having to defeat the sea and death, Yahweh used both as his instruments in destroying the Egyptians (Ex 15:8, 10, 12).[5] His superiority to Baal is obvious.

In celebrating Yahweh's victory Moses described Yahweh's kingship in terms reminiscent of the Baal myth. Yahweh would lead his people across the Jordan River and establish them in the land, called here the mountain of his inheritance, dwelling-place, and sanctuary (Ex 15:16b-18). From there he would rule as eternal king over his people (v. 18). The precise phrase "mountain of inheritance" (v. 17) occurs only here in the Old Testament, but the Ugaritic myths use a semantically equivalent expression (*gr nhlt*) of Baal's throne or place of rule (see *CTA* 3 C 27 and 3 D 64; *CML*, 49, 51). This mountain, which is associated with Baal's victory over Yam and is called his "hill of victory" (*CTA* 3 C 28; *CML*, 49), is "the territory won by the deity through battle" (Gibson 1978:9; Mullen 1980:59, n. 97). Before Baal's battle with

Yam, Kothar-wa-Khasis tells the storm god: "Truly I tell you, O prince Baal, I repeat to you, o rider on the clouds. Now (you must smite) your foes, Baal, now you must still your enemies. You shall take your everlasting kingdom, your dominion forever and ever" (*CTA* 2 iv 7-10; *CML*, 43). Following Baal's victory onlookers declare: "Yam is indeed dead! Baal shall be king!" (*CTA* 2 iv 32; *CML*, 45). Shortly thereafter both Anat and Athirat refer to Baal as an incomparable king (*CTA* 3 E 40-41, 4 iv 43-44; *CML*, 54, 60). In the same way Yahweh had defeated his enemies (Ex 15:6) and would rule forever as incomparable king (vv. 11, 18) from the mountain of his inheritance (v. 17; Habel 1964:61-2; Miller 1973: 116-7; Day 1985:98).

At Sinai Yahweh revealed himself as the victorious warrior-king who claims the allegiance of the people he has delivered. Elements of the storm, including thunder, lightning, and a thick cloud, accompanied his descent upon the mountain, causing it to smolder and shake (Ex 19:16, 18; Dt 4:11-12). The effects of Yahweh's self-revelation at Sinai resemble closely those of Baal's storm theophany following his victory over Yam:

> Baal uttered his holy voice, Baal repeated the (issue) of his lips; (he uttered) his (holy) voice (and) the earth did quake, (he repeated) the issue of his lips (and) the rocks (did quake); peoples afar off were dismayed (. . .) the peoples of the east; the high places of the earth shook. The foes of Baal clung to the forests, the enemies of Hadad to the hollows of the rock (*CTA* 4 vii 29-37a; *CML*, 65).

Baal's theophany from his new palace is a manifestation of his power as a victorious warrior and an assertion of his kingship and right to rule (Habel 1964:77-8). Through his self-revelation at Sinai, Yahweh was again making the exploits of Baal his own. Yahweh, not Baal, really reigned as the victorious king, a fact demonstrated by the manifestation of his power in the theophany.

Additional parallels to the Baal myth appear in Moses' blessing of the Israelite tribes (Dt 33), which combines the themes of Yahweh's kingship (v. 5), incomparability (v. 26), control over the storm (v. 26), and prowess as a warrior (vv. 27-29). Moses depicted the Lord as coming from Sinai (v. 2), the scene of his enthronement over Israel, to bless his people with military victory

(vv. 7, 11, 17, 22-23, 26-27, 29) and agricultural prosperity (vv. 13-16, 28). The concluding stanza, which begins with an affirmation of Yahweh's incomparability (v. 26), calls him "the God" and the "rider of the heavens," an epithet which is very similar to Baal's title "rider of the clouds." As "rider of the clouds" Baal appears as both warrior and bestower of rain, precisely the roles which Yahweh assumes according to verses 26-29. The warrior Yahweh would drive out the Canaanites, enabling Israel to dwell securely in a land blessed with the grain, wine, and dew he provides (cf. *CTA* 16 iii 4-16; *CML*, 98).

To summarize, from the very beginning of Israel's history, Yahweh revealed himself as the incomparable warrior-king. Like Baal he controls the elements of the storm (Ex 9:22-25; 19:16-19) as the rider of the heavens (Dt 33:26) and suppresses all challenges to his rule (Ex 19:4; Dt 33:29). He is sovereign over the sea and death, which he uses as weapons (Ex 15:8, 10, 12). Following Yahweh's victory at the Red Sea, Moses envisioned a time when Yahweh would lead his people to the mountain of his inheritance where he would defeat the Canaanites, abundantly bless his people, and rule over them forever (Ex 15:16-18; Dt 33:26-29). These Baal-like exploits, accomplished in the historical arena for all to see, are proof of Yahweh's incomparability and kingship (Ex 9:14; 15:11; Dt 33:26) and validated his right to demand Israel's exclusive loyalty and worship (Ex 20:2-5).

The Baal Polemic in the Former Prophets

As Israel moved into the promised land and encountered Baalism, Yahweh again proved his superiority to Baal through his mighty deeds and self-revelation in the storm, while Israel's poets continued to affirm his kingship and incomparability in terms reminiscent of the Baal myths.

On several occasions Yahweh revealed his power in the storm in order to defeat challengers to his authority and/or affirm his right to Israel's allegiance. At Gibeon he hurled hailstones down upon the fleeing Amorites (Jos 10:11). According to the Song of Deborah (Jdg 5), a poetic account of Yahweh's victory over the "kings of Canaan" (v. 19), the stars fought for Israel and the Kishon River swept Sisera's army away (vv. 20-21). The language suggests that Yahweh caused a storm and flashflood, an interpretation consistent with the song's introduction, which pictures Yahweh coming in the storm to do battle (vv. 4-5).[6]

In her song of praise following the birth of Samuel, Hannah portrayed Yahweh as a mighty warrior who "thunders against" his enemies and shatters their power (1Sa 2:4, 9-10). Yahweh is the incomparable, transcendent ruler of the world who protects his people (vv. 2, 8b) and dispenses justice by elevating the oppressed and humiliating the proud (vv. 3, 5-10). Yahweh grants fertility (v. 5) and exercises control over the realm of death (v. 6). In short, this poem describes Yahweh in typically Baal-like terms as a warrior-king who controls the storm and is sovereign over death. By declaring Yahweh the incomparable judge of the world (vv. 2, 10), Hannah also directly attributed to Yahweh another of Baal's royal epithets. In the Baal myth Anat declares: "Mightiest Baal is our king, our judge over whom there is none" (*CTA* 3 E40-41; *CML*, 54). Hannah, a barren woman who could have easily succumbed to Baalism in an effort to find divine blessing, knew that Yahweh, not Baal, was the real king who con-trolled fertility.

Years later, following Israel's repudiation of false gods, including the Baals (1Sa 7:4), Yahweh won a great victory over the Philistines as he thundered from the heavens (v. 10). Just as he would do later at Carmel, Yahweh demonstrated that he, not Baal, controlled the storm. In this way he affirmed the wisdom of the Israelites' decision to serve him exclusively and turn from Baalism (cf. v. 3).

In his farewell address Samuel urged the people to renew their covenantal loyalty to Yahweh and reminded them that Yahweh, not their newly appointed human king, was their true sovereign (1Sa 12:14-15). As proof that he possessed the right and power to bless and curse, Yahweh "sent thunder and rain" upon the ready-to-harvest fields of wheat (vv. 16-18a). Samuel then exhorted the people to serve Yahweh wholeheartedly and warned them not to turn to idols (vv. 20-25).

The Baal polemic culminates at Mt. Carmel. Over the past twenty-five years several scholars have pointed to the polemical character of 1 Kings 17-18, which tells of Elijah's encounter with the prophets of Baal and the incidents leading up to this event (Bronner 1968; Fensham 1980; Saint-Laurent 1980; Battenfield 1988). Following King Ahab's decision to promote Baal worship in the heart of the Northern Kingdom (1Ki 16:31-33), Yahweh sent a drought upon Israel and Phoenicia (the homeland of Ahab's queen, Jezebel). This form of judgment was appropriate for the fertility god Baal promised his worshipers agricultural prosperity. Through the prophet Elijah, Yahweh moved into Phoenicia, Baal's backyard, and supernaturally provided the staples of life for a Phoenician widow (1Ki 17:14) and raised her son from the dead (v. 17), thereby demonstrating his superiority to Baal, who was thought to be subject to Mot, the god of death, during times of prolonged drought. The story climaxes with Elijah's challenge to the prophets of Baal at Carmel. Before the eyes of all Israel, Yahweh proved that he, not Baal, controls the elements of the storm. After Baal's prophets unsuccessfully went through their frantic mourning rites in an effort to rouse their god to action (1Ki 18:26-29), Yahweh, in response to Elijah's prayer, sent fire to consume the sacrifice and then caused it to rain (vv. 36-38, 45). Yahweh's victory over Baal climaxed with the slaughter of Baal's prophets at the Kishon River (v. 40), where years before Yahweh had defeated Canaanite armies in Baal-like fashion (cf. Jdg 4-5). By exhibiting his sovereignty over Baal's traditional spheres of authority, Yahweh established his right to Israel's undivided loyalty. Israel must look to Yahweh, the one true God (1Ki 18:24, 37, 39), for the necessities of life. Baalism was not an option.

To summarize, the polemic against Baalism inaugurated in Moses' time gained momentum during the periods of the judges and the early monarchy. Yahweh continued to reveal himself as an incomparable warrior-king who, like Baal, controls the elements of the storm (Jos 10:11; Jdg 5:4-5; 1Sa 2:10; 7:10; 12:16-18), defeats those who challenge his rule (Jos 10; Jdg 5), and exercises dominion over the realm of death (1Sa 2:6). However, there was no danger that Yahweh would be confused with Baal, for Yahweh's self-revelation was designed to demonstrate his incomparability (1Sa 2:2) and his sole right to Israel's allegiance (1Sa 7, 12).

Main Features of Yahweh's Anti-Baal Strategy

Yahweh's polemical attack on Baal must be understood within the framework of Yahwistic exclusivism. Within Yahwism there was no room for other deities or for any form of syncretism. At the same time Yahweh contextualized his self-revelation, usurping Baal's position as king and his role as the sovereign dispenser of human and agricultural fertility. Rather than philosophically denying Baal's existence, Yahweh took a much more practical approach which accommodated the cultural situation of ancient Israel. Through word and deed he demonstrated that he alone could meet the very real needs which Baalism claimed to satisfy. In this way he destroyed any basis or motivation for Baal worship. It was irrelevant whether or not Baal really existed; the important point for Israel was that Baal could not deliver what he promised, while Yahweh could. In short, Yahweh contextualized his self-revelation for maximum effect without compromising to any degree his claim for exclusive allegiance. To put it another way, contextualization compelled one to exclusivism; it did not blur the distinction between Yahweh and Baal and foster syncretism.

Yahweh's War against the Gods of Babylon

Isaiah's Polemic against the Idol-Gods

As the prophet Isaiah addressed the future exiles, he knew they would be discouraged and concerned about their future. Some would think that the Lord had rejected his people or treated them unfairly. Having been defeated by the Babylonians, some might conclude that the Babylonian idol-gods were superior to Yahweh and be tempted to worship them. The prophet's task was to encourage the exiles by reminding them that Yahweh was the incomparable Creator and sovereign Ruler of the world who had temporarily chastised them for their sins, but still held their destiny in his hands. No one, not even the idol-gods of Babylon, would be able to thwart his purposes.

As part of his strategy the prophet taunted the Babylonian idol-gods by emphasizing their manmade status and contrasting them with Yahweh. Human craftspeople make the idol-gods (40:19-20; 41:7), but Yahweh created the craftspeople (54:16). In other words, Yahweh created the creator of the idol-god! A craftsperson makes an idol from wood (40:22), but Yahweh created the trees which supply the wood (41:19) and receives their worship (44:23). All of Lebanon's great trees could not fuel an adequate sacrificial fire for Yahweh (40:16), but an idol is made from the same wood people use to cook their food and warm their hands (44:15). Craftspeople exhaust their strength to form their idols (44:12), but Yahweh can give his weary people supernatural strength (40:29-31). Idol worshipers use the refining process (40:19; 41:7; 46:6) to shape their metallic gods (44:9-10), but Yahweh refines (48:10) and forms (44:2) his people. A worker overlays (Heb. *raqaʿ*) an idol with metal (40:19) and stretches a measuring line over his work (44:13); Yahweh "spreads out" (Heb. *raqaʿ*) the earth (42:5; 44:24) and stretches out the heavens (40:22). People set up (Heb. *kun*) their idols (40:20) in puny little shrines (44:13); Yahweh establishes (Heb. *kun*) the earth (45:18), sits on its horizon, and raises up and brings down kingdoms (40:22). Yahweh frustrates the mere human wisdom and skill that produces an idol (44:25; cf. 40:20). Idols can be carried off into exile (46:1-2), but Yahweh carries and supports his people (46:3-4). In these passages Yahweh is the active king of the world; humanity is the product of his creation and the recipient of his help. By contrast the pagan idol-gods are inactive products of frail human creative efforts and cannot help their worshipers.

Isaiah's polemic against the Babylonian gods accurately reflects the Babylonians' obsession with idols. With regard to Mesopotamian idols, Oppenheim observes: "There are two distinct levels on which the image played a role within the cult life of the sanctuary: it served as the focal point for sacrificial activities, and it was carried in the internal and outdoor ceremonies that related the city to the deity" (Oppenheim 1977:185). He explains that the images "had to undergo an elaborate and highly secret ritual of consecration to transform the lifeless matter into a receptacle of the divine presence. During these nocturnal ceremonies they were endowed with 'life,' their eyes and mouths were 'opened' so that the images could see and eat" (1977, 185-86). The idol-gods were "fed" large quantities of food, requiring a large number of temple personnel, including butchers, brewers, and bakers (1977:188-89; Beaulieu 1993:246-47).

Yahweh versus the Babylonian Diviners

Divination was also fundamental to Babylonian religion.[7] According to Wilson (1980:91-92), there were two underlying components to Babylonian divination theory. First, the Babylonians "saw all aspects of reality as an interlocking totality. Historical occurrences and elements of human experience were not thought to be isolated phenomena but were seen as part of a much larger matrix." If one knew an event's "past context," the event had "predictive potential." Consequently "scribes very early began to catalogue all sorts of unusual occurrences together with the events that accompanied them." Second, the Mesopotamians viewed the gods as "intimately involved in everyday happenings." The gods communicated their will through events. Consequently it was "only necessary to interpret events properly in order for the desire of the gods to be uncovered." In addition to observing casual phenomena, other popular divination techniques included the examination of animals' inner organs and astrological observations.

Because they could discern the will of the gods and control the future, diviners were indispensable to Mesopotamian society. As Wilson observes, the king "required their services in order to make political, religious, and social decisions." He consulted them when making political appointments and formulating battle plans. Diviners would even lead armies on occasion (1980:97-98).

Yahweh announced through Isaiah that he would undermine this entire system and bring the neo-Babylonian empire to its demise. In Isaiah 44:24-25 he declares: "I am the LORD . . . who foils the signs of false prophets and makes fools of diviners, who overthrows the learning of the wise and turns it into non-sense" (cf. also 47:13).[8]

In 539 B.C. Yahweh made this threat reality. A partial eclipse of the moon occurred on June 13, 539 B.C., which must have been interpreted as a bad omen by the moon-worshiper Nabonidus and his astrologers (Beaulieu 1993:260-61). About that same time Nabonidus, aware of the rising Persian military threat, gathered huge quantities of idols into Babylon to prevent their being captured by the invaders and to ensure the protection of the land (Beaulieu 1993:242-43, 257). His efforts failed for Yahweh, the ruler of the world, had signalled and decreed that Babylon would fall and all the idol-gods and astrologers in the world could not change that decision. Shortly thereafter Belshazzar saw Babylon's fate announced by the mysterious "handwriting on the wall." Cyrus conquered the neo-Babylonian empire and decreed that God's exiled people could return to their homeland.

Main Features of Yahweh's Attack on Babylonian Religion

Like his war against Pharaoh and the gods of Egypt, Yahweh's attack on Babylonian religion was direct and hard-hitting. Perhaps Yahweh prefers this approach when his people are in an especially desperate situation and need their faith energized as a prelude to a mighty act of deliverance. At any rate, Yahweh both insulted and injured the Babylonians, sarcastically ridiculing their idol-gods and then causing their religious system to fail. Again we see that Yahweh refuses to share his glory with any other would-be deity (cf. Isa 42:8) and gives his people tangible and incontrovertible evidence of his incomparability and sovereignty.

Concluding Observations and Questions

Based on our survey we can make the following concluding observations:

1) During the Old Testament period Yahweh was active in the world and demonstrated his incomparability in tangible and incontrovertible ways. In the process the pagan gods were revealed to be impotent, unworthy of devotion, and incapable of thwarting Yahweh's purposes.

2) Yahweh demanded exclusive worship and tolerated no rivals. He was unwilling to share his glory with any other "god." One senses that the word "pluralism" does not exist in the divine vocabulary; indeed the spirit of religious pluralism was antithetical to Yahwism.

3) Yahweh sometimes contextualized his self-revelation, but such contextualization had a polemical design and rode on the back of a clearly articulated demand for exclusive allegiance. Contextualization compelled one toward exclusivism; it did not promote syncretism.

Our study and conclusions raise several questions:

1) Does Yahweh engage in a power struggle with paganism today? If so, how? Should we expect him to reveal himself in the same tangible and incontrovertible manner that we see in the Old Testament?

2) Should the proclamation of the gospel be characterized by the same degree of exclusivism that we see in ancient Yahwism?

3) What implications does the Baal polemic have for modern theories and methods of contextualization? While the Baal polemic certainly legitimizes a form of contextualization, is contextualization only legitimate when coupled with exclusivistic demands concerning loyalty and worship?

4) In a polytheistic context should we champion pure monotheism or promote a practical monotheism that emphasizes the incomparability of God?

Notes

[1] This section of the paper is an abridged and revised version of a portion of Chisholm (1994).

[2] Unless indicated otherwise, this paper identifies the mythological texts according to the sigla employed by Herdner (1963, abbreviated *CTA*). Unless indicated otherwise, transla-tions of the texts are from Gibson (1978, abbreviated *CML*).

[3] For a survey of the major interpretations of the Baal cycle, a reading of the myth, and extensive bibliography, see Smith (1986).

[4] Though many acknowledge the close parallels between the biblical account of Yahweh's mighty deeds and the mythological description of Baal's exploits, these same scholars disagree over the significance of these parallels. Some regard the parallels as evidence of a demythologizing phase in Israel's religious evolution, while others attribute them to mere literary borrowing or to a common Semitic literary milieu in which warrior-kings are described in somewhat stereotypical terms. In light of the clear polemical pattern revealed in 1 Kings 17-18 (whereby Yahweh makes Baal's deeds his own and thereby usurps Baal's authority), it is far more likely that the Old Testament in many cases utilized mythological motifs for polemical purposes.

The appearance of incomparability formulae in several pertinent contexts (cf. Ex 9:14; 15:11; 18:11; Dt 33:26; 1Sa 2:2; Ps 18:31) supports this thesis. In ancient Assyro-Babylonian hymns, expressions of incomparability were used of various deities without any notion of exclusivism being implied (Labuschagne 1966:53-54). As such they appear to be, in the words of Labuschagne (1966:66), "nothing more than exclamations of praise without any comparative notion." However, within the framework of the Old Testament's militantly exclusivistic Yahwism (cf. Ex 20:2-5a), such expressions, rather than being idiomatic hyperbole, are inherently comparative/polemical and, in their respective contexts, affirm Yahweh's uniqueness and right to rule over his people (cf. Ex 9:14; Dt 33:26; 1Sa 2:2; 2Sa 7:22; 1Ki 8:23; Ps 86:8; Jer 10:6-7). For a detailed defense of this view, see Labuschagne (1966:64-123). For further discussion of orthodox Yahwism's exclusivism and militant attitude toward other gods, see Block (1988:67-68). Block states: "According to the orthodox Yahwist, the God of Israel would brook no rivals. In this respect the Hebrew view of Israel's relationship to its patron deity differed fundamentally from the perceptions of all of the other nations around."

In this context, where the sea, not the literal ground, engulfs the enemy, it is likely that Heb. *'rṣ* refers to the realm of death. See Cross (1973:129).

In *CTA* 3 B 40-41 (*CML*, 48) the stars are sources of rain. Thus Jdg 5:20 may picture the stars fighting by pouring forth rain and causing the Kishon to flood. For other interpretive options see Craigie (1969:262-63; 1977:33-38).

For a thorough study of Mesopotamian divination and how modern scholars have interpreted it, see Cryer (1994:124-215).

MT's *bdym* (cf. also Jer 50:36 and perhaps Hos 11:6) is problematic. *The Hebrew and Aramaic Lexicon of the Old Testament.* (3rd ed., Eng. version; abbrev. *HAL³*) suggests the word is related to Amorite *baddum*, which they define as "oracle priest" (p. 109). According to the *Chicago Assyrian Dictionary* (2:27; abbrev. *CAD*) *baddu* refers in the Mari correspondence to a military official. In light of the Mesopotamian background of Isa 44:25, it might be preferable to read *brym* "*baru*-priests." *HAL³* (Eng. version, p. 153) offers this as a possibility. See also North (1964:144). These priests were divination specialists. See Oppenheim (1977:212), Wilson (1980:93-98) and *CAD*, 2:121-125.

Reference List

Battenfield, James R.
    1988   "YHWH's Refutation of the Baal Myth through the Actions of Elijah and Elisha." In *Israel's Apostasy and Restoration: Essays in Honor of Roland K. Harrison*. A. Gileadi, ed. Pp. 19-37. Grand Rapids, MI: Baker.

Beaulieu, Paul-Alain
    1993   "An Episode in the Fall of Babylon to the Persians." *Journal of Near Eastern Studies* 52:241-61.

Block, Daniel I.
    1988   *The Gods of the Nations*. ETSMS 2. Jackson.

Bronner, Leah.
    1968   *The Stories of Elijah and Elisha as Polemics against Baal Worship*. Leiden: E. J. Brill.

Chisholm, Robert B.
    1994   "The Polemic against Baalism in Israel's Early History and Literature." *Bibliotheca Sacra* 151:267-83.

Craigie, Peter C.
    1969   "The Song of Deborah and the Epic of Tukulti-Ninurta." *Journal of Biblical Literature* 88:253-65.
    1977   "Three Ugaritic Notes on the Song of Deborah." *Journal for the Study of the Old Testament* 2:33-49.

Cross, Frank M.
    1973   *Canaanite Myth and Hebrew Epic*. Cambridge, MA: Harvard.

Cryer, Frederick H.
    1994   *Divination in Ancient Israel and its Near Eastern Environment*. JSOTS 142. Sheffield, England: JSOT.

Day, John
    1985   *God's Conflict with the Dragon and the Sea*. Cambridge: Cambridge University.

Fensham, F. Charles
    1980   "A Few Observations on the Polarisation between Yahweh and Baal in 1 Kings 17-19." *Zeitschrift für die alttestamentliche Wissenschaft* 92:227-36.

Gibson, J. C. L.
    1978   *Canaanite Myths and Legends.* 2nd edition. Edinburgh: T & T Clark.

Habel, Norman C.
    1964   *Yahweh Versus Baal.* New York: Bookman.

Herdner, Andree
    1963   *Corpus des tablettes en cuneiformes alphabetiques.* Paris: Imprimerie Nationale.

Labuschagne, C. J.
    1966   *The Incomparability of Yahweh in the Old Testament.* Leiden: E. J. Brill.

Miller, Patrick D.
    1973   *The Divine Warrior in Early Israel.* Cambridge, MA: Harvard.

Mullen, E. Theodore, Jr.
    1980   *The Divine Council in Canaanite and Early Hebrew Literature.* Chico, CA: Scholars.

North, C. R.
    1964   *The Second Isaiah.* Oxford: Oxford University.

Oppenheim, A. Leo
    1977   *Ancient Mesopotamia.* Revised edition. Chicago: University of Chicago.

Pope, Marvin and Jeffrey Tigay
    1971   "A Description of Baal." *Ugarit Forschungen* 3:117-30.

Saint-Laurent, George E.
    1980   "Light from Ras Shamra on Elijah's Ordeal upon Mount Carmel." In *Scripture in Context: Essays on the Comparative Method.* C. D. Evans, W. W. Hallo, and J. B. White, eds. Pp. 123-39. Pittsburg: Pickwick.

Smith, Mark S.
    1986   "Interpreting the Baal Cycle." *Ugarit Forschungen* 18:313-39.

Wilson, Robert R.
    1980   *Prophecy and Society in Ancient Israel.* Philadelphia: Fortress.

5

THE CONTRIBUTION OF THE GOSPELS AND ACTS TO A BIBLICAL THEOLOGY OF RELIGIONS

William J. Larkin, Jr.

The Gospels and Acts are uniquely qualified to make a contribution to a biblical theology of religions. Although some are convinced that the Gospels, particularly the synoptic Gospels, do not tell us anything of what Jesus taught about other religions (Schmidt 1992:104-105), there is evidence that Jesus and the gospel writers were very aware of and, to the extent their material and aims allowed, sought to address the first century context of religious pluralism. Though they portray Jesus as Messiah focusing on Israel during his earthly ministry (Mt 15:24; cf. 10:6), they do present his encounters with Gentiles, persons of other religious heritages (Mt 8:5-13/Lk 7:1-10; Mt 15:21-28/Mk 7:24-30; Lk 17:16-19; cf. Jn 12:20-26). They show from their report of Jesus' teaching that he did envision for his disciples a mission to the Gentiles (Mt 24:14/Mk 13:10; Mt 26:13/Mk 14:9; Mt 28:18-20; Lk 24:46-47; cf. Scott 1990). It must be constantly born in mind that these gospel writers and their audiences operate in a religiously pluralistic environment (Carson, Moo, Morris 1992:75-76, 99, 117-118; Ball 1992:80).

The Gospel of John also envisions a Gentile mission (Jn 10:16; 11:52). It too contains Jesus' encounter with those of other religions, including a most extensive dialogue with the Samaritan woman (Jn 4:1-42; 12:20-26). The difference of this gospel's language and style from other New Testament writings indicates

Fensham, F. Charles
    1980   "A Few Observations on the Polarisation between Yahweh and Baal in 1 Kings 17-19." *Zeitschrift für die alttestamentliche Wissenschaft* 92:227-36.

Gibson, J. C. L.
    1978   *Canaanite Myths and Legends.* 2nd edition. Edinburgh: T & T Clark.

Habel, Norman C.
    1964   *Yahweh Versus Baal.* New York: Bookman.

Herdner, Andree
    1963   *Corpus des tablettes en cuneiformes alphabetiques.* Paris: Imprimerie Nationale.

Labuschagne, C. J.
    1966   *The Incomparability of Yahweh in the Old Testament.* Leiden: E. J. Brill.

Miller, Patrick D.
    1973   *The Divine Warrior in Early Israel.* Cambridge, MA: Harvard.

Mullen, E. Theodore, Jr.
    1980   *The Divine Council in Canaanite and Early Hebrew Literature.* Chico, CA: Scholars.

North, C. R.
    1964   *The Second Isaiah.* Oxford: Oxford University.

Oppenheim, A. Leo
    1977   *Ancient Mesopotamia.* Revised edition. Chicago: University of Chicago.

Pope, Marvin and Jeffrey Tigay
    1971   "A Description of Baal." *Ugarit Forschungen* 3:117-30.

Saint-Laurent, George E.
    1980   "Light from Ras Shamra on Elijah's Ordeal upon Mount Carmel." In *Scripture in Context: Essays on the Comparative Method.* C. D. Evans, W. W. Hallo, and J. B. White, eds. Pp. 123-39. Pittsburg: Pickwick.

Smith, Mark S.
    1986   "Interpreting the Baal Cycle." *Ugarit Forschungen* 18:313-39.

Wilson, Robert R.
    1980   *Prophecy and Society in Ancient Israel.* Philadelphia: Fortress.

5

THE CONTRIBUTION OF THE GOSPELS AND ACTS TO A BIBLICAL THEOLOGY OF RELIGIONS

William J. Larkin, Jr.

The Gospels and Acts are uniquely qualified to make a contribution to a biblical theology of religions. Although some are convinced that the Gospels, particularly the synoptic Gospels, do not tell us anything of what Jesus taught about other religions (Schmidt 1992:104-105), there is evidence that Jesus and the gospel writers were very aware of and, to the extent their material and aims allowed, sought to address the first century context of religious pluralism. Though they portray Jesus as Messiah focusing on Israel during his earthly ministry (Mt 15:24; cf. 10:6), they do present his encounters with Gentiles, persons of other religious heritages (Mt 8:5-13/Lk 7:1-10; Mt 15:21-28/Mk 7:24-30; Lk 17:16-19; cf. Jn 12:20-26). They show from their report of Jesus' teaching that he did envision for his disciples a mission to the Gentiles (Mt 24:14/Mk 13:10; Mt 26:13/Mk 14:9; Mt 28:18-20; Lk 24:46-47; cf. Scott 1990). It must be constantly born in mind that these gospel writers and their audiences operate in a religiously pluralistic environment (Carson, Moo, Morris 1992:75-76, 99, 117-118; Ball 1992:80).

The Gospel of John also envisions a Gentile mission (Jn 10:16; 11:52). It too contains Jesus' encounter with those of other religions, including a most extensive dialogue with the Samaritan woman (Jn 4:1-42; 12:20-26). The difference of this gospel's language and style from other New Testament writings indicates

John was confronted by a new world of religion and thought with which he was trying to communicate (Vellanickal 1987:116).

Acts alone of the New Testament writings describes the early church's evangelistic efforts in a religiously pluralistic context. It is the only New Testament work other than 1 Corinthians to give us any extended description or assessment of non-Christian religions.

In sum, the Gospels and Acts give us an understanding of the gospel in the context of religious pluralism. They teach that the gospel is unique and its reception indispensable for salvation. And they give us an understanding of religions in the context of the gospel. Finally, Acts gives us a model for evangelistic approach to non-Christian religions: how to make contact with respectful integrity; how to contextualize the message through constructive and corrective engagement with the non-Christian worldview; and how to call for conversion with a particular gospel which makes a universal offer.

The Gospels

When we ask the gospel writers how the gospel, the Christian plan of salvation, should be understood in the context of religious pluralism, they say it is at the same time universal and unique, exclusive. The synoptic writers promote its universality by beginning their works with genealogies of Jesus, the messianic Savior, which contain Gentiles (Mt 1:1-17; Lk 3:23-38) and showing Gentiles as the first to worship him (Mt 2:12). They declare Jesus' ministry as the fulfillment of the Old Testament Scriptures' promise that the nations will be the recipients of God's salvation, light, hope through Messiah (Lk 3:6/Is 40:5; Mt 4:15-16/Is 9:1-2, cf. Lk 2:32; Mt 12:21/Is 42:4). They portray masses from Gentile territory (Mt 4:24-25; Mk 3:7-12; Lk 6:17-19) or individual Gentiles coming to Jesus for help (Mt 8:5-13/Lk 7:1-10; Mt 15:21-28/Mk 7:24-30; Lk 17:16-19; cf. Jn 12:20-26; cf. a Gentile confession at the climax of Mark, Mk 15:39).

Jesus' teaching, especially at the end of his earthly ministry and during his resurrection appearances, contains the evangelistic mission of the church to all nations (Mt 24:14/Mk 13:10; Mt 26:13/Mk 14:9; Mt 28:18-20; Lk 24:46-47; cf. Mt 10:18; Jn 10:16; 11:52). And when he deals with Israel's rejection of his mission, it is often in the context of statements about the receptivity of the

Gentiles to God's message and saving work whether in the past (Mt 12:41-42; Lk 11:29-32; 4:25-27) or the future (Mt 8:11-12; Lk 13:28-29; Mt 21:41/Mk 12:9/Lk 20:16; Mt 22:1-14; Lk 14:15-24; cf. Mk 11:17). In all these ways, the gospel writers clearly set forth the universality of God's plan of salvation (cf. Pinnock 1992:30 for further evidence).

But what is offered universally is unique and therefore exclusive. It is a unique salvation accomplished through a particular person, Jesus Christ (Mk 10:45; Mt 26:28/Mk 14:24). Its blessings are proclaimed as received exclusively on the authority of this particular name (Lk 24:47; cf. Mt 28:18-20). Ariarajah's claims that, while there may be such exclusivist claims in the Gospel of John (Jn 3:16, 18; 14:5-6), the Jesus of the Synoptics is God-centered leaving to the Father the mediation of salvation (Mk 10:38-41; 1985:20-22). The passage Ariarajah cites, however, deals with rewards in the kingdom not with reception of salvation.

Jesus explicitly recognizes the exclusiveness of the salvation he offers through two types of imagery: the narrow gate and the wedding banquet (Mt 7:13-14; Lk 13:22-30; Mt 22:11-14; cf. Lk 14:15-24). It does not do justice to the application of the image which immediately follows: "only a few find it," to say that Jesus is emphasizing the necessity of choosing the arduous path (as Pinnock 1992:154; note he does call this a "text about fewness"). Parrott (1989:119) presents an incomplete understanding of the image's thrust when he says it specifies a rejection of the majority choice but does not thereby specify a particular minority position.

The question which triggers the "narrow gate" statement in Luke: "Lord, are only a few people going to be saved?" indicates that there was an exclusiveness, a restrictiveness, at work in Jesus' teaching (Lk 13:23-24; Bock 1994:244). It is true that Jesus does not answer this question directly, but rather gives a warning about the existential importance of entering the narrow gate (Marshall 1978:565). Jesus does this because what prevents entrance into the gate is a lack of repentance (Stein 1992:379). The second clause of the warning, however, does contain an implicit answer: "because many...will try to enter and will not be able to" (Lk 13:24). The answer is a restrictive "Yes." Only by focusing on the form of the reply, a warning not a direct answer, and arguing from silence that Jesus does not tell us that that warning must be heeded in this life (as Sanders 1992:105) can one claim that there is no restrictiveness taught here.

Though the Matthean "marriage feast" parable seems to deal only with Israel (Ballard 1972), still its surprise ending and final "punchline"—"Many are invited, but few are chosen" point to the exclusiveness of God's salvation. Even if we see the parable as distinguishing between the large number of false disciples and the fewness of true disciples (Gundry 1982:441), the exclusiveness still comes through. The exclusion of the person who does not have proper wedding banquet attire (Mt 22:12-13) only heightens the importance of meeting the conditions for entering the kingdom and challenges any kind of Christian pluralistic inclusivism (Lemcio 1986:21).

Of the passages throughout the Gospel of John which point to the exclusive particularity of Christ and his salvation (Jn 1:14, 18; 3:18, 36; 17:3; the "I am" passages), none says it more forcefully than John 14:6. "Jesus answered, 'I am the way and the truth and the life. No one comes to the Father except through me'." Pinnock (1992:79) contends that what John 14:6 affirms is not a denial of John 1:9, understood as an enlightenment of all who enter the world, or of the view that God is at work savingly in a wider sphere beyond Palestine and before Christ's own time. Yet, to claim this is to participate in the most basic of contradictions and not to let the explanatory second affirmation—"No one comes to the Father except through me" have its full force. Some seek to raise the concepts of "way" and "truth" to a transcendent cosmic level so that all religious traditions somehow participate in that one supreme dominating Way which is Jesus (Cracknell 1986:85) or may be sources of genuine truth to be discovered in dialogue (Peters 1986:885). To do so is to violate the thrust of the immediate and larger contexts of John's writing in which he quite emphatically maintains that Jesus "alone is the link between God and men" (Barrett 1978:458; Jn 14:8-9; 1:51; 3:13). Indeed, the absolute "I am" affirmations (8:18, 24, 28, 58) and the "I am" sayings with predicates, when understood in the light of their Isaianic background (Is 44:6, 8; 45:5, 6, 18, 21-22; 46:9) posit an exclusivity expressly in the context of religious pluralism. John, then, portrays Christ as the one who takes on himself the exclusive words of Yahweh who 'alone is God in contrast to the so-called gods of the various peoples of the world'" (Ball 1992:80).

Parallel to the exclusiveness of Christ's work in the accomplishment of salvation is the fact that the reception of the gospel about this saving work is indispensable if a person is to have that salvation applied to him. John clearly points this out in his consistent use of "Jesus" as the object of *pisteu_* in describing faith that brings salvation (e.g., Jn 3:16, 18; 20:31; cf. 14:6, 9). Some who desire to deny this indispensability may affirm the ontological necessity of Christ's saving work, i.e., the uniqueness of Christ in accomplishing salvation. But they will drive a wedge between this ontological necessity and the epistemological necessity of hearing and believing in Jesus in order to apply that salvation to oneself. Further, they will argue that the exclusivist texts are silent concerning the fate of those who do not have opportunity to hear the gospel (Sanders 1992:64). Such reasoning fails to take into account that in each statement ontological necessity and epistemological necessity are inextricably bound together. Explicit belief in Jesus is the condition for applying to oneself the salvation blessings that his redeeming work makes possible (Jn 1:12; 6:40; 11:25).

Finding "Pagan Saints" and a different basis for salvation (Mt 25:31-46; Lk 12:10) in the synoptic Gospels are two other ways some have maintained that this portion of Scripture opens a wider hope, a hope of salvation for those who have not heard (Pinnock 1992:27; Sanders 1992:221; Meier 1986:397; Donahue 1986; Ukpong 1992; Lewis 1970:111). Jesus' encounter with Gentiles who approached him (Mt 2:1-12; 8:5-13/Lk 7:1-10; Mt 15:21-28/Mk 7:24-30; Lk 17:16) or his reference to responsive Gentiles in his teaching (Mt 12:38-42, cf. Lk 11:29-32) consistently demonstrates the opposite lesson. Gentiles are declared to be positive examples of what God delights in as they come to the God of Israel and his Messiah for saving help.

The "Parable of the Sheep and the Goats" (Mt 25:31-46) does not provide a criterion for salvation for those who have not heard of Christ: "care for the poor and needy" (i.e., understanding the "least of these my brethren" in this sense, Hunter 1960:90; Jeremias 1963:207). In Matthew, Jesus identifies his brethren as those who are related to him spiritually through a life of discipleship, doing the will of God (Mt 12:46-50; 28:10). Because of the kind of care shown to them and the parallel sayings of Mt 10:40-42, Jesus' parable is probably describing Christians' evidencing their faith by a charitable treatment of missionaries or other suffering members of the Christian community (Michaels 1965:28; Ladd 1974:197). They do not recognize Christ as the recipient of their kindness in that the glorious exalted Son of Man manifests himself through the suffering community and in that sense is hidden (Donahue 1986:14). It is interesting to note that the eschatological framework in which this parable of the last judgment is spoken includes the affirmation of Matthew 24:14, "And this gospel of the kingdom will be preached in the whole world as a testimony to all nations, and then the end will come." This leads at least one commentator to observe that "those who haven't heard" is not within the purview of Matthew's presentation of salvation history when he presents all the nations, who have all received a gospel witness, now gathered for judgment (Donahue 1986:14).

Blasphemy against the Son of Man which may be forgiven (Lk 12:10) does not mean "Honest rejection of Christ, however mistaken, will be forgiven and healed" (contra Lewis 1970:111). Marshall (1964:67) notes there is no distinction in the passage between the sins of Christians and non-Christians. The emphasis is on the culpability of those who blaspheme the Spirit guided and empowered witness of saints undergoing persecution.

The pattern of interaction between Jesus and those of other religions is not dialogue but proclamation (Marshall 1992). In the synoptic Gospels the question and answer style in pronouncement stories and the telling of parables is not "a 'dialectical' means of progress in understanding where both sides grow in understanding, are partners in a common search for truth" (Marshall 1992:35). Rather, Jesus is always the teacher who knows the answers. If he asks questions, it is to help or force his hearers to see things in a new light. His interaction with Gentiles: the centurion, the Syrophoenecian woman, the Samaritan leper, manifests no different pattern. To reach back to Jesus' childhood (Lk 2:47) for a model for dialogue (Pinnock 1992:130) is to fail to see what Luke wanted his readers to see in this incident: the unique wisdom of God's Son, as revealed in both his questions and answers (Stein 1992:122).

The Gospel of John for all its many dialogue situations presents a picture entirely consistent with the Synoptics. The dialogue with the Samaritan woman begins and continues with Jesus pointing out her deficiency. She does not know the way of salvation (Jn 4:10, 22). Jesus does not actually dialogue with the Greeks who approach him (12:20-26), though some try to see the situation as an example of it (Pathrapankal 1985:394). In fact, the Greek's approach evokes an affirmation about Jesus' exalted position from which he draws all men to himself (Jn 12:32). This points away from a dialogical stance (Jn 12:32).

In the Gospels the consistent stance of Jesus in the communication of the gospel is proclamation (Mt 4:17; 9:35; 11:1; Mk 1:14, 38-39, 45; 5:20; Lk 4:18-19, 44; 8:1). And this is what his disciples will do (Mt 24:14; 26;13; Mk 13:10; 14:9; Lk 24:47).

When we consider religions in the context of God's salvation plan, we note that the Gospels give us little on how God the Creator, especially through general revelation, relates to persons of other religions. Jesus in the Sermon on the Mount says God "causes his sun to rise on the evil and the good, and sends rain on the righteous and the unrighteous" (Mt 5:45). But he does not describe or evaluate their religious response. John's prologue declares that in the Word "was life, and that life was the light of men...The true light that gives light to every man was coming into the world" (Jn 1:4, 9). Here is a Logos Christology which points to Christ as the only source of humanity's existence in its fullness and meaning (Schnackenburg 1980:241). But these two verses together do not establish the claim that, either imperfectly or adequately, the truth in non-Christian religions is the Word's light by which practitioners may, without knowledge of the gospel, return to God (contra Vellanickal 1987:122-126; Cracknell 1986:106; Sanders 1992:238). Rather, the "giving light" of John 1:9 is not a personal saving illumination but an outward "shedding of light, bringing to light, making visible." It refers to the judgment Jesus' presence in the world brings as some repent and come to the light and others continue to love the darkness (3:19-21; Barrett 1978:161). John's assertions which immediately follow John 1:4 and 1:9 certainly confirm this. He says that Jesus' "shining" takes place in darkness which cannot overcome it and that the world "did not recognize him" (1:5, 10; Morris 1971:83).

The Gospels consistently evaluate non-Christian religions negatively as either blind ignorance or willful rebellion. Salvation and the Savior as light to the Gentiles (Lk 2:32; Mt 4:15-16; Jn 1:9-11) assumes a darkness of ignorance in religious practice. When the Gentiles make long prayers hoping to find the right words which will manipulate the deity into compliance they exhibit a lack of knowledge of the one true God who knows a human's needs before he or she asks (Mt 6:7). In fact, the pagans run after material security, but Christians need not because of the assurance of the care of a heavenly Father who knows what they need (6:32; Lk 12:30). Presumably, if pagans knew and trusted that same heavenly Father, they would show the same trust.

In John's Gospel Jesus declares that the world neither sees nor knows the Spirit of God (Jn 14:17). As for the Samaritans, they worship what they don't know, "for salvation is from the Jews" (4:22).

Ignorance extends to Judaism. Jesus' woes on the Pharisees reveals their blindness in using perverse logic to figure out how to so frame the application of the letter of the law in oath-taking that they maximize personal advantage (Mt 23:16-22). They prove to be "blind guides" in their evangelism and as they master adherence to the externals of ritual purity and piety, yet live immoral lives when it comes to "justice, mercy, and faithfulness" (Mt 23:15, 23-29; Lk 11:39-44).

The Pharisaic practitioners of Jewish religion show themselves to be in willful rebellion against God when they hypocritically, for their own advantage, use their casuistical applications of God's law to set aside obedience to its commands (Mt 15:1-20/ Mk 7:1-23). Their ostentation, even in lengthy prayers, and their desire for praise of people mask lives of socio-economic oppression (Mt 23:1-14/Mk 12:38-40/Lk 20:45-47). Religionists have been and will be the source of persecution of God's people, especially witnesses to the gospel (Mt 23:29-36; Lk 11:47-50; Mt 10:17; cf. Mk 13:9/Lk 21:12).

Acts

As Luke presents in Acts the gospel in a context of religious pluralism, he grounds the salvation accomplished in the uniqueness of Christ (Lk 24:46-48; Acts 4:12). The gospel message's content: "This is what is written: The Christ will suffer and rise from the dead on the third day, and repentance and forgiveness of sins will be preached in his name to all nations" combines particularity of achievement and universality of offer. In so doing it proclaims the uniqueness of Christ to provide salvation. A particular Messiah suffers and in his name repentance and forgiveness is to be preached to all persons in all nations, no matter their religious background.

Before the Sanhedrin Peter declares, "Salvation is found in no one else, for there is no other name under heaven given to men by which we must be saved" (Ac 4:12). This is not an isolated text, as Ariarajah (1985:20) contends, or even one which must be limited in its application to the early church"s anti-Jewish polemic, as Cracknell (1986:108) argues. Rather, a study of "salvation" words in Acts shows that Luke stresses time and time again the uniqueness of the salvation to be found in Jesus. He not only says the salvation is explicitly for Israel (5:31; 13:23, 26; 2:47), he presents it as for the Gentiles, even those adhering to other religions (10:36; 13:47; 26:23; 28:28; cf. 11:14; 14:7, 15; 16:31). At points he will say it is for both (15:11) or even, as here, leave the recipient undesignated in terms of ethnic status (4:12; 2:21; 10:43). To say that the "salvation" of Acts 4:12 is "messianic salvation," which does not exclude other types, and that its claims to uniqueness "no other name" are simply ways of making a qualitative statement, "No one can save like Jesus" (Pinnock 1992:78) fails to take into account some of the details in Peter's contention. No other name "under heaven, given to men" by which we must be saved is an exclusive name which admits no other options. The statement is quantitatively exclusionary in scope, not just an assertion of qualitative superiority. If the salvation referred to is just "physical healing" (Forward 1985:9), then the natural first referent of the statement—spiritual salvation—is passed over and a play on words is lost.

The emphasis on "the name" is a focus on the particu-larity, a basis for the exclusive uniqueness of Jesus Christ. In fact, this emphasis consistently comes out as Gentiles are presented with the gospel (10:36, 43; 13:12, 48-49; 16:31; 17:30-31; 18:11; 28:28, 31).

To drive a wedge between ontological and epistemological necessity at Acts 4:12 and say it teaches the former but not the latter (Sanders 1992:62) is again to misunderstand the text. If Luke did not have both in mind why did he talk about the name as "given to men," and the means "by which we must be saved?" In fact, Acts consistently contends that the gospel's salvation can only be applied when the particular savior is proclaimed and the person, no matter his religious background, responds in repentance and faith in Christ (2:21, 38; 3:19-20; 10:43; 11:17; 13:12, 38; 15:11; 16:15, 31; 17:3, 18; 19:13; 20:21; 22:16; 24:24; 25:19; 26:23). This evidence answers Sanders' (1988:247) assertion that "calling on the name" is simply relying on God's authority in granting salvation.

Some see the Cornelius episode as proof that Luke in Acts did not believe that one had to hear and believe the gospel in order to be saved. After all wasn't Cornelius declared as "acceptable" to God before he heard the gospel (10:35; Anderson

1970:102)? The "acceptability" referred to, however, was not a regenerate status. Otherwise, why did the angel tell him in summoning Peter that the apostle will bring "a message through which you and all your household will be saved" (Ac 11:14; Fernando 1987:133)? Why did he have to receive the Spirit (10:44-45)? Not only is the whole episode superfluous if Cornelius already has salvation, he is not an appropriate model for today's non-Christian religions. The God he fears is the one true God. The works of righteousness which he does are according to piety derived from the Old Testament law. What Cornelius does teach us is that God does work in hearts among pagans and honors their Spirit-prompted response to the light which they have, by providing them with more light, the light of the gospel message (cf. Shaw 1983:61).

Acts, as the Gospels, presents the gospel in a context of religious pluralism as offering a salvation which is uniquely accomplished in Christ and indispensably known through the Christian witness. The gospel messenger's stance, here also is necessarily proclamation. The risen Lord so commanded (Lk 24:47, "repentance and the forgiveness of sins is to be preached"; Ac 10:42) and the first Christians so bore witness, even to those of another religion ("preached," 19:13; 20:25; 28:31; "announced," 15:36; 17:23; 26:23; "told the good news," 11:20; 14:15; 17:18). The role of "dialogue" must always be understood within this proclamation context (Hesselgrave 1978:233). Though Acts may use *dialegomai* to describe the activity of discussion and dialogue (cf. 17:2-4), it is interesting that many times it simply refers to "speaking a religious lecture or sermon" without any indication of interaction (17:17; 18:4, 19; 19:9-10; 24:25). The other terms in the immediate context, used to describe the same activity, often point to a proclamation stance (17:18; 19:10; 24:26). Where dialogue does occur it is never of the twentieth-century variety. The dialogue partner from the non-Christian religion does not set the agenda. The Christian does not enter the dialogue hoping to learn more of God's truth (contra Cracknell 1986:27, 30). Rather, Acts presents the Christian witness as setting the terms for the discussion by proposing a point for investigation such as the scriptural prophecy of Messiah's death and resurrection (17:2-4). The purpose of entering into discussion is to overcome a misunderstanding of the Scriptures so that the audience may be persuaded that the Jesus whom the witness announces to them is indeed the Messiah. Or the disputation issues from the proclamation (Marshall 1992:31). Correctly Marshall concludes, "There is not the slightest suggestion that the church and the world conversed as equal partners in the search for truth" (Marshall 1992:45).

When we consider Acts' assessment of non-Christian religions, i.e., religions in the context of God's plan of salvation, we must begin again with their relation to the God of Creation and Revelation. God has taken the initiative and relates to humanity as transcendent creator of all things (17:24; 14:15). He is the creator of humanity and the providential sustainer of all cultures in their appointed geographical locations and seasons (17:26-27). His purpose is for humans to seek him. God as Revealer has left a witness through nature to humans in every culture (14:17; Peters 1979:292). He is a beneficent God, who is the source of fruitful seasons which sustain human life even in abundance and joy. Part of that witness points to the relationship of dependence humans have on him (17:28). Because of the limited content of the witness: "a Beneficent Creator God exists, upon whom humans are dependent for their physical life"; because of the negative evaluation of the human religious response to such a "revealed witness," we must not conclude that Acts sees the witness as providing saving knowledge (contra Idowu in Igenoza 1988:267).

Acts characterizes the human religious response negatively. As in the Gospels, it is blind ignorance and foolish rebellion. In the very midst of setting out God's purpose in the creation of humankind and the providential ordering of human life in cultures, namely "to seek God," Paul introduces the concept of "groping, and perhaps finding" him. Far from pointing to a divine pattern for successfully finding God and salvation, apart from hearing the gospel (as Osburn 1989:372), this feature points to sin's intervention so that all humans become as those who are blind in their search for God (Caragounis 1988:230). The fact that God is not very far away, as the next phrase contends, shows that the human lack of success is not a function of how God has set up the search, but of an intervening factor, sin. We find throughout the Areopagus speech the theme of human religion as ignorance. Paul's point of contact is an admission of ignorance by the Athenians, their worship of "An Unknown God" (17:23). Paul's transition to proclamation with the use of neuter instead of masculine pronouns clearly shows that he is not simply going to proclaim to them the identity of the one whom they worship ignorantly. Here is no basis for contending that non-Christian religionists, who are seeking him but don't know his name, are in a saving relation with God (contra Pinnock 1990:364; Richardson 1981, chapter 1; Erickson 1983:172). Rather Paul is arguing from what that particular Athenian god represents (see Diogenes Laertes, *Lives of the Eminent Philosophers* 1:110 for the origin of the inscription within an animistic polytheistic environment), human ignorance to what the gospel message makes known (Legrand 1981:165). In fact, the whole era and context of religions is the "times of ignorance" (17:30).

For Acts human religion is foolish rebellion since what is worshipped is *mataios*, futile (14:15). The idols cannot produce what they promise. Further thought about the accouterments and practice of religious worship, especially in the light of the central truths of general revelation, show how irrational such worship is. Gods made with hands are no gods at all, for the divine nature of the one who created and sustains all things giving breath of life even to humans, should not be thought to be like inanimate objects of "gold or silver or stone—an image made by man's design and skill" (17:29; cf. 19:26). He does not dwell in temples made with human hands. He is not serviced, sustained, by the offerings of human beings (17:24-25).

Non-Christian religious worship is also rebellious. The revealed witness is enough for someone to know that their metaphysical dependence is on the transcendent Creator God (Demarest 1989:335). Greek poets have said as much when declaring, "We are his offspring" (17:28; Aratus via Aristobolus, fr. 4 in Eusebius, *Preparation for the Gospel* 666b-d; Edwards 1992:266-269). But human religion turns away from the worship of the true God to idols. No wonder Paul and Barnabas tear their clothes at the blasphemy of being the objects of such false worship (Ac 14:14; cf. Mt 26:65; 2Ki 18:37; 19:1). No wonder the "forest of idols" at Athens deeply disturb Paul (Ac 17:16; cf. Is 65:2-3; Ps 106:28-29; Wycherly 1968:619).

Such rebellion is each culture going its own way, autonomously developing its religion without reference to the one true God and his general revelation (Ac 14:16). This foolish rebellion is culpable, because of that witness (14:17). If this were not so, the "times of ignorance" would not have had to be overlooked. Paul's message would not have climaxed in a call to repentance (17:30). As Acts assesses it, "religion represents a rebellious response to God whose glory is arrayed before them in nature, history and conscience" (Shaw 1983, 55).

Though Paul in his writings explicitly links human religion and the demonic (1Co 10:20), Luke in Acts makes only oblique references. The general call to the unconverted is to come out from under the "authority of Satan" (Ac 26:18). Power encounters with Satan or the demonic in Samaria (8:7, 9-13); on Cyprus (13:6-12); at Philippi (16:16-18) and Ephesus (19:13-16) take place within a more or less explicitly religious environment. What is clear is that human religion will oppose the gospel in a number of ways. There may be an attempt to co-opt the power of the gospel as Simon Magus and the sons of Sceva tried to do (8:18-20; 19:13-16). There may be a discrediting of the gospel by telling half-truths as the slave girl with the "spirit Python," i.e., of the Pythian Apollo, did (16:16-17). To polytheistic pagan ears the declaration, "These men are servants of the Most High God, who are telling you the way to be saved" meant that the Christian witnesses were messengers of whatever god the pagan considered supreme, since that was a title commonly used by henotheistic pagans for their "high god" (Trebilco 1989:60). And the "way of salvation" was release from the powers governing the fate of humanity and of the material world. Finally, there may be direct opposition such as Elymas's attempts to turn the provincial governor away from the faith (13:8, 10). Acts also tells us of direct opposition to the gospel from religionists, without referring to demonic forces. Because of a threatened loss of economic livelihood and the source of ethnic and regional pride, Demetrius, a silversmith in support of the Artemis cult, stirs up Ephesians against Paul (19:23-34; cf. 16:19-22).

With such a negative relation between religion and God's plan of salvation, it is good news that religionists can be positively related to Jesus as Savior. Their blind ignorance can be taken away if they will allow the Christian message: the light declared to the nations, to turn them from darkness to light, from Satan's authority to God (13:47; 26:18, 23). Then they will know forgiveness of sins, and more, an inheritance among those who are sanctified by faith in Christ (26:18; 10:45).

And since human religion is also foolish rebellion, this turning must be a repentance (17:30; implied in 14:15). Jesus, Lord of all, is the risen and coming judge (10:36, 42-43; 17:31). Luke presents a clear warning that if Jesus is not received as savior now, the religionist must face him as judge at his return.

Luke's evangelistic approach to non-Christian religions takes into account all the factors discussed so far. His stance as he makes a point of contact is "respectful integrity." His common ground with the religionist is not as a fellow religious person but as a fellow human being. In the face of worship directed to them at Lystra, Paul and Barnabas cry, "We too are only men, human like you" (14:15). This becomes the basis for an appeal to turn from futile idols to the living God. Similarly at Athens, after establishing, even with the aid of one of their poets, that humans are "God's offspring," appeal is made to see how humanly illogical idolatry is in the light of that truth. If the mutual respect of fellow human beings is the basis on which appeals to turn away from idolatry can begin to be made, then humanity's religion must be treated in such a way that no initial offense is rendered. Thus, initial references to religiosity are general and often ambiguous. The Athenians are *deisidaimotesterous*. This may be translated "very religious" or "very superstitious" (17:22; cf. Aristotle *Politics* 5:11 p. 1315a; Plutarch *Moralia* 164E-171F). The Ephesians know that Paul has preached the principle: "Gods made with hands are no gods at all" (19:26). Yet, the town clerk can dismiss the tumultuous assembly saying that the Christian missionaries are neither blasphemous nor robbers of temples (19:37). Acts seems to avoid two extremes: direct confrontation with the particulars of a religion and treating the religion as fulfilled in Christianity (Legrand 1981:166). A definite integrity of the gospel is preserved as well, for in making contact no essential truths are compromised. Its incongruence with the non-Christian worldview is so evident that pagan hearers will either mock the gospel as nonsense or not understand it. So at Athens Epicureans, atomistic empiricists, mock when they hear of bodily resurrection and pantheistic Stoics think Paul proclaims two deities, Jesus and his consort Anastasis, resurrection (17:18, 32).

To contextualize the message to religionists requires both a constructive and corrective engagement of the non-Christian worldview. At Lystra in an encounter with polytheistic animists, who saw the missionaries as epiphanies, there must be immediate correction concerning the true source of power to heal, create physical well being (14:15-17). It is the transcendent, living Creator God who "does good." And there is constructive engagement followed by correction. The pagans are right to see divine power as the source of fertility. But they have gone their own way and worship Zeus as the weather god, the god of thunder and rain. Yet, there is a God in heaven who "has shown kindness by giving you rain from heaven and crops in their seasons; he provides you with plenty of food and fills your hearts with joy" (14:17). This is the witness to his existence for which they are responsible.

On Mars Hill the Epicureans will agree with Paul in his critique of building temples for the gods or service maintenance of idols. For them too the deity is self-sufficient (Winter 1992:137; Philodemus, *Pros eusebeias* fr. 38, "God has no need of human things"). But Paul will move on to correction for he speaks of a God who is near humankind and desires to enter into a personal relationship of accountability. This the deity of the Epicureans, living as it does in supreme undisturbed blessedness, never would. Epicurus writes Meneoceus, "the statements of the many about the gods are not conceptions derived from sensation, but false suppositions, according to which the greatest misfortunes befall the wicked and the greatest blessings [the good] by the gift of the gods." As for a final judgment by a risen judge this is the proper subject of mockery (17:32) for those whose founder said, "when death comes, then we do not exist" (Epicurus, *Epistle to Menoeceus* 123ff.).

The Stoics will agree with Paul about Divine Providence (17:25-26; cf. Seneca the Younger, *De Providentia*; Winter 1992: 133-136). But when it comes to the nature of the relationship between God and humanity in creation and providence, Paul introduces a fundamental correction. Stoics, pantheistic materialists, believe that *logos*, the rational principle which orders the universe, i.e., "God," indwells humans. Posidonius states, "The cause of...the unhappy life—is that men do not follow absolutely the demon that is in them, which is akin to, and has a like nature with the Power governing the whole cosmos" (cited in Barrett 1961:65). But Paul says, "For in him we live and move and have our being. As some of your own poets have said, 'We are his offspring'" (Acts 17:28, quoting Aratus, *Phaenomena* 5). He corrects pantheistic materialism with immanental theism. Humans should not claim to have God in them, but recognize that they are sustained by an immanent, as well as a transcendent, God.

Such contextualized constructive engagement and correction necessarily leads to a call for conversion. For Luke, with his understanding of human religion as blind ignorance and foolish rebellion and his heralding of a gospel, grounded in the uniqueness of Christ, the knowledge of which is indispensable for salvation, the appeal for repentance involves "a rejection of the pluralistic perception of divinity present in an epiphany or in any idol"

(Winter 1992:142). According to Luke in Acts, them, this particular gospel, centered in suffering, risen and coming savior and judge, the Lord Jesus, must be offered to all people everywhere (17:30-31; 14:15-17; 19:10; 20:21). It is the only light which can permanently dispel the darkness of the context of religious pluralism (13:47; 26:18, 23). The Gospels in their presentation of the mission and message of Jesus the Messiah and Savior of the world certainly concur (Mt 12:21; Mk 10:45; Lk 19:10; Jn 4:42).

Reference List

Anderson, James N. D.
    1970   *Christianity and Comparative Religion*. London: Tyndale.
Ariarajah, S. Wesley
    1985   *The Bible and People of Other Faiths*. Geneva: World Council of Churches.
Ball, David M.
    1992   "'I am..:' The 'I am' Sayings of Jesus and Religious Pluralism." In *One God, One Lord: Christianity in a World of Religious Pluralism*. Bruce W. Winter and Andrew D Clarke, eds. 2nd edition. Pp. 65-84. Grand Rapids, MI: Baker.
Ballard, Paul H.
    1972   "Reasons for Refusing the Great Supper (Mt 22:1-14; Lk 14:14-24)." *Journal of Theological Studies* 23:341-350.
Barrett, Charles K.
    1961   *The New Testament Background: Selected Documents*. New York: Harper and Row Publishers.
    1978   *The Gospel according to Saint John*. 2nd edition. Philadelphia: Westminster.
Bock, Darrell L.
    1994   *Luke*. IVPNTC. Downers Grove, IL: InterVarsity.
Caragounis, Chris
    1988   "Divine Revelation." *Evangelical Review of Theology* 12: 226-240.

Carson, D. A., Douglas J. Moo, and Leon Morris
    1992   *An Introduction to the New Testament.* Grand Rapids, MI: Zondervan.
Cracknell, Kenneth
    1986   *Towards a New Relationship: Christians and the People of Other Faiths.* London: Epworth.
Demarest, Bruce A., and Richard J. Harpel
    1989   "Don Richardson's 'Redemptive Analogies' and the Biblical Idea of Revelation." *Bibliotheca Sacra* 146: 330-340.
Donahue, John R.
    1986   "The 'Parable' of the Sheep and the Goats: A Challenge to Christian Ethics." *Theological Studies* 47:3-31.
Edwards, M. J.
    1992   "Quoting Aratus: Acts 17:28." *Zeitschrift für die neutestamentliche Wissenschaft* 83:266-269.
Erickson, Millard J.
    1983   *Christian Theology.* Grand Rapids, MI: Baker.
Fernando, Ajith
    1987   *The Christian's Attitude toward World Religions.* Wheaton, IL: Tyndale.
Forward, Martin
    1985   "Pilgrimage: Luke/Acts and the World of Religions." *King's Theological Review* 8:9-11.
Gundry, Robert H.
    1982   *Matthew: A Commentary on His Literary and Theological Art.* Grand Rapids, MI: Eerdmans.
Hesselgrave, David J.
    1978   "Interreligious dialogue—Biblical and Contemporary Perspectives." In *Theology and Mission.* David J. Hesselgrave, ed. Pp. 227-240. Grand Rapids, MI: Baker.
Hunter, Archibald M.
    1960   *Interpreting the Parables.* Philadelphia: Westminster.
Igenoza, Andrew O.
    1988   "Universalism and New Testament Christianity." *Evangelical Review of Theology* 12:261-275.
Jeremias, Joachim
    1963   *The Parables of Jesus.* Revised edition. New York: Scribner.

Ladd, George E.
　1974　"The Parable of the Sheep and the Goats in Recent Interpretation." In *New Dimensions in New Testament Study*. Richard N. Longenecker and Merrill C. Tenney, eds. Pp. 191-199. Grand Rapids, MI: Zondervan.

Legrand, L.
　1981　"The Unknown God of Athens and the Religions of the Gentiles." *Indian Journal of Theology* 30(3):158-167.

Lemcio, Eugene E.
　1986　"The Parables of the Great Supper and the Wedding Feast: History, Redaction, and Canon." *Horizons in Biblical Theology* 8:1-26.

Lewis, C. S.
　1970　*God in the Dock: Essays on Theology and Ethics*. Grand Rapids, MI: Eerdmans.

Marshall, I. H.
　1964　"Hard Sayings [Lk 12:10]." *Theology* 67:65-67.
　1978　*The Gospel of Luke: A Commentary on the Greek Text*. NIGTC. Grand Rapids, MI: Eerdmans.
　1992　"Dialogue with Non-Christians in the New Testament." *Evangelical Review of Theology* 16:28-47.

Meier, John P.
　1986　"Matthew 15:21-28." *Interpretation* 40:397-402.

Michaels, J. Ramsey
　1965　"Apostolic Hardships and Righteous Gentiles: A Study of Matthew 25:31-46." *Journal of Biblical Literature* 84:27-37.

Morris, Leon
　1971　*The Gospel According to John*. NICNTC. Grand Rapids, MI: Eerdmans.

Osburn, Evert D.
　1989　"Those Who have Never Heard: Have They No Hope?" *Journal of the Evangelical Theological Society* 32:367-372.

Parrott, Rod
　1989　"Entering the Narrow Door: Mt 7:13-14/Lk 13:22-24." *Forum* 5:111-120.

Pathrapankal, Joseph
　1985　"Jesus and the Greek: Reflections on a Theology of Religious Identity." *Journal of Dharma* 10(4):392-403.

Peters, George W.
    1979   "Missions in a Religiously Pluralistic World."
            Bibliotheca Sacra 136:294-301.
Peters, Ted
    1986   "A Christian Theology of InterreligiousDialogue."
            Christian Century 103:883-885.
Pinnock, Clark H.
    1990   "Toward an Evangelical Theology of Religions."
            Journal of the Evangelical Theological Society 33:359-368.
    1992   *A Wideness in God's Mercy: The Finality of Christ in a World of Religions.* Grand Rapids, MI: Zondervan.
Richardson, Don
    1981   *Eternity in Their* Hearts. Ventura, CA: Regal.
Sanders, John E.
    1988   "Is Belief in Christ Necessary for Salvation?"
            Evangelical Quarterly 60: 241-259.
    1992   *No Other Name: An Investigation in the Destiny of the Unevangelized.* Grand Rapids, MI: Eerdmans.
Schmidt, Frederick W.
    1991   "Jesus and the Salvation of the Gentiles." In *Through No Fault of Their Own: The Fate of Those Who have Never Heard.* Wm. V. Crockett and J. G. Sigountis, eds. Pp. 97-105. Grand Rapids, MI: Baker.
Schnackenburg, Rudolf
    1980   *The Gospel According to Saint John.* 3 vols. New York: Seabury.
Scott, J. Julius
    1990   "Gentiles and the Ministry of Jesus: Further Observations on Matthew 1:5-6; 15:21-28." *Journal of the Evangelical Theological Society* 33:161-169.
Shaw, Mark
    1983   "Is There Salvation Outside the Christian Faith?"
            East Africa Journal of Evangelical Theology 2(2):42-62.
Stein, Robert H.
    1992   *Luke.* NAC. Vol. 24. Nashville: Broadman.
Trebilco, Paul R.
    1989   "Paul and Silas: Servants of the Most High God (Acts 16:16-18)." *Journal for the Study of the New Testament* 36: 51-73.

Ukpong, Justin S.
   1992   "The Immanuel Christology of Matthew 25:31-46 in African Context." In *Exploring Afro-Christianity*. J. Pobee, ed. Pp. 55-64. Frankfurt am Main: Peter Lang.

Vellanickal, M.
   1987   "Biblical Background of Inter-religious Dialogue." *Biblebhashyam* 13:105-127.

Winter, Bruce
   1993   "In Public and in Private: Early Christians and Religious Pluralism." In *One God, One Lord: Christianity in a World of Religious Pluralism..* Bruce W. Winter and Andrew D Clarke, eds. 2nd edition. Pp. 125-148. Grand Rapids, MI: Baker.

Wycherly, R. E.
   1968   "St. Paul at Athens." *Journal of Theological Studies* 19:619-624.

6

THE APOSTLE PAUL AND FIRST CENTURY RELIGIOUS PLURALISM

Don N. Howell, Jr.

When the apostle Paul launched his evangelistic and church planting ministry into the urban centers of the eastern Mediterranean he encountered a world of "many gods and many lords" (1Co 8:5). The pantheon of Olympian gods presided over by Zeus had, since the earth-shaking conquests of Alexander the Great and the subsequent rise of Rome to political dominance, become incorporated with Roman and Egyptian deities, both local and domestic, to produce a vast and confusing array of religious alternatives (Aune 1993; Gill 1992). The political conflicts and disturbances of power created a world of fear and uncertainty, accounting for the rapid spread of the mystery religions which offered, through elaborate rituals of initiation, the promise of salvation—health and prosperity in this life and immortal bliss in the afterlife (Meyer 1987:1-13).

Added to the mix was the Roman imperial cult, particularly strong in Asia minor, which, in order to bolster social and political stability, enforced the worship of divinized emperors such as Julius Caesar and Augustus. Paul's dismay at Athens as a city "full of idols" (Ac 17:16) and his perception of the Athenian philosophers as "in every way very religious" (Ac 17:22) could apply equally to many of the major cities and their inhabitants to whom he introduced the Christian gospel—Tarsus, Syrian Antioch, Pisidian Antioch, Philippi, Thessalonica, Corinth and Ephesus. In the multi-cultural city of Corinth, for example, worshippers streamed to the temples of Apollo, Tyche, goddess of good fortune, Aphrodite, goddess of love and fertility, Poseidon, the sea god, and to the sanctuaries of Asclepius, the god of healing, the

Greek mystery cult of Demeter and Kore, and the Egyptian mystery cults of Isis and of Sarapis (Furnish 1984:15-20).

Into such an environment came the Apostle to the Gentiles proclaiming the gospel of God's righteousness through Jesus Christ to all who believe (Ro 1:16-17). The extant letters of Paul are pastoral communications to the emerging churches designed to instruct believers in Christian doctrine and exhort them toward authentic Christian living and witness in a hostile pagan setting. How did Paul view the non-Christian religions of the Greco-Roman world? What were his underlying convictions and approach in dealing with congregations struggling to maintain their Christian identity against the gravitational pull of idolatry and syncretism? Can we discover in Paul a paradigm for contemporary contextualization of the Christian message to the equally pluralistic world of the approaching twenty first century (Mather and Nichols 1993)? Such is the scope of the present inquiry into Paul's encounter with the religious pluralism of his day, considered under four areas: A Theocentric Christology, The Employment of Pagan Religious Terminology, Idolatry and the Church in Corinth, and Syncretism and the Church in Colossae.

A Theocentric Christology

The starting point in any discussion of Pauline thought must be his Jewish concept of God (*theos*). The fundamental Jewish confession captured in the Shema—"Hear, O Israel: The Lord our God is one Lord" (Dt 6:4)—though christologically reformulated in light of the resurrection and exaltation of Jesus Christ as Lord (1Co 8:6; 12:4-6; Eph 4:4-6), remained as the essence of Paul's understanding of God to the end of his life. Unlike the lifeless images and limited deities worshipped by Greeks and Romans, Paul proclaimed the one and only Creator and Redeemer of all peoples (Ro 3:30; 1Co 8:4, 6; Gal 3:20; 1Ti 2:5), the living and true God (Ro 9:26; 2Co 3:3; 6:16; 1Th 1:9; 1Ti 3:15; 4:10; cf. Ac 14:15), the Sovereign One "able to" initiate, execute and consum-mate his redemptive purposes for his people (Ro 11:23; 16:25; 2Co 9:8; Eph 3:20; 2Ti 1:12). Concisely put, Paul is fundamentally theocentric, God-centered, in that he views God as the origin, mediator and goal of creation and redemption (Ro 11:36; 1Co 8:6).

Modern religious pluralists such as John Hick and Paul Knitter have attempted to set such theocentrism (of Paul and the other New Testament writers) over against christocentrism in order to establish a paradigmatic shift away from the traditional exclusivist model of Christian proclamation. The shift from christocentrism to theocentrism is for Hick the "Copernican revolution" of modern religious understanding: as Copernicus recognized that the sun and not the earth was the center of the universe, so our ultimate attention must be shifted away from Jesus Christ to God, the "originative source of light and life, whom all the religions reflect in their own different ways" (Hick 1980:18, 70-71). Similarly, Knitter argues for a shift in focus from Christ as the indispensable guide to God, to God as the key for interpreting the Christ event (Knitter 1985). Though he concedes that the exclusivistic character of Christian faith resides in its doctrine of the incarnation of the Son of God, Knitter believes that this can be overcome by a theocentric model which makes God, not Christ, the essence of truth.

One scholar has provided a brief but incisive critique of Knitter's logic and appeal (Heim 1987; see further, Carruthers 1990). In the repeated progressive jumps to a broader and more expansive center, the content of God—*theos*—becomes practically indeterminate. By removing *theos* from its christological orientation so that it can incorporate anything and everything, Knitter in effect ends up with a centerless center, that is, a center without location. If *theos* is everything, it is nothing. But in the New Testament, and in Paul's letters in particular, *theos* is the term of signification for God, the Father (*pater*) of the Lord Jesus Christ (Ro 15:6; 2Co 1:3; 11:31; Eph 1:3, 17; Col 1:3). If biblical parameters are to be brought into the equation at all—and this Knitter (unlike Hick) seeks to do—the term God must be given a clearly delimited reference point, namely the planning, superintendence and consummation of the redemptive program focused exclusively in Jesus Christ. Heim captures the dilemma created by Knitter's model: "The problem is that for there to be a theocentric Christology there must first be a theocentric theology. In it, presumably, *theos* will be the norm for defining . . . Theos. What does or can this mean?" Knitter and Hick never really provide any content to the center around which their new paradigm revolves.

Theocentrism and christocentrism should not be played off against one another as competing alternatives. Pauline christology is theocentric and Pauline soteriology is christocentric: "God was in Christ reconciling the world to himself" (2Co 5:19a).

By a theocentric christology, then, we mean that behind the Christ event is the person of God the Father and that only in the broader redemptive historical and eschatological purposes of God the Father can Pauline christology be satisfactorily integrated. By a christocentric soteriology we mean that the executor of the Father's redemptive program is exclusively the person of the Lord Jesus Christ, full participant with God the Father and the Holy Spirit in the nature and prerogatives of deity (Howell 1993). Jesus Christ is the preexistent Son of God (Ro 1:3-4; Gal 1:16; 1Co 15:28), the exalted Lord over his church (Ro 10:9; 14:9; 1Co 12:3; Php 2:9-11) and sovereign ruler over the created universe of which he is both mediator and goal (Col 1:15-20).

The Employment of Pagan Religious Terminology

At the heart of Paul's message to his beloved Greeks was the lordship of Jesus Christ. The title par excellence for Jesus Christ in the Pauline literature is *kyrios*. Of approximately 270 total occurrences of *kyrios* in Paul (of 717 total occurrences in the New Testament, or 38 percent) 246 are used as a christological designation. The Pauline usage of *kyrios* reveals a marked emphasis on Jesus as the risen and exalted One, sovereign over the church and the world, a powerful presence among his people, and the soon returning judge of humankind and the consummator of redemption. The risen Lord Jesus, whose presence is effectually mediated by the Spirit (1Co 15:45; 2Co 3:17-18), is powerfully manifest in the assembled church (1Co 5:4) and in the believer's walk of faith (Eph 6:10; Php 3:10). After conquering death the Lord ascended to heaven (Eph 4:8-10; 1Ti 3:16) and was exalted to the right hand of God the Father (Ro 8:34b; Eph 1:20; Col 3:1), in fulfillment of Psalm 110:1. He has assumed both now, and will in the age to come a place far above every class of spiritual power (1Co 15:24-28; 2Co 2:14; Eph 1:21-22; 4:8; Php 3:21; Col 2:10, 15) and all sentient beings (Php 2:9-11), in fulfillment of Psalms 8:6; 68:18. "Jesus is Lord" is the basic confession of the Pauline congregations (Ro 10:9; 1Co 12:3), very likely a primitive *homologia* inherited from the pre-Pauline Palestinian church (Ac 2:36; cf. Ac 13:32-33; Ro 1:3-4). In contradistinction to the multiple lords of the Gentile world, Jesus is the exclusive and undisputed Lord (1Co 8:6b; Eph 4:5), the one Lord of both Jew and Gentile (Ro

10:12), of both the dead and the living (Ro 14:9). He is the "Lord of glory," the descriptive genitive (*doxes*) attested in the Old Testament (Ps 24:7-10; cf. Ac 7:2) and Pseudepigrapha (1En 22:14; 25:3, 7; 27:3-4; 66:2; 75:3) as a qualifier of God.

In order to account for this high Christology of the New Testament authors, especially Paul and John, the proponents of religious pluralism draw on the arguments of *Religionsgeschichte* (history of religions or comparative religions). This school of thought—though it has lost much of its force in recent years with the increasing appreciation of the Jewishness of the New Testament—strives to demonstrate the continuity of Christianity with the Hellenistic and/or oriental religious traditions prevalent in the first century. Gnosticism, the mystery religions, Greek mythology, oriental mysticism, Mithraism and many others are mined for parallels to New Testament teaching. Verbal parallels are quickly transformed into conceptual parallels and these in turn are said to be sources of such foundational Christian doctrines as redemption, vicarious atonement, resurrection, baptism and the eucharist, lordship, and the new birth.

Perhaps the most impressive attempt to establish organic connections between the Pauline kerygma and Hellenistic religion is that of W. Bousset who in his famous work *Kyrios Christos* (1913) sought to explain Paul's lordship Christology as a product of his contact with the mystery cults of Hellenistic Antioch. The simpler faith of the primitive Jerusalem church in Jesus as the coming apocalyptic Son of Man suddenly made a quantum leap, when it entered the Greek world, into the category of exalted *Kyrios*. With consummate skill Bousset explored the Hermetic literature, Philo, Gnostic documents, and the mystery cults of Isis, Osiris, and Orphis. In the process he discovered conceptual "parallels" with Paul's Christ mysticism (*en Christo*), doctrine of the Holy Spirit, Christ-Adam theology, cross and sacrament, and the dying-rising Redeemer. Bousset's theory was embraced by the representative par excellence of the history of religions' approach, Rudolf Bultmann (1951:1.51-53, 121-33), and continues to have advocates in a modified form (Dunn 1990:50-54).

With respect to the Pauline concept of Christ's lordship, several decisive objections have rendered the Bousset-Bultmann hypothesis all but obsolete: (1) The deeper ontological element resident in several key synoptic passages (Mt 7:21; Mk 11: 3; and esp. Mk 12:35-37; Mt 22:41-45) could easily extend, in the aftermath of Christ's resurrection and exaltation, into the fuller, more developed Christology of Paul and John. (2) There is strong evidence in the preservation of the Aramaic liturgical formula maranatha in 1 Corinthians 16:22 that the acclamation of Jesus as exalted Lord reaches back to the Palestinian church (Fitzmyer 1981). (3) It is a fundamental non sequitur to argue that since *kyrios* was a prominent title for divinity in the Greco-Roman world (the same can be said for *theos, soter* and *huios theou*) the apostle Paul must have adopted not only the term but also its pagan content. Is it not highly unlikely, indeed unthinkable, that the Paul of the "no other gospel" of Galatians 1:6-9 would have borrowed the essence of his message from the very people among whom he worked? There is a failure here to distinguish terminological from conceptual correspondence, as Wedderburn (1987) has impressively shown with respect to Pauline teaching on baptism and resurrection (esp. Ro 6:3-10) over against the teaching of the mystery cults of the first century. That Paul was aware of the pagan usage of *kyrios* is clear from 1 Corinthians 8:5 where he refers to the *kyrioi polloi* of the contemporary world (cf. Gal 4:8). Is it not self-evident, however, that this Jewish Christian missionary, committed to the purity of his gospel, employed current terms in order to establish an area of commonality with his listeners, while confronting their deep rooted value systems with a christological reformulation and redefinition of these same terms (1Co 8:6)?

The present writer has struggled over the past fifteen years as a missionary in Japan with how to contextualize the gospel in order to make it understandable to a people immersed in Shinto and Buddhist traditions. *Kami*, the Japanese term for God, connotes "that which inspires, illumines or stimulates harmony with nature" such as a lake, sunset, rock formation, venerated ancestor or simply one' inner feelings. *Tsumi*, the word for sin, possesses social (horizontal) not theological (vertical) coordinates; to commit sin is to violate the norms of one's group, whether it be the family, the company, the neighborhood association, or society at large. *Megumi*, or grace, is the granting of favor to one out of a sense of duty or appreciation for favors received; unmerited favor granted freely and without some sort of external constraint is without precedent in Japanese culture. Far from adopting wholesale the available terminology and its accepted cultural meaning, the missionary committed to the proclamation of biblical truth (and who would not place Paul in this category?) takes the current linguistic vehicle and pours into it new semantic content, carefully redefining and explaining his or her terms as he or she expounds the gospel. "*Kami*," the missionary proclaims, "is the sovereign Creator of the earth and the heavens, transcendent over the created world, invisible and immaterial; he is a person who knows and deeply cares for people that he made like himself with the capacities of mind, will and emotion. It is to reestablish harmony with him, broken by disobedience of his law (*tsumi*), that he sent Jesus into the world, whose death and resurrection provides a new relationship to God as Father and fellow-believers as brothers. This new relationship is freely bestowed (*megumi*) on those who forsake other gods and receive Jesus as their only Lord and Savior." Like Paul, the modern missionary realizes that the meaning of a message is determined not by the sender but by the receptor who filters it through his worldview and life experiences. Charles Corwin's (1967) analysis of key biblical themes (e.g. faith, sin, truth, righteousness, eternity) in which he compares and contrasts the Japanese understanding of these concepts with their biblical counterpart has been a source of inestimable help to missionaries in the land of the rising sun.

In order to penetrate the hearts and minds of his pagan listeners the apostle Paul used well-known Greek terms but appropriated them as vehicles for the communication of biblical truth. In the Hellenistic world *mysterion* denoted the secret customs and ceremonies of those mystery religions into which its devotees were initiated. The cults of Isis, Attis, Mithras, Cybele, Adonis, Demeter, and Dionysus shared this common feature. In later Gnosticism, which had primitive roots in the New Testament period, the *mysteria* were secret revelations granted only to the perfect (*teleioi*) that issued in salvation. The elitist and secluded character of the mystery is pronounced. For Paul, however, *myste l rion* is a salvation historical term. Unlike the esoteric secrets of the mystery religions where only a privileged elite were initiated into their benefits, the Pauline *mysterion* is God's salvific plan formerly concealed but now revealed in Jesus Christ for all to know, understand and embrace (Ro 11:25; 16:25; 1Co 2:1, 7; 4:1; 15:51; Eph 1:9; 3:3, 4, 9; 5:32; 6:19; Col 1:26, 27; 2:2; 4:3; 1Ti 3:9, 16). Here is the christological reinterpretation and reformulation of pagan religious data, not its unaltered borrowing or acceptance. Similarly, *sophia* and *gnosis* are employed by Paul of God's wisdom and knowledge in Christ crucified (1:18-3:23) over against the Hellenistic propensity to inflate rhetorical skill and reasoning powers; *teleios* in 1 Corinthians 2:6; 14:20; Philippians 3:15; Ephesians 4:13; Colossians 1:28 refers not to a spiritual elite who have attained moral perfection but to those in Christ who are in the maturation process of being conformed to his glorious image.

Returning to the term *kyrios* (Lord), it draws its defining moment not from the Greco-Roman mystery cults but from the Greek Old Testament where it translates the covenant name Yahweh over 6000 times. Paul repeatedly associates Yahweh with the Lord Jesus Christ in his use of the Old Testament. One should compare such passages as Romans 10:13 (Joel 2:32); 1 Corinthians 1:31 and 2 Corinthians 10:17 (Jer 9:24); 1 Corinthians 2:16 (Isa 40:13; the same text is applied to God in Ro 11:34); 1 Corinthians 10:9 (Nu 21:5-9): 1 Corinthians 10:26 (Ps 24:1); 2 Corinthians 3:16 (Ex 34:34); Eph 4:8 (Ps 68:18). Perhaps the most impressive application of the covenant name of Yahweh to Jesus is Philippians 2:10-11. In describing Jesus' exaltation, the Apostle borrows his language from Isaiah 45:23, situated in a polemical context (45:1-25) where the singularity and uniqueness of the one true Lord God of Israel, sole Creator and Savior, is contrasted with the pagan gods of the surrounding nations (O'Brien 1991:238-43). In Romans 14:11 the same Old Testament text is applied to the worship of God the Father. Even as Paul reformulates the Shema (Dt 6:4) to encompass the lordship of Christ in 1 Corinthians 8:6 (Wright 1992:120-36) so he applies to his Lord the prerogative of worship that belongs to God the Father (Php 2:11). In summary, the employment of pagan religious terminology by the apostle Paul demonstrates his communicative skill in proclaiming a distinctively christocentric message to his Greek listeners. What we have here, in the words of one scholar, are Greek words with Hebrew meanings (Hill 1967).

Idolatry and the Church in Corinth

When the delegation from the church in Corinth led by Stephanus came to Paul in Ephesus they brought a letter of questions regarding issues in the church that demanded urgent attention (1Co 16:15-18; cf. peri de: 7:1, 25; 8:1; 12:1; 16:1. 12). One such issue was relational division in the church over the consumption of meat that had been offered to idols (*eidolothytos*: 8:1, 4, 7, 10; 10:19; *hierothytos*: 10:28). In light of 8:10 *(eidoleion)*, we are inclined with Fee (1987:357-63; contra Fisk 1989) to see Paul first addressing the problem of participation in feasts in pagan temples (8:1-13; 10:1-22) before later turning his attention to the eating of meat sold in the marketplace that had been offered on a pagan altar (10:23-30).

In a Greek city such as Corinth with its multiplicity of pagan temples and sanctuaries most if not all of the meat sold in the marketplace for general consumption had been butchered by pagan priests and placed on pagan altars before being carted off to the macellum or meat-market. Further, as has been demonstrated from the primary sources (Willis 1985:7-64), temples served as the focal point for both religious and social life in the community with the lines separating idolatrous worship from social engagement practically nonexistent. While (1) the feasts in a pagan temple did not necessarily take on the sacramental character of granting the participant special spiritual powers or status, and (2) the social dimensions of the feast—good food, good company, fulfillment of relational obligations—were pronounced, the participants still formally acknowledged the reality of the deity in whose presence they ate. One typical invitation to a meal in a pagan temple reads: "Chaeremon requests your company at the table of the lord Sarapis at the Sarapeum tomorrow, the 15th at 9 o'clock" (Poxy 1.110). As a focus for social occasions such as birthday parties and family gatherings, such temple feasts would have been difficult to avoid without incurring misunderstanding and ridicule from friends and relatives. We can understand the dilemma that Christians faced in their new allegiance to Jesus Christ as the one and only Lord (1Co 12:2-3). A contemporary example from Japan is the author Kosuke Koyama (1985) who, like many believers in that country, finds it an almost intolerable tension to maintain his Christian identity in a society so pervaded by idolatry.

Apparently some of the believers (the so-called "strong") in Corinth had resumed participation in temple feasts, justifying their conduct on the fact that the idols in whose presence they ate were nonexistent (8:4) and that food in and of itself was a neutral matter (8:8). Since idols do not exist and food is no more than a material substance it must matter to God neither what is consumed nor where it is eaten. Similar logic is followed today by the mainline Protestant and Catholic churches of Japan to support the supposedly innocuous character of Christian believers maintaining the Buddhist family altar with its regular material offerings to departed ancestors and full participation in the annual

Obon festival, celebrated in July and August, where families gather at the ancestral grave to offer flowers, incense and small sweets to the spirits of their deceased loved ones. As with the Corinthians of old it is maintained that such activities have no inherent religious meaning but are expressions of family solidarity and social communion which, in fact, by virtue of his or her loving involvement actually enhance the believer's testimony to family and friends.

How did the Apostle respond to such a sensitive issue in which the religious and social dimensions were so intertwined? While pious Jews faced the religious pluralism of their day by (1) abstaining from all food, previously marketplace meat, that had been offered to idols, (2) proscribing all entry into idol sanctuaries, and (3) banning the sale of animals to Gentiles, especially at the time of pagan religious festivals (Winter 1990:218-19), Paul drew the Rubicon separating acceptable social engagement from idolatrous compromise differently. He addresses this delicate problem with boldness as well as sensitivity, preserving the biblical tension between truth and grace. His argument is grounded in both theological convictions—the oneness of God (8:6), God's judgment against idolatry (10:1-13), the meaning of the Lord's Supper (10:14-22), the goodness of the created order (10:25), the glory of God (10:31)—as well as in concrete relational concerns—the sensitive conscience and vulnerability of the weak brother (8:7-13), the priority of edification over liberty (10:23-24, 32-33), and attention to how one's actions are interpreted by outsiders (10:27-30).

In broad terms we can identify three fundamental convictions that guided the Apostle's approach to the encroachment of idolatry in the church at Corinth. First, Paul sides with the strong in their contention that idols have no real, objective, ontological existence. "We know," Paul says in agreement, "that an idol is nothing at all in the world and that there is no God but one" (8:4). Later Paul adds rhetorically, "Do I mean then that a sacrifice offered to an idol is anything, or that an idol is anything?," to which he responds negatively before qualifying his answer, "No, but . . . " (10:19-20a). Idols do not exist and their images are powerless and lifeless material objects. Such an appraisal of idolatry Paul inherits from Old Testament poets and prophets (cf. Ps 115:4-7; 135:15-17; Isa 44:9-20; 46:1-7; also 1Co 12:2, "mute idols"; Rev 9:20).

There are two corollaries to this first principle. (1) Incidental contact with idolatry and idolaters is both unavoidable and harmless. Paul had written a previous letter to Corinth in which he urged believers to separate from those who professed the faith but engaged in immorality and idolatry. The Corinthians, however, had misunderstood the letter to mean that they must separate from all people engaged in such activities. No, Paul clarifies, I was not referring to the people of this world who are immoral, greedy, swindlers, drunkards, idolaters, for "in that case you would have to leave this world" (1Co 5:9-11). Separation involves disassociation from Christian believers engaged in such conduct, not monastic retreat from engagement with the people of this world. Witness to the world without conformity to the world is the Pauline model. (2) The consumption of meat that has been offered on a pagan altar is not in and of itself harmful. Since an idol is nonexistent the meat is unaffected by being placed before the lifeless image of an idol. Paul enjoins the Corinthians, in light of the goodness of the Lord's created order (quot. Ps 24:1), to freely buy and eat the meat sold in the marketplace without making it a matter of conscience (10:25). Such freedom to eat applies whether the setting is one's own house or a private meal to which one is invited by an unbelieving friend (10:27), though the latter, as we shall see, may be qualified by other considerations (10:28-30). Paul, then, draws the lines of separation more broadly then the conservative Jew of his day. He will not restrict activity which is not inherently idolatrous so as to hamper the normal activities of believers in a city permeated by images, idols, altars and temples. The modern missionary to Japan would have almost no room to maneuver if such incidental contact with idolatry was forbidden—he could enter no public building nor visit almost any private home since they have been invariably dedicated by Shinto priests to the gods and contain ancestral altars and god-shelves.

Second, while idols have no ontological existence they most certainly do possess phenomenological or perceptual reality in the minds of their devotees. Pastor Nobuji Horikoshi of Tokyo has documented how the perceived reality of idols in the minds of Japanese Buddhists dominates every facet of life (1986). In fact, Horikoshi shows, from the idol worshipper's point of view it is the scornful secular minded Westerner who lacks the spiritual capacity to perceive and experience the very real spiritual realities behind the seemingly lifeless images chiseled by human hands. Paul acknowledges the many "so-called" (*legomenoi*) gods and lords of his day (8:5), indicating that such deities are embraced and worshipped popularly but erroneously (Winter 1992:143-45). The phenomenological existence of idols is so powerful that the conscience of the weak could be defiled by eating food as part of a temple banquet (8:7, 12), resulting in his or her irreparable spiritual harm (8:9, 11, 13; cf. Ro 14:15, 20, 21). In spite of a head knowledge that denies the objective existence of the gods in whose honor they dine, these believers are "so accustomed to idols" (8:7) in their experiential past that to eat such idol meat would be to ignore the delicate voice of conscience and damage a part of their human makeup essential to spiritual health.

Such perceived reality underscores the gravity of protecting the conscience (*syneidesis*) both of oneself and others, evident in such passages as Romans 9:1 (the conscience as the locus of the Spirit's work), 2 Corinthians 1:12 (the conscience witnesses to one's integrity), 2 Corinthians 4:2 and 5:11 (the conscience the place of appeal to the truth of one's message), 1 Timothy 1:5, 19; 3:9 (a good and clear conscience essential for spiritual leaders), 1 Timothy 4:2 and Titus 1:15 (spiritual bankruptcy for the one who sears the conscience). Paul will not allow the strong, who are apparently urging the weak to participate in idol feasts in order to strengthen their weak consciences (8:9-10), to act in such a potentially destructive manner.

One corollary of this second principle is the qualification in 10:28-30 of the believer's freedom to eat whatever one's host prepares in a private meal (10:27). If one's host, or perhaps a fellow guest who is not a believer, offers a cautionary word that the meat has been offered to an idol, then the believer should abstain "for the sake of the other person's conscience," that is, so as not to damage the high moral expectations the informant has of Christians (10:29a). The unbelieving informant would, albeit ignorantly, interpret such eating on the part of the believer as a weakened stance toward idol worship. So the believer should refrain rather than send the wrong message. Again there is behavioral modification springing from others' perceptions and the impact one's actions will have on others. Paul will go on to proscribe participation in idol feasts on creedal grounds (10:1-22) but initially he sets the matter in its relational framework (8:7-13). It is their lack of love for their brothers, a love that can forego the insistence on perceived rights for the sake of others (supported by Paul's example in Ch. 9), that lies at the heart of the problem.

Third, while idols have only perceptual, not objective existence, behind the worship of idols is the activity of demons (10:20). The elaborate systems of idol worship centered in temple activities are not neutral social events the believer may freely dabble in. There are dark spiritual forces ultimately at work behind the most frivolous of ceremonies, capturing the allegiance of people and leading to spiritual ruin. This explains Paul's consistent stance in his letters that the worship of the true God and the worship of idols are mutually exclusive (1Co 10:14-22; 2Co 6:15-18; 1Th 1:9). Idolatry not only robs God of the devotion and glory that is his due but leads to moral and spiritual reprobation (Ro 1:18-32; 1Co 5:10-11; 6:9; Gal 5:20; Eph 5:5; Col 3:5). Wilderness Israel is the prime example of a people who, although the recipient of abundant spiritual privilege (1Co 10:1-4), by engaging in idolatry both in the golden calf incident (Ex 32:1-6) and with the Baal of Peor (Nu 25:1-9) subjected themselves to demonic influence (implicit reference to the tempter in 1Co 10:13; cf. 7:5b; 1Th 3:5) and incurred God's judgment (1Co 10:1-13). The new union of the believer with Christ and solidarity with other believers in the worship of Christ, celebrated in the Lord's Supper, rules out participation (*koinonia*) in temple feasts which binds the person to the other participants in the worship of demons (1Co 10:14-22). Behind the festive social occasion, Paul says, are evil spiritual beings beckoning the time and attention of the celebrants.

Whether in the form of temple banquets (1Co 10:19-21), magic (Gal 5:20, *pharmakeia*; cf. 2Ti 3:13; Ac 13:6-12; 19:13-20), empty philosophical speculation (Col 2:4, 8, 20-23) or false doctrine (1Ti 4:1-3), Paul clearly believes in the ontological reality and intense activity of malevolent spiritual beings under the hegemony of Satan that seek to capture people's minds and divert them away from God's salvation in Christ (1Co 5:5; 2Co 4:4; 11:3, 13-15; Eph 2:2; 6:12, 16; 1Th 2:18; 3:5; 1Ti 1:20; 3:6, 7; 4:1; 5:15; 2Ti 2:26). The Apostle employs a number of terms for various classes of evil angelic beings that inhabit the heaven and earth and aggressively work to frustrate God's redemptive purposes in Christ: (i) *archai* or "rulers" (Ro 8:38; 1Co 15:24 [s.]; Eph 1:21 [s.]; 3:10; 6:12; Col 1:16; 2:10 [s.], 15); (ii) *exousiai* or "authorities" (1Co 15:24 [s.]; Eph 1:21 [s.]; 2:2 [s.]; 3:10; 6:12; Col 1:16; 2:10 [s.], 15); (iii) *dymaneis* or "powers" (Ro 8:38; Eph 1:21 [s.]); (iv) *kyriotetes* or "lordships" (Eph 1:21 [s.]; Col 1:16); (v) *thronoi* or "thrones" (Col 1:16); (vi) *kosmokratores tou skotous toutou* or "cosmic rulers of this darkness" (Eph 6:12); (vii) ta *pneumatika tes ponerias en tois epouraniois* or "spiritual forces of evil in the heavenly realms" (Eph 6:12); (viii) *angeloi* or "angels" (Ro 8:38; cf. 1Co 6:3; Col 2:18). Several texts have inclusive phrases which refer to every imaginable category of being, good and evil (Ro 8:39; Col 1:16; Php 2:10; Eph 1:21). For Paul, the watershed event is the cross, where Christ decisively defeated all these forces (Col 2:15) and is now exalted to a position of unrivaled sovereignty (Eph 1:20-22). United with the exalted Lord the believer engages in spiritual warfare from the vantage point of eventual but certain victory (1Co 15:24, 27-28; Ro 16:20), seeking to disarm all thought systems that challenge the supremacy of the one Lord Jesus Christ (2Co 10:3-5; O'Brien 1984; Arnold 1992; Reid 1993).

Syncretism and the Church in Colossae

The small town of Colossae, situated in the Lycus valley of the province of Asia, was evangelized along with Laodicea and Hierapolis during Paul"s extended stay in Ephesus (Ac 19:10) through the efforts of Epaphras, a native of Colossae (Col 1:7-8; 4:12-13). The pluralistic religious character of the town is evidenced by Colossian coins that have been discovered bearing the images of such deities as Isis, Sarapis, the Ephesian Artemis, the Laodicean Zeus, Demeter, Men, Selene and Helios (Arnold 1992:139). From the content of the letter to the Colossians we can safely infer that nearly all of the believers were Gentile converts from a pagan background (cf. 1:12-14, 21-22, 27; 2:13; 3:5-7). Some years after its founding a destructive heresy had begun to tear away at the spiritual fabric of the church. Epaphras brought news of the church to Paul, now under house arrest in Rome (Ac 28:30-31), and the Apostle penned the letter to the Colossians.

Though the exact nature of the heresy is uncertain, four of its basic features can be reconstructed from Paul's language: (1) a Greek tendency toward the elevation of knowledge and revelatory experiences (1:26-27; 2:2; 4:3: mysteries; 2:3, 23: wisdom and knowledge; 2:4, fine-sounding words; 2:8, philosophy; 2:18b, fleshly mind puffed up by visions; 2:18a, 23: delighting in false humility); (2) a Jewish orientation toward legalistic prescriptions (2:11-13, circumcision; 2:14, regulations of the written code; 2:16, 21: requirements about eating, drinking, festivals, new moons, Sabbaths, touching, tasting, handling; and even rigid asceticism

[2:23b], yet without effective power to restrain the sinful nature [2:23c]); (3) its essentially human, worldly origins (2:8, traditions of humans and elementary principles of the world; 2:22, human commands and teachings; 2:23, self-imposed form of worship); (4) a patently defective christology that apparently conceived of Christ as part of the *ple | ro | ma* or mediatorial expanse between God and the material world that included angelic powers (2:10b, 15, 18b). There is a growing consensus that the Colossian heresy was an amalgam of Jewish and Gnostic elements, either a judaized gnosticism or a gnosticized Judaism, that above all denied the supremacy of Christ and his sufficiency to mediate redemption between God and people (O'Brien 1982:xxx-xxxviii).

Faced with such teaching Paul expounds the supremacy and sufficiency of the Lord Jesus Christ. Christ himself is the mystery (2:2), the storehouse of wisdom and knowledge (2:3), the *pleroma* of deity (2:9), the reality over against the shadow (2:17), the head from whom these believers are in jeopardy of losing connection (2:19). The christological response to the heresy in the polemical section of Colossians (2:8-23) flows out of the magnifi-cent hymn of 1:15-20 where Christ is praised as Lord over the created universe (1:15-17)—image of God, mediator, goal and sustainer of creation—and Lord of the church whom he reconciled to God through his death on the cross (1:18-20). Far from seeking common ground with the incorporationist religions of Colossae the Apostle is intent on driving them out of the church through his explication of the unrivaled supremacy of the person of Jesus Christ. Instead of rapprochement or accommodation there is displacement. Here is the dividing line for Paul, that is, anything that deprecates the full deity of Jesus and the adequacy of his redemptive work must be steadfastly rejected. Though the most flexible of people when it comes to nonessentials (1Co 9:19-23)—circumcision (1Co 7:19; Gal 5:6; 6:15; cf. Ac 16:3), Jewish food laws (Ro 14:1-4, 21-22), calendrical distinctions (Ro 14:6a), performance of Jewish vows and/or sacrifices (Ac 18:18; 21:22-26), the eating of meat sold in the marketplace that had been offered on a pagan altar (1Co 10:23-27)—the Apostle will not suffer any rival claimant to the believers' allegiance other than the one Lord Christ.

Critical scholars such as J. C. Beker (1980:160, 163, 214, 278, 303-4, 335, 365) reject the Pauline character of Colossians and the closely related Ephesians (written, according to Arnold (1989), to believers who came out of a background of involvement in magical practices and participation in the cult of the goddess Artemis as described in Acts 19, though his thesis is generally considered overdrawn (Lincoln 1990:lxxxi) on the ground that their pronounced christology and its expansion into the metaphysical domain is substantively discontinuous from the functional, soteriological christology of the authentic Pauline letters. But it has been demonstrated that such cosmic parameters are more than anticipated in the uncontested Pauline literature (cf. Ro 8:18-25; 14:9; 1Co 8:6; 15:28; Phil 2:9-11; 3:21) and that the christological hymn of Colossians 1:15-20 is an intensification and development with organic continuity of Paul's earlier teaching (Helyer 1994). Heresy, then, becomes the stimulus and catalyst for Paul's deeper reflection on the meaning of Christ's exalted lordship so that the dimensions of his preeminence are explicitly extended to the fullest expanse of the created universe. Doctrinal aberration becomes an opportunity for Paul to expound the protological dimensions of Christ's person and work. His positive exposition of Christ reveals both his foundational theological convictions as well as a pastor's heart aroused by godly jealousy to present the church a pure virgin to her one husband, Christ (2Co 11:2).

Conclusion

We conclude this study of the apostle Paul's approach to the religious pluralism of his day by identifying three general findings which arise from the data. (1) The Pauline letters provide no encouragement for the inclusivistic "theocentrism" posited by the modern proponents of religious pluralism. When the churches were besieged by alien ideologies that compromised the exclusiveness of the one true and living God or the sufficiency of the person and work of his Son, sole mediator of redemption (1Co 8:6; 1Ti 2:5), the Apostle responded with sharp and incisive countermeasures. What conditioned Paul's response to the religious pluralism of his day, whether in evangelistic or pastoral ministry, was his Old Testament view of God (Guthrie and Martin 1993)— Creator of the universe (Ro 1:20, 25; 11:36; 1Co 8:6; 11:12; 2Co 4:6; Eph 3:9; 1Ti 4:3-4), sovereign Ruler of his world (1Ti 1:17; 6:15), righteous Judge (Ro 1:32; 2:5; 3:4-6, 8; 2Th 1:5-6), Redeemer and Savior whose love (Ro 5:8), mercy (Ro 15:9; Tit 3:5), compassion (Ro 12:1; 2Co 1:3), kindness (Ro 2:4; 11:22), forbearance

(Ro 2:4; 3:26) and long-suffering (Ro 2:4; 9:22) are extended in salvific blessing to humankind through Jesus Christ. Above all, the God Paul preached is the Father of the Lord Jesus Christ (Ro 15:6; 2Co 1:3; 11:31; Eph 1:3; Col 1:3) who planned, directs, and will one day consummate the redemption of the cosmos (Ro 8:18-25).

(2) The church is called to be fully engaged in its witness to people enmeshed in idolatrous cultures without compromising its spiritual integrity. The Apostle denies the objective existence of idols while at the same time recognizing their perceptual reality in the minds of idolaters. The mature believer will demonstrate a sensitivity to those in the church whose conscience has not been fully liberated from past associations. Further, the "liberated" believer must never underestimate the essentially demonic character of systems of worship focused on something other than the one Lord of the church (1Co 8:6; Eph 4:5). The line between acceptable engagement and idolatrous compromise may not always be easy to draw but that does not mean there is no line.

(3) Sensitive to his listeners, the Apostle employed the Greek language with which they were familiar in order to gain a hearing, while redefining those terms within the conceptual framework of the gospel. However, even where syncretism had crept into the church, as at Corinth and Colossae, Paul addresses the believers as saints (1Co 1:2; Col 1:2), confident in the Holy Spirit's ability to preserve the church in purity until Christ returns (Php 1:6). Grace under pressure, or one might say pastoral admonition without panic, characterizes the Apostle's approach to churches struggling to swim upstream against the prevailing idolatrous current. Is this not a worthy model for the modern apostle-church planter whose high calling is, like Paul, to establish living congregations in the still unreached areas of the world (Ro 15:20-21)?

Reference List

Arnold, Clinton E.
    1989   *Ephesians: Power and Magic. The Concept of Power in Ephesians in Light of its Historical Setting.* Society for New Testament Studies 63. New York: Cambridge.
    1992   *Powers of Darkness: Principalities and Powers in Paul's Letters.* Downers Grove, IL: InterVarsity.

Aune, D. E.
    1993   "Greco-Roman Religions." In *Dictionary of Paul and His Letters.* G. F. Hawthorne and R. P. Martin, eds. Pp. 786-96. Downers Grove, IL: InterVarsity.

Beker, J. Christiaan
    1980   *Paul the Apostle. The Triumph of God in Life and Thought.* Philadelphia: Fortress Press.

Bousset, W.
    1970   *Kyrios Christos. A History of the Belief in Christ from the Beginnings of Christianity to Irenaeus.* John E. Steely, trans. Nashville: Abingdon. (Original: 1913.)

Bultmann, Rudolf
    1951   *Theology of the New Testament.* Kendrick Grobel, trans. Two vols. in one. New York: Charles Scribner's Sons.

Carruthers, Gregory H.
    1990   *The Uniqueness of Jesus Christ in the Theocentric Model of the Christian Theology of World Religions: An Elaboration and Evaluation of the Position of John Hick.* Lanham, MD: University Press of America.

Corwin, Charles
    1967   *Biblical Encounter with Japanese Culture.* Tokyo: Christian Literature Crusade.

Dunn, James D. G.
    1990   *Unity and Diversity in the New Testament.* 2nd edition. Philadelphia: Westminster.

Fee, Gordon D.
    1987   *The First Epistle to the Corinthians.* NICNT. Grand Rapids: Eerdmans.

Fisk, Bruce N.
    1989   "Eating Meat Offered to Idols: Corinthian Behavior and Pauline Response in 1 Corinthians 8-10" (A response to Gordon Fee). *Trinity Journal* 10 NS:49-70.

Fitzmyer, Joseph A.
    1981   "New Testament *kyrios* and *maranatha* and Their Aramaic Background." In *To Advance the Gospel*. J. A. Fitzmyer. Pp. 223-29. New York: Crossroad.

Furnish, Victor Paul
    1984   *2 Corinthians*. The Anchor Bible. Garden City, NY: Doubleday.

Gill, David W. J.
    1992   "Behind the Classical Facade: Local Religions of the Roman Empire." In *One God, One Lord: Christianity in a World of Religious Pluralism*. A. D. Clarke and B. W. Winter, eds. 2nd edition. Pp. 85-100. Grand Rapids, MI: Baker.

Guthrie, D., and R. P. Martin
    1993   "God." In *Dictionary of Paul and His Letters*. G. F. Hawthorne and R. P. Martin, eds. Pp. 354-69. Downers Grove, IL: InterVarsity.

Heim, S. Mark
    1987   "Thinking About Theocentric Christology." *Journal of Ecumenical Studies* 24(1):1-16.

Helyer, Larry L.
    1994   "Cosmic Christology and Colossians 1:15-20." *Journal of the Evangelical Theological Society* 37(2):235-46.

Hick, John
    1980   *God Has Many Names: Britain's New Religious Pluralism*. Philadelphia: Westminster.

Hill, David
    1967   *Greek Words and Hebrew Meanings: Studies in the Semantics of Soteriological Terms*. Cambridge: University Press.

Horikoshi, Nobuji
    1986   *Nihonjin no Kokoro to Kirisutokyo* (Christianity and the Heart of the Japanese). Tokyo: Word of Life.

Howell, Don N., Jr.
    1993   "God-Christ Interchange in Paul: Impressive Testimony to the Deity of Jesus." *Journal of the Evangelical Theological Society* 36(4):467-79.

Knitter, Paul
    1985   *No Other Name? A Critical Survey of Christian Attitudes Toward the World Religions.* New York: Orbis.

Koyama, Kosuke
    1985   *Mount Fuji and Mount Sinai: A Critique of Idols.* Maryknoll, NY: Orbis.

Lincoln, Andrew T.
    1990   *Ephesians.* Word Biblical Commentary 42. Dallas, TX: Word.

Mathers, George A., and Larry A. Nichols, eds.
    1993   *Dictionary of Cults, Sects Religions and the Occult.* Grand Rapids, MI: Zondervan.

Meyer, Marvin W.
    1987   *The Ancient Mysteries. A Sourcebook.* San Francisco: Harper and Row.

O'Brien, Peter T.
    1982   *Colossians, Philemon.* Word Biblical Commentary 44. Waco, TX: Word.
    1991   *The Epistle to the Philippians. A Commentary on the Greek Text.* NIGTC. Grand Rapids, MI: Eerdmans.
    1984   "Principalities and Powers: Opponents of the Church." In *Biblical Interpretation and the Church: The Problem of Contextualization.* D. A. Carson, ed. Pp. 110-50. Nashville: Thomas Nelson.

Reid, D. G.
    1993   "Principalities and Powers." In *Dictionary of Paul and His Letters.* G. F. Hawthorne and R. P. Martin, eds. Pp. 746-52. Downers Grove, IL: InterVarsity.

Wedderburn, A. J. M.
    1987   *Baptism and Resurrection: Studies in Pauline Theology Against Its Graeco-Roman Background.* WUNT I.44. Tübingen: J. C. B. Mohr.

Willis, W. L.
    1985   *Idol Meat at Corinth: The Pauline Argument in 1 Corinthians 8 and 10.* Society of Biblical Literature Dissertaton Series 68. Chico, CA: Scholars.

Winter, Bruce W.
    1992   "In Public and In Private: Early Christians and Religious Pluralism." In *One God, One Lord: Christianity in a World of Religious Pluralism.* A. D. Clarke and B. W. Winter, eds. Pp. 125-48. Grand Rapids, MI: Baker Book House.
    1990   "Theological and Ethical Responses to Religious Pluralism—1 Corinthians 8-10." *Tyndale Bulletin* 41:209-26.

Wright, N. T.
    1992   *The Climax of the Covenant: Christ and the Law in Pauline Theology.* Minneapolis: Fortress.

7

THE CONTRIBUTION OF THE GENERAL EPISTLES AND REVELATION TO A BIBLICAL THEOLOGY OF RELIGIONS

Andreas Köstenberger

It should be acknowledged at the outset that the writings grouped together rather amorphously under the heading "general epistles," as well as the book of Revelation, do not self-consciously address the issue of religious pluralism, at least not in terms akin to the modern use, where "pluralism" has come to denote a construct of often rather abstract philosophical or religious sets of beliefs. Even where the issues entailed by a plurality of conflicting worldviews are in view, such as in the book of Revelation, the discourse is conducted largely on a practical rather than doctrinal level, and the prevailing concern is for the spiritual purity of believers rather than for the formulation of apologetic rationales for the purpose of religious dialogue.

The present study should therefore be launched on the basis of the observation that, in the writings under consideration, the presence of other worldviews and religious beliefs is presupposed rather than addressed directly. To what extent can one therefore speak of a contribution made by these books to a biblical theology of religions? Foremost of all, one should avoid overstating one's case by claiming that they reflect a consciously worked out Christian theology and response to religious pluralism in their day—in the opinion of this writer, they do not. Conflicting truth claims are rather brought to the fore by religious persecution and the challenge of formulating a believing approach to it. The New Testament data should not be intellectualized, and one should not claim a greater degree of deliberateness or sophistication than the evidence bears out. Moreover, owing to the occasional nature of these writings, much of the relevant material is incidental rather than systematic, so that many insights can be gained on the level of inference or implication rather than by explicit reference or direct injunction.

In the light of these caveats, do the general epistles and Revelation provide any information regarding a proper Christian response to other religious faiths? What can we learn from these writings about dealing with other religions? First, we can observe how the biblical authors themselves dealt with other religions. Second, we may ask how these writings provide any other helpful material for interacting with other faiths, such as teaching on the unique person and work of Christ, on Christians' identity in the world, and on the church's relationship to the world, particularly with reference to mission.

In the following discussion, emphasis will be given to Hebrews and the Petrine and Johannine material, since James yields little helpful information, and much of Jude is reapplied to a similar context in 2 Peter and can be subsumed under the discussion there. The writings considered here share in common the general backdrop of the dominant political power of the day, i.e. the Roman Empire, and the impending or real suffering of persecution by believers, especially in Rome and Asia Minor. The relationship between Judaism and Christianity is still a vital issue (Hebrews, Revelation), and proto-gnosticism rears its head as an early Christian heresy (1-3Jn). The world's hostility toward the Messiah sent by God, i.e. Jesus, had resulted in Jesus' crucifixion and continued to find expression in the persecution of his followers, just as Jesus himself had predicted (Jn 15:20; 16:33).

Hebrews

This "word of exhortation" (13:22; the only other instance of this phrase in Ac 13:15 refers to a homily) deals with one aspect of religious pluralism, i.e. the relationship between Judaism and Christianity, perhaps shortly before the destruction of the Jerusalem temple in 70 C.E. (note the reference to Timothy in 13:23 and the conspicuous absence of any reference to the destruction of the temple, a fact that, if it had already occurred at the time of writing, would have been highly significant for the writer's argument). The letter is probably addressed to a Jewish-

Christian congregation in Rome (13:14) where the threat of religious persecution tempted segments of the church to defect from Christianity back to the safe confines of Judaism (cf. e.g. 12:4-13), while perhaps revealing that others may never have fully embraced the Christian faith in the first place (cf. the "warning passages" in 2:1-3; 3:6b--4:13; 5:11--6:8; 10:19-39; 13:14-29).

In this time of transition where the lines between Christianity and Judaism were not always neatly drawn (Blomberg 1994:76), the unknown author, probably a second-generation believer (cf. 2:3; perhaps Apollos), keenly accentuates the differences between the old and the new covenant system. He points to a typological correspondence between events in the history of the Old Testament people of God such as Israel's unbelief during her wilderness wanderings subsequent to the exodus (3:7-4:10) and the situation of some in his audience, seeking to show that faith in God also entails faith in Jesus, the person through whom God revealed himself "in these last days" (1:1-4). Faith in Jesus, according to the author, is therefore not an optional appendage to Judaism, but essential, since Judaism, as a religious system, has been eclipsed by Christianity. Inherent in the claim to Jesus' superiority over previous mediator figures, such as angels, Moses, Joshua, or the Old Testament priesthood, is the assertion of the exclusivity of salvation in Jesus, the antitype of these various preceding persons and institutions.

The Supremacy of Jesus

What are the claims made regarding Jesus in the Book of Hebrews? The book opens with several striking assertions of the supremacy of the revelation brought by Jesus, and of the superior nature and work of Jesus (1:1-3). God's revelation in Jesus is superior, since God in ancient days spoke through prophets, while, in the last days, he spoke to us in "son"-revelation (1:1-2), a divine self-disclosure that exceeds that of the giving of the Law which had been mediated by angels (2:2; cf. Ac 7:38,53; Dt 33:2). Jesus' work is superior, since, through Jesus, God made the ages. Jesus also made purification from sin, and sat down at the right hand of the majesty on high (1:2-3). Jesus" nature, too, is superior, since Jesus is the effulgence of God's glory and the exact representation of his nature (1:3). Apparently, no tension is felt between these assertions and monotheism (cf. already the increasing emphasis on mediator figures in the intertestamental literature and the role of wisdom in creation according to Pr 8:22-31; see also Rev below). Finally, Jesus is superior to other spirit beings (i.e. angels, including Satan; see 2:14), in nature, calling, and authority (1:4-2:18). In an age where there is a sharp rise in the interest in angels, Hebrews' emphasis on the supremacy of Jesus is timely indeed.

Jesus is also presented as the great high priest (1:3; 2:9-18; 4:14-10:39; cf. 2:17) who was given an eternal priesthood according to the order of Melchizedek (5:1-7:28) and who instituted a new, superior covenant (8:1-10:39). The writer of Hebrews draws the implication that when Jesus "sat down" (1:3; 8:1; 10:12; 12:2), this indicated that there remained no further need for sacrifice. Complete atonement had been rendered (9:23-28). The question of how to deal effectively with sin is crucial for all world religions. Hebrews provides a powerful answer: Jesus has dealt once and for all decisively with sin. He has overcome the power of Satan. Regarding Judaism, the extensive quotes of Jeremiah 31:31-34 and 31:33 with reference to Jesus (cf. 8:8-12; 10:16-17) imply that, now that a "new" covenant has been made, the "old" covenant is obsolete and no longer effective, so that Jews should find the fulfillment of God's promise of an eschatological covenant in Jesus.

The Identity of Believers

Believers' dealings with other faiths need to be undergirded by an accurate understanding of their own identity, both individually and as a community. According to the author of Hebrews, Christians are pilgrims, exiles in search of a homeland and of a better country, i.e. of "a city prepared by God" (11:13-16; cf. 12:22; Johnsson 1978; Käsemann 1984; Grässer 1986). The pilgrimage to an earthly sanctuary is replaced by the pilgrimage to a lasting heavenly home (6:19-20); Israel's unbelief during the exodus is to serve as a warning against the Hebrews' lack of faith during their new exodus (3:7-4:11; cf. 1Co 10:6,11). Abraham is presented as a model pilgrim: he set out not knowing where he was going, acting upon nothing but God's word of promise, living in tents like a foreigner, looking ahead to a permanent home, not in Palestine, but in heaven (11:8-10). Moses, likewise, scorned the fleeting pleasures of this world (11:24-29). According to the pat-tern set by Abraham and Moses, the readers of Hebrews were to be sojourners embarking on a new exodus, with their way led, not by Joshua (Greek: *Iesous*) but by Jesus (cf. 2:10; 12:2). As the author of Hebrews argues, the Old Testament already contains the acknowledgment that, even after Israel had entered the Promised Land, there remains a "rest" for God's people, i.e. hea-ven (3:7-4:11; cf. Ps 95:7-11; cf. also 11:13-16; Attridge 1980).

The climactic exhortation of the entire book, transcending even 12:1-3, is found in 13:13. After affirming that Jesus suffered outside the gate, the author exhorts his audience, "Therefore let us go out to him, outside the camp, and bear the abuse he endured" (cf. 10:25-26). Remarkably, conceptualizations involving the "temple" have been eclipsed in Hebrews by "tent" and "camp" terminologies. Christians are to count it a privilege to follow the one "who for the joy set before him endured the cross, despising the shame" (12:2). Their mission is to have its root in this radical discipleship which reveals itself in believers' close association with Christ, not just in his glory, but also in his sufferings (cf. also 1Pe 1:11-12; 5:1).

Believers' Relationship to the World

In Hebrews, "witness" terminology is never applied to believers in the active sense of the term, i.e. as a call for them to bear witness. Rather, it is God who bears witness to the faith of previous believers (11:2,4,5,39; 12:1). The many verbal and allusive parallels to the intertestamental book of 2 Maccabees in 12:1-3 indicate, together with the exhortation of 12:4, that the author conceives of the Christian "witness" as one who is prepared to "resist to the point of shedding blood." This certainly was true for many of the believers mentioned in 11:32-38 as well as for the martyrs of the Maccabean period. When facing the prospect of persecution, the Hebrew believers should therefore be inspired by the "great cloud of witnesses" who had gone and suffered before them (12:1), with Jesus, "the pioneer and perfecter of our faith . . . who endured such hostility from sinners against himself," as the supreme forerunner (12:1-3; cf. also 2:10; and 6:20).

The epistle's equivalent to the "witness" terminology found in other writings may be the references to believers' "confession" (*homologia*: 3:1; 4:14; 10:23). The Jewish Christians to whom the epistle is addressed, are to hold fast to their confession, not throwing away their "assurance" (*hypostasis*: 3:14; 11:1), "confidence" (*parresia*: 3:6; 4:16; 10:19,35), or "faith" (*pistis*: 4:2; 6:1, 12; 10:22, 38, 39; 11:1,3,4,5,6,7 [bis], 8, 9, 11, 13, 17, 20, 21, 22, 23, 24, 27, 28, 29, 30, 31, 33, 39; 12:2; 13:7). Moreover, by using the metaphor of a "race," even that of a marathon, the author urges his audience to view suffering as a form of divine discipline designed to perfect them as sons (12:5-11; quoting Pr 3:11-12), just as Jesus himself learned obedience through suffering (cf. 2:10,17-18; 5:7-9). This mindset would help believers persevere in their struggle as they "ran the race" by fixing their eyes on Jesus, just as he had fixed his eyes on God. Christians' primary focus should therefore not be on the world, but, in Jesus, on God.

Implications

The book of Hebrews contributes to a biblical theology of religions its unequivocal assertion of the supremacy of Christ and the finality of God's revelation in him, the "Son." This speaks decisively against all claims by later so-called "prophets," be it Mohammad, Joseph Smith, or others, to have received further direct revelation from God that in effect sets aside or contradicts God's revelation in Jesus Christ. How can anyone, in the light of the assertions made in Hebrews 1:1-2, claim to provide divine revelation beyond Christ without being subject to the charge of blasphemy? This, of course, is also expressed in the warning of Revelation 22:18-19.

The writer's exhortation to believers to go to Jesus "outside the camp" and to bear suffering with him accentuates the call to Christians to be "outsiders," choosing, not the easy road of material prosperity, but the path of the cross, of self-denying, death-defying discipleship and, if called for, even social ostracism. This letter's message will be especially meaningful for the church in a time and place where it is called to suffer for Christ's sake, and where it is tempted to engage in religious compromise in order to escape severe persecution. Of course, the message of Hebrews should not be taken to imply that it is always inappropriate for Christians to exercise influence on society's government and structures. Where this is possible, there appears no reason to preclude such efforts. This involvement, however, should not be coupled with religious compromise or merely be used as an excuse for self-aggrandizement.

1 Peter

Peter's first epistle appears to have been written to believers "dispersed" in Asia Minor at the onset of a major persecution in the early 60s C.E. Peter probably wrote from Rome (5:13), where such a persecution may already have started, in order to prepare his readers for imminent suffering (4:12: "do not be surprised at the fiery ordeal among you . . . as though some strange thing were happening to you"). By referring to the location where he lives at the time of writing as "Babylon" (5:13), Peter symbolically relates Rome to the nation that was responsible for Israel's exile, a metaphor developed even more fully in Revelation (O'Connor 1991:17-26; contra Prete 1984:335-52). Peter, who identifies himself as a "fellow-witness of Christ's sufferings" (5:1), would soon be martyred himself, providing, like Jesus, an example in his sufferings that others could follow (cf. also Jn 21:15-23). In the light of the explicit claims of 1:1 and 5:1, not to mention numerous other factors, Petrine authorship appears certain (see Guthrie 1990:762-81; Carson, Moo, and Morris 1992:421-24; contra Senior and Stuhlmueller 1983:298,302).

Despite 1 Peter 3:15 (and 2:9), there are no elaborate strategies for verbal gospel proclamation in the Petrine literature. The first epistle calls believers to a godly response to imminent suffering, while the second letter reapplies parts of Jude's epistle to Peter's concerns in the context of a "reminder" of the first letter (2Pe 1:12; 3:1). While the author of Hebrews accentuates the new covenant brought by Jesus, thus highlighting elements of discontinuity between Old Testament and New Testament, Peter focuses more on the continuity between Old Testament Israel and the New Testament people of God. In both cases, the salvation-historical character of Christianity, as the culmination of God's revelatory and redemptive patterns begun in Old Testament times, roots believers' faith deeply in one particular trajectory reaching from Old Testament Israel over Jesus to the church comprised of both Jews and Gentiles. The question whether other religious faiths have any revelatory or redemptive value is not directly addressed and may not have been asked in such terms by the authors of the books under consideration. Peter views his faith in deeply personal terms, i.e. both as the fulfillment of Old Testament prophecy (1Pe 1:10-12; 2Pe 1:19-21) and as the result of his personal acquaintance with Jesus (2Pe 1:16-18) rather than merely as the adherence to an abstract system of truth claims.

Peter describes people's lives before their Christian conversion in the following ways: those believers had been pursuing "the passions of former ignorance" (1Pe 1:14; see also 2:11; 4:2), living according to "the futile ways inherited from the forefathers" (1Pe 1:18), and walking in "darkness" (1Pe 2:9; 2Pe 1:14). The people of God have "escaped from the corruption of the world and its passions" (2Pe 1:4) and "defilements" (2Pe 2:20). The response to which Christians are called is described primarily in behavioral and attitudinal terms: they are to "maintain good conduct among the Gentiles" (1Pe 2:12), to "live lives of holiness and godliness" (2Pe 3:11), and to keep themselves "without spot or blemish" (2Pe 3:14). Nevertheless, references to verbal witness are not entirely absent: believers, in analogy to Old Testament Israel, are to proclaim the excellencies of God (1Pe 2:9 alluding to Isa 43:21), and they are to be prepared to give a defense (*apologia*) of their hope (1Pe 3:15). Even the latter reference, however, should not be understood in terms of elaborate interreligious dialogue or the detailed engagement of other world views, but as satisfying the curiosity aroused by Christians' godly response to unjust suffering. To reassure believers, God is presented both as a Father and as a righteous Judge. The final judgment is a recurring theme in Peter's letters (see 1Pe 1:17; 2:12,23; 4:7,17; 5:4; 2Pe 2:1-3:13).

Jesus the Example in Suffering

Who is Jesus, and is he the only Savior? By applying to Jesus numerous Old Testament passages in Messianic fashion, Peter clearly affirms Jesus' uniqueness and exclusive saving role (cf. e.g. 1Pe 2:6-8,21-25). These teachings, however, are not ends in themselves but rather serve the purpose of instructing believers on how to respond to persecution. Like the author of Hebrews, Peter holds up Jesus as believers' example in suffering (1Pe 2:21-25 echoing Isa 53; cf. Heb 12:1-3). Patient suffering on the part of Christians may even lead some to God. This is the implication of Peter's explanatory statement, "For Christ also died for sins once for all, the just for the unjust, *in order that he might bring us to God*" (1Pe 3:18), in connection with the exhortation to suffer for doing what is right (1Pe 3:17). While Peter's focus is on Christians' appropriate attitude toward, and response to, suffering, he does not therefore neglect to point to their need of being prepared to give an answer to those who ask them (1Pe 3:15).

While this approach may be considered to be more defensive than, for example, the "Great Commission" in the Gospel of Matthew, it is an appropriate, as well as realistic, perspective on possible missionizing in the context of persecution. As in 1 Peter 2:9-12, verbal proclamation is linked with the necessity of a holy life: believers are to "set apart the Lord Christ in their hearts" (1Pe 3:16). Like Noah, Christians are to bear bold witness in the midst of hostile unbelievers (1Pe 3:19-20). Moreover, even in a context of persecution, believers are to practice love and hospitality (1Pe 4:8-9; cf. Heb 13:1-2), and to exercise their spiritual gifts, be it those of speaking or serving, to the glory of God in Christ (1Pe 4:10-11). Simply put, believers are to "do good" (1Pe 2:12,15,20; 3:6,11,17; 4:19).

The Identity of Believers

According to Peter, believers are sojourners, "resident aliens" (1:1 *parepidemois;* 1:17 *paroikias*; 2:11 *paroikous kai parepidemos*; cf. also Heb 11:13 *xenoi kai parepidemoi*; Heb 11:9 *parokesen*; and Phil 3:20 *politeuma en ouanois*; cf. Elliott, 1966; id., 1982; Wolff 1975:333-42; Chin 1991; Feldmeier 1992; Schutter 1994). A strong eschatological component flavors the entire epistle, especially in the light of the church's suffering and persecution (cf. also 1:7,9,13; 2:12; 4:7,11,13,17; 5:1,10). Peter reminds Christians in the diaspora of their imper-ishable inheritance kept in heaven (1:4), assuring them that they are, by the power of God, guarded through faith for a salvation to be revealed on the last day (1:5). Thus believers are to rejoice in their hope, even though they have to endure various trials in this world, "for a little while, if necessary" (1:6). Christians are, however, not alone in their sufferings; there is a solidarity of brotherhood in all the world (5:9; cf. also 5:1; and 2:21-25).

Peter's message to his readers is that their "home," i.e. their identity, is found in the "household of God" (*oikos tou theou* 4:17), i.e. the fellowship of God's people, a "spiritual house" (*oikos pneumatikos*, 2:5; cf. O'Connor 1991:20). Paradoxically, these "resident aliens" are also God's "chosen race" (2:9; cf 1:1-2). Peter's charac-terization of his recipients' identity in those terms represents an effort to equip the church in his sphere of influence for the fulfill-ment of its mission. Rather than being discouraged by their powerlessness, uprootedness, and abuse from the world, Chris-tians are given hope and are strengthened in their faith and vision (O'Connor 1991:20). Thus empowered, believers are read-ied to minister to an often abusive world rather than adopting a defensive "siege mentality" (Senior and Stuhlmueller 1983:299). God's people rather are to be "involved strangers," showing "critical solidarity" with the world (Botha 1988:27-37), loving their enemies (cf. Mt 5:44; see Piper 1980:212-31).

God's promises to his Old Testament covenant people of a physical land, inheritance, and descendants are transformed in 1 Peter into expectations of eternal realities, thus putting exper-iences in this life into an eschatological perspective. Likewise, categories reserved in the Old Testament for Israel are now freely transferred to the church (2:9-10; cf. Steuernagel 1986:8-18). It appears that Peter's entire vision of the church's mission takes its cue from the Old Testament concept where Israel was to be a mediatorial body, a light to the nations, thus revealing God's glory (cf. Ex 19:6 and Isa 43:20 quoted in 1Pe 2:9; cf. also Isa 49:6). The implication of Peter's incorporation of the Old Testa-ment concept of mission into the new covenant community points to the essential continuity between these missions, contrary to some who exclusively stress the discontinuity between the dyna-mics involved in the Old Testament and New Testament.

Analogous to Israel's intended function, Peter perceives the church's presence in the world from the vantage point of mis-sion, stressing its identity as a witnessing community (Robinson 1989:176-87). The transferal of covenant categories from God's old to his new covenant community in 2:9-10 is linked with the climactic purpose statement in 2:9, "that you may proclaim the excellencies of him who called you out of darkness into his mar-velous light," quoting Isaiah 43:21. Immediately following this, the epistle's recipients are exhorted to keep their behavior excel-lent among the nations "so that in the things they slander you as evildoers, they may on account of your good deeds, as they ob-serve them, glorify God in the day of visitation" (2:12). The pro-clamation of God's excellencies thus must be undergirded by "ex-cellent behavior," now not by Old Testament Israel among the Gentiles, but by the new covenant community in the unbelieving world surrounding it.

Believers' Relationship to the World

As one writer contends, "[No] part of the NT speaks out more eloquently . . . on [the] theme of holiness of life as a way of Christian witness [as does 1 Peter]" (O'Connor 1991:17). The entire section of 1:13-2:10 is devoted to Peter's exhortation to his readers to live a holy, spiritually set-apart life. This injunction is grounded in God's command to the people he called out from slavery in Egypt to be holy and set apart for him (1:15-16 quoting Lev 11:44,45; 19:2; and 20:7). While the external expressions of such distinctness, i.e. dietary, ritual, and ceremonial laws, have since largely been rendered obsolete, there remains a need for God's people to live a distinct Christian lifestyle and to abstain from both physical and spiritual adultery (1:14,18; 2:1,11-12; 4:3-4,15; cf. Mt 5-7). By living holy lives, Christians reveal to their surrounding world God's very own nature, just as Israel was called to do. A failure to do so, today as then, amounts to a failure of the mission of the church of Christ, regardless of its verbal gospel proclamation. Notably, the power for living a holy life is not drawn from one's own moral capacity, but derives from Christ's redemption (1:18-23).

Not only this, even believers' submission to earthly authorities, be they civil, economic, familial, or ecclesial (cf. 2:13,18; 3:1; 5:1,5), is necessary ultimately for its witness to the world, a frequently overlooked fact. The obligation to be God's representatives does not only provide a powerful rationale for the necessity of submission to governing authorities (2:13) or economic superiors (2:18), but also for wives to husbands (3:1) and for younger men in the church to elders (5:5). In each case, the same word, *hypotasso*, is used (this is given inadequate consideration by Senior and Stuhlmueller 1983:300-301, 310-11 and Richardson 1987:70-80). Christian wives may hope to win over any unbelieving husbands by their submissive behavior "without a word" (3:1). In a society where women were usually expected to adopt their husband's religion, Christian wives in mixed marriages were in a very vulnerable position indeed (Balch 1981). Husbands, in turn, are to treat their wives with understanding, as fellow-heirs of grace (3:7), while the entire congregation is to humble itself under God (5:6). Indeed, Christ, the powerful one who became weak (cf. 1Co 1:25-29; 2Co 8:9; Php 2:6-8), is more than able to strengthen those in minority positions, be it Christian citizens in an ungodly society, Christian slaves suffering from the abuse of people in authority over them, or Christian wives who have to live with their unbelieving husbands. According to Peter, the church is the place where exemplary relationships in proper submission are to be lived out before a watching world.

Implications

Peter's teaching on believers' relationship to the world does not focus on the verbal proclamation or defense of the gospel but rather on Christians' distinctive living out of their roles in their families, workplace, society, and Christian communities. Lofty Christian concepts and virtues are brought down to earth and applied to everyday relationships. No sphere of life is to be exempt from obedience to Christ. This vision was revived during the Protestant Reformation. If there is no difference between Christians and non-Christians in the way they live (as is all too often the case in contemporary North American society), their witness will remain ineffectual. There will be no reason for questions concerning the hope of Christians (3:15). Peter believes that the Christian lifestyle has certain unique qualities which will render the gospel proclamation attractive, but only if a holy lifestyle is maintained and not compromised.

John

The first epistle of John can only be adequately understood against the backdrop of a proto-Gnostic heresy which had entered the church through some who had since left it (1Jn 2:19). The letter was apparently written in an effort to undo the harm done by those false teachers and to reassure the members of the congregation that were left behind bewildered and confused (Carson 1992). Thus the epistle provides, not an example of interreligious dialogue, but a pattern of dealing with Christian heresies or cults.

The letter's argument may best be traced by the claims it seeks to refute: (1) the claim that those teachers "walked in the light" while living immoral lives (1:6); (2) their claim to have no sin (1:8,10); (3) their claim to know Jesus while disobeying his commandments (2:4,6); (4) their claim to love God while hating their brother (4:20; see also 2:9,11; 3:10,12,15); and (5) their claim to special divine revelation (2:20,27). These tenets appear to reflect some form of early gnosticism, a Greek philosophy that was rooted in neoplatonic dualism, fostering a dichotomy between matter and spirit, considering the former evil and the latter good. Significantly, the appropriate Christian response to such an infiltration of concepts incompatible with true Christianity is spelled out not so much on the level of verbal argumentation (except for leaders such as the author of the epistle) as in terms of proper living: believers are not to "love the world" (2:15-17) and they should love their fellow-believers (3:16-18). Then they can be fully assured that they have the Spirit (2:20,27), that they are born of God and know God (3:1-2,9-10; 4:4-5; 5:18-19), and that they have eternal life (5:11-12).

Christians, according to John, are not to "engage" the world, but rather to "overcome" both the evil one (2:13-14) and the world (4:4-5), a victory that is assured by believers' spiritual birth and by their faith in Jesus who had come to destroy the works of the devil (3:8). In fact, John asserts that the whole world is under the power of the evil one (5:19) so that God's people should keep themselves from idols (5:21). When John affirms that believers in Jesus know the truth, he does so, similarly to Peter, in deeply personal terms: they "know him who is true" and "are in him who is true" (5:20). The world is merely temporary and will pass away (2:17). It is already "the last hour" (2:18), and the spirit of the antichrist is at work in the false teachers (2:18; 4:1-6; see also 2Jn 7) whose judgment is sure (2:28).

The Uniqueness of Jesus

John's major christological and soteriological emphases are, in interaction with proto-Gnostic challenges, twofold: first, Jesus came in the flesh (1:7; 4:2; 2 John 7), rather than having merely had a phantom spiritual existence as the Docetists would hold; and second, Jesus made atonement for the sins of the entire world (2:2; cf. 4:10), contrary to those who conceived of religious experience merely in terms of esoteric divine revelation. Whether it was docetism, Cerinthianism, or some other form of early gnosticism that provided the major target for John in his epistles (for an overview, see Carson, Moo, Morris 1993:452-55; Schnackenburg 17-24; Marshall 1978:14-22; Stott 1988:44-55), these assertions of Christ's full humanity and the universality of his atonement effectively countered the notion that Christianity could merely mediate a higher knowledge of the divine, or a more profound spiritual union with God, without first dealing with sin and providing salvation and forgiveness (cf. Jn 20:23; 1Jn 1:9; 2:1). A full-fledged, entirely orthodox Christology and soteriology are thus crucial and indispensable in dealing with other religions which may be open to *aspects* of Christian teaching, such as in the ethical realm, or which may be willing to acknowledge that Jesus was a prophet from God, while refusing to embrace biblical christological and soteriological teaching in its entirety.

The Identity of Believers

John's message to believers is deeply reassuring. He focuses primarily on the ontological realities that are beyond question for all true believers, such as their regeneration ("child-ren of God": 3:1-2,10; "born of God," "of God": 3:9; 4:4,6; 5:18-19; cf. also Jn 3:3,5) and possession of the Holy Spirit (2:20,27), the availability of forgiveness of sin (1:9; 2:1), or their eternal security (5:11-12). In dealing with adherents of other religions, therefore, Christians need not be in the least intimidated by other forms of spirituality that claim intimate knowledge and communion with God (Carson 1994). Christianity is a religion for everyone, not merely for a spiritual elite initiated into certain religious rites or blessed with esoteric knowledge of divine secrets, as was the case in the mystery religions that flourished in that day (Köstenberger 1991:80-83).

Various tenets of mystery religions and different strands of Greek religion and thought have been incorporated into modern movements such as the New Age movement or other forms of an emerging Western neo-paganism. Thus it is highly relevant to learn how biblical writers such as John deal with challenges proceeding from such faiths.

Believers' Relationship to the World

We find in John's letters no strategy or call to a direct verbal engagement or dialogue with the world. This may be owing to John's realization that the world is caught up in its sinful blindness and hardened in its opposition to Christ, to believers, and to the gospel, so that John appears less optimistic regarding the possibility of successfully engaging other belief systems by way of religious dialogue (cf. 2:15-17). Indeed, to challenge or to change a commitment to other religions entails not merely more education, information, or arguments, but repentance, i.e. a changing of one's mind, especially regarding the person and work of Jesus Christ. John's message to his readers is, not an exhortation to enhanced apologetic efforts, but a call to perseverance, holiness, full assurance, and brotherly love. Prophetically, John insists that a person's true beliefs will be apparent in that person's actions, be they good or evil. Truthful lives thus make a telling statement to the surrounding world, while people living a lie invalidate their words by their deeds. This approach brings the issue of the credibility of the church's and of individual believers' witness into proper focus.

Implications

John's concern for the purity of the church, which is shared by other New Testament writers such as Paul accentuates the need for distinguishing Christian teaching clearly from syncretistic elements. In North America, there is generally far too little concern for the purity of the local church, and, paradoxically, missionary efforts are often far too removed from local churches. In an age of pragmatism and pluralism, John calls the church to a return to the simplicity and clarity of biblical teaching on the Christian faith. Believers should not merely engage in interaction with other world religions, but also be concerned with preserving the internal purity of the Christian faith and make every effort to purge it from syncretistic elements and mere nominalism. This necessitates more emphasis on being than doing, and a renewed concern for believers' true identity in Christ in contrast to the surrounding world. John is not hostile to the world, but he reminds us that the world is ultimately hostile to us as Christians. This should warn us both against a complacent accommodation to the world and against undue optimism in engaging the world.

Revelation

The churches in Asia at the end of the first century were apparently plagued by opposition both from within and from without. Believers were called to resist both pressures. On the one hand, the Roman Empire is cast as the very personification of evil in its perpetration of religious persecution (cf. e.g. 17-18). On the other hand, numerous false teachers are named, some apparently Jewish: the Nicolaitans (2:6,15); the so-called "synagogue of Satan" (2:9; 3:9; cf. also 2:24); some perpetrating the "teaching of Balaam" (2:14; cf. 2Pe 2:15-16; Jude 11); and the "woman Jezebel" (2:20).

Of these forces, i.e. the Domitian persecution (81-96 C.E.) and Jewish opposition, the Romans are the ultimate threat. The Jews are merely opportunistically collaborating with the Romans to secure a relatively autonomous fragile coexistence with the powers that be. This spirit of accommodation and compromise, already evident in the political maneuvering of the Pharisees and Sadducees in Jesus' and Paul's day, is strongly condemned in Revelation and clearly presented as unacceptable for Christians. Such accommodation is not a solution for Christians. The role of the Vatican and the state churches of Germany and Austria during the rise and rule of Hitler in Nazi Germany, for example, illustrates both the danger and the reality of the temptation faced by the institutional church in times of persecution. Genuine believers only have the choice of separating themselves in such times from apostate bodies and banding together in underground resistance movements, though whether this should entail the use of force is disputable.

John's vision presents the Messianic community as a woman who, after having given birth to a son (i.e. Christ), flees into the wilderness to escape persecution, but there is nurtured by God (12:1-17). Satan is cast as a dragon (cf. Satan as a roaring lion in 1Pe 5:8; deSilva 1991:185-208). "Babylon," i.e. Rome, is powerfully portrayed as "the great harlot" with whom the kings of the earth committed acts of immorality, "the scarlet woman . . . drunk with the blood of the saints, and with the blood of the witnesses of Jesus" (17:1-6). Witness in such a context must not lead to defilement (cf. 14:4). While Peter's first epistle still emphasizes discriminate participation in society, the seer here focuses on non-participation in activities associated with the pervasive emperor cult. Revelation may thus be likened to a subversive underground tract, seeking to strengthen believers against the controlling power by holding before them a vision of the end, where, in a complete reversal of contemporary circumstances, Rome will get her due while Christians will be completely vindicated. Only faith could sustain a vision so entirely contrary to people's current experience. As in Hebrews and 1 Peter, only infinitely more gloriously, Jesus is presented as believers' supreme example in suffering.

John's Prophetic-Apocalyptic Political and Social Analysis

Rome's depiction in Revelation as a dragon (12:3-18), a beast (13:1-18), and as a whore (17:3-18), seeks to underscore its usurpation of Christ's power and its promotion of false, counterfeit worship that detracts from the worship of the one true God. Political power and the materialistic amassing of earthly wealth are seen to be at the heart of the self-serving spirit driving the ambitions of the citizens of this worldly empire. John thus attempts a social critique of the society of his day. He provides this analysis, however, not in an effort to evangelize or to dialogue, but merely in order to open the eyes of believers who are tempted to compromise. After all, this compromise may perhaps be due merely to the failure to see clearly the demonic underpinnings of the world system, with the result that those believers think they can combine the securing of their own well-being with their religious commitment. John excludes this possibility. His predominant concern is for the purity of the communities of believers and of individual believers in partially apostate bodies rather than for the development of an elaborate apologetic for the Christian faith as such.

There is evidence that the Roman emperor insisted on being addressed as *dominus et deus*, i.e. as "Lord and God" (Suet. *Dom.* 13; Mart. *Epig.* 9.56.3). Revelation itself may provide evidence for the escalation of a "polemical parallelism" (Deissmann's term) between the titles and institutions in Rome and the church. Jewish synagogues introduced the curse of the Minim into the "Eighteen Benedictions" in about 90 C.E. (Hemer 1986:216) as a means of detecting Christians in the synagogues. The lack of explicit evidence for outright persecution of Christians under Domitian points to the possibility that persecution took on the form of a systematic and deliberate exploitation of pressures inherent in people's existential circumstances, be it social, economic, political, or religious (Hemer 1986:11), a powerful lesson for Christians even today. Owing to heavy taxation of Jews, many appear to have left the synagogues in order to avoid paying tribute to the Romans, a practice met by the Jews' occasional disclosure of their bona fide members to the Roman authorities.

Christians thus were caught between two alternatives if they wanted to avoid persecution for their faith: to associate with paganism by participating in the emperor cult ("Nicolaitanism"; see below), or to find shelter in the confines of the local synagogue, which implied, besides heavy taxation by the Romans, also at least implicit denial of the Lord Jesus Christ, especially after 90 C.E. Believers' commitment was thus severely tested, and the temptations to compromise were many. The flawed rationale for any of these false alternatives, however, needed to be fully exposed in order to open up for believers the glorious vistas of eternal heavenly worship of the glorious Christ. His sole worthiness of worship, and the absolute necessity of holiness and spiritual purity, needed to be held squarely before struggling believers in order to confirm their resolve to face even death rather than the loss of eternal blessedness with Christ. The latter, in the ultimate analysis, was by far the worst option.

These alternatives, then as today, are not always as clearly in view as might be desirable. Then as today, it is the prophetic responsibility of those so called within the Christian church, to expose potential areas of moral and practical compromise for believers and to clarify the choices that are required, if severe eternal consequences should be avoided. The book of Hebrews provides an early example of this issue. The question of whether or not people who had fallen away from the faith during persecution should afterwards be reinstated in the church in later years likewise shows that this continued to be a vital issue in the church.

The Christian Community's Enemies

It is now necessary to return in more detail to the specific enemies of the faith named in the seven letters. It appears that these opponents of believers should be divided into two distinctive threats: on the one hand, Jewish antagonists, i.e. the "synagogue of Satan"; on the other hand, antinomian tendencies, i.e. the Nicolaitans perpetrating "the teaching of Balaam," and the "woman Jezebel." We may begin with the latter phenomena.

Who were the Nicolaitans (Hemer 1986:87-94)? It appears that this movement, possibly founded by a certain Nicolaus, was based on a misrepresentation of Pauline teaching on Christian liberty (cf. 1Co 8:1-13; 10:20-30; see also 2Pe 3:15-17?). Thus believers were tempted to violate the spirit of the apostolic decree cited in Acts 15:20,29 which explicitly forbade Gentiles in mixed communities to commit fornication and to eat meat offered to idols. Such partaking may also have been viewed as participation in the emperor cult, thus raising acutely the choice faced by many between Christ and Caesar. Balaam, the Jewish prophet, whose counsel was traditionally seen as contriving the Israelites' sin with the daughters of Moab, may here be viewed typologically as a tempter of God's people to both literal and figurative, i.e. spiritual, immorality (cf. Nu 25:1-2; cf. also Jude 11 and 2Pe 2:15).

The exalted Jesus, according to John, demanded that the churches of Asia Minor be purged from such influences, since these would make individual believers and entire communities more susceptible to spiritual compromise, watering down the churches' distinctness, and forging unholy links between believers and the emperor worship. Significantly, the distortions of Christian teaching associated with Nicolaitanism are primarily practical, not doctrinal, in nature. They involve no extensive apologetic dimension but rather have serious behavioral implications. There is no hint regarding the need to engage the world view of Nicolaitanism by individual believers or even entire communities beyond the prophetic denunciation of the teaching by Jesus himself as reported by John.

Similar to Balaam, Jezebel was considered to have induced Israel into idolatry (1Ki 16:31-33; 21:25-26). Hemer considers the teaching of Jezebel in Thyatira to have been a reapplication of Nicolaitanism to a different context. While elsewhere the lives of Christians were at stake, here it was their livelihood. The "woman Jezebel," it may be conjectured, argued that it was possible for believers to join a guild and to participate in its feasts in order to secure their business interests without compromising their faith (Hemer 1981:123). By claiming to know "the deep things of God" (cf. 1Co 2:10?), this teaching may have sought support from Paul's dealing with a similar situation in Corinth, while conveniently setting aside the apostolic degree of Acts 15. This kind of rationalization and ethical accommodation to lower pagan standards would certainly have been tempting where people's livelihood was at stake and where compromise may at the outset have appeared harmless and inconsequential. Jesus' prophetic counsel, however, drew a sharp line between the worship of God and participation in practices perpetrated in a society pervaded by Satan. A clear choice was required; such lukewarmness would not be tolerated by the Lord Jesus Christ.

In the light of these pressures, John emphasizes the following truths (Osborne 1993): (1) Jesus' supreme worthiness of allegiance; (2) the confidence that people adhering to conflicting truth claims will be judged by God at the final revelation of Jesus Christ and that believers will ultimately be vindicated by a sovereign, just God; (3) that believers are to entrust themselves to God in their suffering; (4) the conviction that the world's opposition to Christ and his people is ultimately satanically inspired. Once again, truth is personalized in Jesus. A person's relationship to Jesus is the crucial issue, not merely beliefs about him.

The book's categories are black and white, and the need for an uncompromising attitude is stressed (cf. e.g. 18:4). Angel worship is discouraged (19:10). The world is characterized as given to spiritual fornication and blasphemy (17:2-3), as drunk with the blood of martyrs (18:6), as the dwelling place of demons (18:2), the source of material enrichment for some who absorb its values (18:3). Just as Satan is a liar, the world he controls is a counterfeit system. Jesus, on the other hand, is faithful and true (19:11), the Word of God (19:13), and the King of kings and the Lord of lords (19:16).

Overall, it appears that the greatest problem faced by believers at the time when Revelation was written was not the question of how to dialogue with adherents of other faiths, but rather the issue of how they could keep their Christian practice clean from associations with their pagan environment. The solution was spiritual separation rather than compromise and accommodation. Prophetically, Jesus calls for a clear choice between Christ and Caesar, excluding the possibility of a middle ground.

The Portrayal of Christ

The Christophany of chapter 1 presents Jesus as the faithful witness, the proto-martyr (see below), as the firstborn from the dead who is preeminent in his church, and as the ruler of the kings of the earth, thus fulfilling Jewish Messianic expectations (cf. 1:5). Jesus is the lion (5:5; cf. Ge 49:9) turned lamb (*to arnion* 5-7; 12:11; 13:8; 14:1,4,10; 15:3; 17:14; 19:7,9; 21:9,14,22, 23,27; 22:1,3), an image that combines paschal imagery with the notion of the warrior-lamb prominent in apocalyptic literature. By relating Isaiah 11:1 to Isaiah 53:2,7 (with possible overtones of Zec 3:8-10), and by adding to those passages the notion that Jesus was the warrior-Messiah who would execute God's judgment, John portrays Christ's death as the decisive victory over Satan and death without stopping there. Jesus is also the fulfillment of Jewish hopes of a powerful, reigning king: "John, rather than reinterpreting the Messianic hopes of Judaism solely along the lines of a cosmic victory accomplished at the cross, fully expected the hopes to be fulfilled and that victory to be prosecuted on earth at the return of Christ" (Hultberg 1994:16; cf. Ac 1:6).

Besides the Christophany of chapter 1 and the image of the lion turned lamb, perhaps the most powerful depiction of Christ in Revelation is that of the rider on the white horse, as the one who is called "faithful" and "true" (ch 19). One further notes that John deliberately blurs the images of God and Christ (cf. Rev 1:14 which portrays Jesus in terms of the "Ancient of Days," i.e. God, in Da 7:9; cf. also the development of Da 7:13 in Rev). Christ is clearly portrayed as divine (cf. e.g. the use of the term "the first and the last" for Christ: 1:8,17; 21:6-7; 22:13), and the book vividly depicts the dual worship of God and Christ (cf. e.g. 5:8-14)

The Christian Community's Witness

Are the believers to whom the book of Revelation is addressed thus to be merely indifferent toward the destiny of people in the surrounding world? This appears to be precluded by the presence of the "witness" motif (Poucouta 1988:397-405), a term that undergoes a permutation from "testimony" to a person's dying for the faith, i.e. as a "martyr" (cf. Heb 12:1,4; see Holtz 1962:55; Filippini 1990:401-49; Vassiliadis 1985:129-34; von Campenhausen 1936).

As a matter of fact, Bauckham has recently argued persuasively that the queston of the conversion of the nations is at the center of the prophetic message of Revelation (Bauckham 1993). This becomes apparent especially by a close study of the book's Old Testament allusions. This author draws attention particularly to the following passages which he considers crucial: (1) 14:6-7 where the usual terminology, "the inhabitants of the earth," is changed to "those who sit on the earth," thus indicating that the latter group, unlike the former, is still a potential prospect for conversion; the passage also contains an allusion to Psalm 96:2b, with Psalm 96 being the first of a string of psalms celebrating Yahweh's universal lordship; (2) the account of the two witnesses (cf. esp. 11:5-6) where Moses and Elijah, both of whom confronted pagan rulers and religions, serve as the Old Testament models, but where the two witnesses transcend both, since they die a martyr's death while neither Moses nor Elijah did, with Elijah (and Moses according to tradition) not having died at all; (3) the vision of the grain harvest (14:14-16), an image, not of judgment, but of the gathering of converted nations into the kingdom of God; and (4) the Song of Moses (15:2-4), a piece of careful exegesis of Exodus 15:1-18 with reference to Psalms 86:8-10; 98:1-2; 105:1; Jeremiah 10:6-7; and Isaiah 12:1-6. As Bauckham contends, in this final period, God does not deliver his faithful people by the slaughter of their enemies, as he did in order to bring the nations to repentance and faith. In this way, those ransomed by the sacrifice of the Lamb now themselves are called to sacrifice in order to participate also in his victory, giving it universal effect.

Thus believers' witness is the quintessential prerequisite for the conversion of the nations. At this "climax of prophecy," suffering and martyrdom are placed in an eternal perspective. Jesus is the prime witness, the proto-martyr (1:5; 3:14; cf. also 11:3; 14:6; 17:6; 19:11; 22:16, 20). Reference is also made to Antipas, "the faithful witness" (2:13), and to the "two witnesses" who testify before the inhabitants of the earth for 1260 days and then are killed on account of their testimony (11:3,7). John the seer, too, is said to testify (1:2; 20:18).

John, similar to Peter, introduces himself as a "fellow-sharer in the tribulation and kingdom and endurance in Jesus" (1:9; cf. 1Pe 5:1-2). "The testimony of Jesus" (1:2,9; 12:17; 19:10 [bis]; 20:4), i.e. believers' testimony *to* Jesus (objective genitive: Filippini 1990:401-49; contra Ford 1990:141-46), with a possible martyrological nuance, i.e. "unto death" (Vassiliadis 1985:129-

34), is presented as a prophetic act that discloses God's truth in a world adamant in its opposition to God. In the final days, it is not active outreach, but "holding to the testimony of Jesus" that is needed, for "the one who overcomes" and "has endurance" is the one who will be rewarded eternally ("overcomes" *nikao*, cf. 2:7,11, 17,26; 3:5,12,21 [bis]; 21:7; "endurance" *hypomone*, 1:9; 2:2,3,19; 3:10; 13:10; 14:12; cf. Heb 10:32,36; 12:1,2,3,7; 1Pe 2:20 [bis]).

Nevertheless, "witness" terminology clearly involves, not mere indifference to the world's fate, but the proclamation of a divine message (cf. 14:6 where an angel proclaims an eternal gospel to all nations). Also, exhortations to repent for five of the seven churches, or individuals in them, clearly indicate that the seer still allows room for conversions (2:5,16,21-22; 3:3,19). The unrepentant attitude of those confronted with the gospel in Revelation also functions as the foil for John's "justification of God," i.e. theodicy (cf. Osborne 1993:63-77; Yarbro Collins 1989:729-50). Finally, the church is, as in 1 Peter, presented as a kingdom of priests (1:6; 5:10; 20:6; cf. Ex 19:6; Isa 61:6; cf. also 1Pe 2:5,9), indicating its mediatorial function for the world (Bandstra 1992: 10-25).

Implications

The book of Revelation is supremely concerned with the difference between true and false worship (Peterson 1992). When dealing with other religions, this book will be supremely relevant regarding the nature and proper object of worship as well as regarding the meaning of martyrdom and believers' future hope.

According to the author of Revelation, it is ultimately Satan himself who stands behind the forces conspiring against Christians. Nevertheless, the church is called to witness until the end, even in the midst of fierce and deadly persecution. It should discern, and expose, the unholy allegiances and ungodly compromises that tempt believers to drift away from their complete allegiance to Christ in this world. A person's Christian commitment is not merely a system of beliefs to be upheld, but an allegiance to be maintained in the face of constant opportunities for compromise. In the post-Christian West at the dawn of the third millennium after Christ, where, according to Francis Schaeffer's prophetic words, personal peace and affluence reign, even in segments of the evangelical subculture, this is a timely message indeed.

Conclusion

The general epistles and the book of Revelation deal with a variety of pastoral concerns and issues of vital interest to the recipients of those writings. Many of these entail the unique and supreme role of Jesus in the Christian faith and life, the identity of believers, and their relationship to the surrounding world, especially in regard to persecution. Conflicting world and religious views are touched upon primarily from the vantage point of their potential for distorting the purity of the Christian faith. The author of Hebrews asserts that the entire old covenant system was merely a model of the life of the new covenant inaugurated by the once-for-all sacrifice of Jesus. Judaism is thus shown to cling to the mere preparatory edifice of which Jesus has become the fulfillment. The Petrine epistles challenge believers to maintain a godly life witness, involving proper submission to authority, in order to render the gospel message attractive. The Johannine correspondence seeks to safeguard its readers from competing views such as proto-gnosticism, in an effort to protect believers from doctrinal and moral compromise. The book of Revelation, finally, presents a vision of believers' future that dramatically reverses their present experience: suffering will turn to glory, and the now powerless will rule with Christ.

The writings considered here do not self-consciously map out a strategy of engaging other religions. Their thrust is primarily defensive, seeking to preserve the purity of individual believers and of entire congregations, while calling believers to hold fast to their confession (Hebrews), witnessing by their entire lives and words (1 Peter), and persevering until the end (Revelation). The book of Revelation, with its contrasting scenes of true and false worship, evokes powerful images etching into our minds crucial importance of choosing the proper object of worship.

Reference List

Attridge, Harold W.
    1980   "'Let us strive to enter that rest': The Logic of Hebrews 4:1-11." *Harvard Theological Review* 73: 279-88.

Balch, David L.
    1981   *Let Wives Be Submissive: The Domestic Code in 1 Peter.* SBLMS 26. Chico, CA: Scholars.

Bandstra, A. J.
    1992   "A Kingship and Priests: Inaugurated Eschatology in the Apocalypse." *Calvin Theological Journal* 27:10-25.

Bauckham, Richard
    1993   "The Conversion of the Nations." In *The Climax of Prophecy. Studies on the Book of Revelation.* Pp. 238-337. Edinburgh: T & T Clark.

Blomberg, Craig
    1994   "Critical Issues in New Testament Studies for Evangelicals Today." In *A Pathway into the Holy Scripture.* Philip E. Satterthwaite and David F. Wright, eds. Grand Rapids, MI: Eerdmans.

Botha, J.
    1988   "Christian and Society in 1 Peter: Critical Solidarity." *Scriptura* 24:27-37.

Carson, D. A.
    1992   "Reflections on Christian Assurance." *Westminster Theological Journal* 54:1-29.
    1994   "When is Spirituality Spiritual? Reflections on Some Problems of Definition." *Journal of the Evangelical Theological Society* 37:381-94.

Carson, D. A., Douglas J. Moo, and Leon Morris
    1992   *An Introduction to the New Testament.* Grand Rapids, MI: Zondervan.

Chin, M.
    1991   "A Heavenly Home for the Homeless. Aliens and Strangers in 1 Peter." *Tyndale Bulletin* 42:96-112.

deSilva, David A.
    1991   "The 'Image of the Beast' and the Christians in Asia Minor: Escalation of Sectarian Tension in Revelation 13." *Trinity Journal* 12 NS:185-208.

Elliott, John H.
  1966   *The Elect and the Holy*. Leiden: E. J. Brill, 1966.
  1982   *A Home for the Homeless. A Sociological Exegesis of 1 Peter, Its Situation and Strategy*. London: SCM.
Feldmeier, Reinhard
  1992   *Die Christen als Fremde: Die Metapher der Fremde in der antiken Welt, im Urchristentum und im 1. Petrusbrief*. WUNT 64. Tübingen: J. C. B. Mohr (Paul Siebock).
Filippini, R.
  1990   "La forza della verità. Sul concetto di testimonianza nell'Apocalisse." *Rivista Biblica* 38: 401-49.
Ford, J. M.
  1990   "Persecution and Martyrdom in the Book of Revelation." *Bible Today* 28:141-46.
Grässer, Erich
  1986   "Das wandernde Gottesvolk. Zum Basismotiv des Hebräerbriefes." *Zeitschrift für die neutestamentliche Wissenschaft* 77:160-79.
Guthrie, Donald
  1990   *New Testament Introduction*. 4th edition. Downers Grove, IL: InterVarsity.
Hemer, Colin J.
  1986   *The Letters to the Seven Churches of Asia in their Local Setting*. JSNTSS 11. Sheffield: JSOT.
Holtz, Traugott
  1962   *Die Christologie der Apokalypse des Johannes*. Berlin: Akademie.
Hultberg, Alan D.
  1994   *The Christology of the Revelation to John*. Seminar paper presented at Trinity Evangelical Divinity School, 1994. Deerfield, IL.
Johnsson, William G.
  1978   "The Pilgrimage Motif in the Book of Hebrews." *Journal of Biblical Literature* 97:239-51.
Käsemann, Ernst
  1984   *The Wandering People of God*. Roy A. Harrisville and Irving L. Sandberg, trans. Minneapolis: Augsburg.

Köstenberger, Andreas J.
    1991   "The Mystery of Christ and the Church: Head and Body, One Flesh." *Trinity Journal* 12 NS: 79-94.

Marshall, I. Howard
    1978   *The Epistles of John*. NICNT. Grand Rapids, MI: Eerdmans.

O'Connor, Dan.
    1991   "Holiness of Life as a Way of Christian Witness." *International Review of Mission* 80:17-26.

Osborne, Grant R.
    1993   "Theodicy in the Apocalypse." *Trinity Journal* 14 NS:63-77.

Peterson, David L.
    1992   *Engaging with God. A Biblical Theology of Worship*. Grand Rapids, MI: Eerdmans.

Piper, John
    1980   "Hope as the Motivation of Love: 1 Peter 3:9-12." *New Testament Studies* 26:212-31.

Poucouta, P.
    1988   "Mission-teamoignage dans l'Apocalypse." *Spiritus* 29:397-405.

Prete, B.
    1984   "L'espressione he en Babyloni syneklekte di 1 Pt. 5,13." *Vetus Christus* 21:335-52.

Richardson, R. L.
    1987   "From 'Subjection to Authority' to 'Mutual Submission': The Ethic of Subordination in 1 Peter." *Faith and Mission* 4:70-80.

Robinson, P. J.
    1989   "Some Missiological Perspectives from I Peter 2:4-10." *Missionalia* 17:176-87.

Schnackenburg, Rudolf
    1992   *The Johannine Epistles*. Reginald and Ilse Fuller, trans. New York: Crossroad.

Schutter, William L.
    1994   Review of *Die Christen als Fremde: Die Metapher der Fremde in der antiken Welt, im Urchristentum und im 1. Petrusbrief* by Reinhard Feldmeier. *Journal of Biblical Literature* 113:743-45.

Senior, Donald and Carroll Stuhlmueller
    1983   *The Biblical Foundations for Mission*. Maryknoll, NY: Orbis.

Steuernagel, V. R.
    1986   "An Exiled Community as a Missionary Community. A Study based on 1 Peter 2:9,10." *Evangelical Review of Theology* 10:8-18.

Stott, John R. W.
    1988   *The Letters of John*. TNTC. Revised edition. Grand Rapids, MI: Eerdmans.

Vassiliadis, P.
    1985   "The Translation of MARTYRIA IESOU in Revelation." *Bible Translator* 36:129-34.

von Campenhausen, Hans
    1936   *Die Idee des Martyriums in der alten Kirche.* Göttingen.

Wolff, C.
    1975   "Christ und Welt im 1. Petrusbrief." *Theologische Literaturzeitschrift* 100:333-42.

Yarbro Collins, Adela
    1989   "Persecution and Vengeance in the Book of Revelation." In *Apocalypticism in the Mediterranean World and the Near East*. 2nd edition. David Hellholm, ed. Pp. 729-30. Tübingen: J. C. B. Mohr (Paul Siebeck).

PART II

HISTORICAL AND DOCTRINAL PERSPECTIVES

8

CHRISTIANITY AND THE RELIGIONS IN THE HISTORY OF THE CHURCH

James F. Lewis

The title "Christianity and the religions in the history of the church" suggests an ambitious task. An encyclopedic work might succeed in describing how Christianity as a whole has related to and interacted with other religions as whole entities. But this is clearly impossible in such a short scope. In fact, even in more extensive works such topics as "Christianity and Hinduism" or "Christianity and Islam" would require a daunting grasp of the diversity that is Christianity in its interaction with the diversity of these religious entities. In any case I believe the best I can do is to offer a brief account of how certain individuals have thought about and interacted with religious others and the consequences of those developments.

The history of Christian-religious other interaction is more than the history of how thinkers, churches and communities have viewed the discrete religions. It is also a history of how Christians have come to understand religion as a human phenomenon. As we shall see in the last section of the paper, Christianity helped to stimulate the modern academic study of religion experiencing both positive and negative outcomes in its understanding of its relationship with the religions.

The individuals I have selected to carry the narrative have been chosen either for the significance of what they did and/or thought or for what I think they symbolized. Accordingly, I have chosen the apostle Paul for his role in leading the Jesus movement out of Judaism to gain an identity of its own. Tertullian was one of several outstanding apologists who sought to offer early formal responses to pagan folk religion and the classical intellectual tradition in which Greco-Roman life was rooted.

William of Rubruck's debate (1254 C.E.) with Buddhists symbolizes the difficulty Christians had (and continue to have) in understanding important segments of the religious world. Luther's attitudes to Islam are examined and shown to be a response based not so much on reliable information about Muslims as on theological and geopolitical concerns.

In the modern period I wish to show how the missionary movement played a small but important part in the rise of the academic study of religion and how that development is impacting Christian self-understanding and interreligious views.

The Period of Apostolic Foundations: From Insiders to Outsiders to Newcomers in the Religious World: to 100 C.E.

Referring to the first century Andrew Wall says, "For one brief, vital period, Christianity was entirely Jewish" (Wall 1990:17). This period saw the emergence of a Christian community that at first was socially and religiously tied to a Palestinian Jewish world. Until about 50 C.E. almost all Christians were Jews or had been converts to Judaism. These followers of a Jewish Jesus practiced Judaism while gradually but painfully and inexorably revising and transcending their Jewish heritage. Their Jewish heritage, especially the acceptance of the Old Testament, provided them with the first paradigms for dealing with religious others.

As the Christians moved outside Jewish enclaves they very naturally viewed religious others as similar to the Jewish division of humanity into Jews, Greeks and Barbarians. Thus Christians inherited a bi-polar way of conceptualizing religious outsiders. Greeks stood for culturally sophisticated pagans and the barbarians the uncultured. In some form, this "we-they" conception was to be the typical and largely unchallenged Christian attitude toward other religious communities until the late twentieth century.

Paul's response to the first century religious world was at each of the levels of his contact with it: Judaism, classical paganism, and pagan folk practices. The Judaism of Paul's time was confident of two things, each of which evoked different responses from Paul. They held that God was one and could only be worshipped spiritually without the aid of manmade images. Paul stood foursquare behind this truth and made it a fixed point in his preaching to pagans (Ac 17). But secondly, according to the Jewish mind, followers of the Jesus movement seriously threatened the unicity of God. Paul's response to this was unaccommodating: Jesus is "image of the invisible God" (Col 1:15) yet in such a way that did no violence to that unity. Jesus is the "fullness of the Godhead bodily" (Col 2:9). Paul agreed with his Jewish contemporaries in their message about one God. But he radically departed from that heritage in regarding Jesus as God. The Apostle asserts twin doctrines: God is one and Christ is God. In promoting these doctrines, Paul and the other apostles launch a new religion in human history.

One other point about Paul and Judaism. Though he grieves over their rejection of Messiah, he foresees a future for them. They will be co-inheritors of the eternal ages as a result of a supernatural operation which will enable them to accept the Lord Jesus whom they have so recently rejected (Ro 9-11).

Paul's writings and recorded experiences at Lystra, Athens and Ephesus demonstrate a thorough knowledge of the pagan Roman world and the Hellenistic culture embraced by it. He knows some classical poetry and is able to carry on dialogue with contemporary philosophers (Ac 17). He seems to find no place to incorporate ideas from writings of classical Greek philosophers and moralists. Rather, he treats non-Jewish religion, both in its philosophical and more popular forms, with sternness. In 1 Corinthians the wisdom of the Greeks is regarded as foolishness. The popular pagan rituals and beliefs, occult practices of spiritism, divination, spell casting and spirit possession are opposed, excised and exorcised. In Romans 1 he condemns pagan morality as moving away from the truth and descending into self-destructive spiral.

Yet there are glimpses of a kinder and gentler side too. When Paul compares the moral Greek to the self-righteous Jew, he seems to suggest the moral Greek may be less severely judged (Ro 2). But in all, Paul seems to draw a sharp contrast between the gospel and the beliefs and practices of the non-Jewish world. Paul's motto relative to the full range of religious beliefs and practices around him might well have been his words in 1 Corinthians 2:2: "I resolve(d) to know nothing while I was with you except Jesus Christ and him crucified."

In sum, Christians in this period first gain their identity vis-a-vis Judaism and then go on to sharpen that identity even while contextualizing the message in terms understandable to the broader Roman world. The most fundamental material product of this period is the emergence of the New Testament, a scriptural corpus which became the touchstone to guide subsequent inter-religious relationships.

The Patristic Era: Christianity moves from being a Struggling Newcomer to a Self-assured Resident: 100-400 C.E.

Andrew Walls notes that the most significant internal religious development for Christianity at this time is the rise of orthodoxy. "Of all the new religious ideas which entered with the Christian penetration of Hellenistic culture, one of the most permeative for the future was that of orthodoxy, a canon of right belief, capable of being stated in a series of propositions arrived at by a process of logical argument" (Wall 1990)

The Christians were faced with religious communities, pagan and Jewish, which had already worked out some systematization of their beliefs. This was clearly true of classical paganism which included the writings of Plato and Aristotle and their various spin-offs. It was also true of Judaism, to some extent, with its rabbinical schools. In view of these realities there was a need to attend to Christian systematics and the result during this period was "orthodoxy, a logically expounded belief set in codified form, established through a process of consultation and maintained through effective organization" (Wall 1990:18).

In this setting Patristic apologists sought to defend their beliefs and state their views against contenders in the marketplace of religious ideas. In dealing with Judaism, the apologists could turn to the New Testament to guide their ideas. But there was comparatively less to draw on from the New Testament in dealing with the philosophies of classical thought. "[T]heologians had almost no biblical precedent for their apologetic to pagan thought" (Pelikan 1971:27).

The early church fathers also had to respond to Roman state religion which called on Christians, like other citizens, to worship the Emperor. But according to George Williams, they were less concerned with the contemporary religions of their own day than they were with classical Greek paganism and pre-Christian Judaism. In dealing with these entities this "new community of faith which thought of itself as a third race, neither Jew nor Gentile, neither Barbarian nor Greek," developed eight distinct positions to explain how these religions related to the revelation of truth through Christ (Williams 1969:322-3). The views are as follows:

1. The view that there might be a few *individuals* elected from amidst the vast numbers of pagan lost. The religions, qua religions, however, were false religions (Williams 1969:323).

2. Some were possibly saved who could be called "Friends of God" who were heirs to limited portions of the primal Edenic message that had survived and been passed down to certain pagans.

3. Through the influence of the eternal *Logos*, some of the classical Greek moralists and philosophers had received divine guidance in working out their philosophy. This ubiquitous influence of the pre-incarnate Christ was a downpayment on the "plentitude of the revelation of the Word as incarnate in Jesus Christ" (Williams 1969:323). Justin was foremost among those who saw a connection between the philosophers and the preexistent Logos who "enabled pagan thinkers like Socrates to see dimly what came to be clearly seen through the revelation of the Logos in the person of Jesus" (Pelikan 1971:32).

4. There was good in the religions. However, whatever was good had been borrowed (or stolen) from either the Hebrews and/or the Christians. This is the most widespread interpretation of the church fathers. Christians were here taking the same approach which many Jewish apologists, for example Josephus, had taken against the Christians. Specifically apologists alleged pagans read Moses (Justin) and plagiarized scriptures (Theophilus of Antioch).

5. The religions were counterfeits deliberately spun by Satan to tempt the weak and sinful to embrace them rather than the true faith.

6. National angels guided all people toward the truth which they experienced in various stages and degrees of obedience and disobedience.

7. The non-Judaeo-Christian religions were a judgment on various people for having rejected Edenic monotheism and the perfect worship enjoyed by Adam in his pre-fallen state.

8. Finally, there is a universalistic strain in the writings of a few of the apologists: "God intended the salvation of all men and would eventually bring about a *restitutio omnium* (Acts 2:21), including the fallen angels" (Williams 1969:323).

In a general way these theories echo with a theme of opposites: old vs. new; the before vs. the after; the imperfect vs. the perfect; and the lost vs. the restored (Williams 1969:320).

Even so, it seems relatively clear that there is no absolute uniformity in the above schematization of the apologists regarding the relationship of Christian truth to the non-Christian religions. In the above there are some polar opposites. Numbers one and five are nearly entirely negative: religions are false and/or Satanic counterfeits. Number eight proposes an eschatological universalism. Somewhere in the middle is the view there may be limited numbers in the religions that could be saved though this was due to factors extrinsic to the pagan religions themselves: numbers two, three and six.

In selecting a representative for this period one might choose a spokesman for either the more generous or more conser-vative of the above polarities. Origen certainly has been a favorite source for modern exponents of a universalist view. He was regarded by Byzantine Christianity to be the most creative of apologists. But on the other hand the Byzantine theologian Psellus was probably right when he said: "the famous Origen...was the pioneer of all our theology and laid its foundations, but on the other hand, all heresies find their origin in him" (Pelikan 1974:244). Tertullian, on the other hand, according to Pelikan, ranks with Augustine and outweighed all the Greek apologists (Pelikan 1971:28).

Tertullian was concerned to speak to two bodies of religious literature from the past and those who continued to draw on that wisdom to shape their religious conceptions. First, he addressed the philosophers such as Socrates and Plato and other classical pagan religious thinkers. Second, he reached back to the "poets" of Greece's antiquity, not so much for the purposes of arraying a separate Christian critique against them as to use them against the philosophers. In his view, it was equally unreasonable to follow either the philosophers or the poets in their theology. Thirdly, he is aware of the day-to-day idolatrous practices and traditions regarding deities in his native north Africa, as well as abroad in the empire in such places as Boeotia, Syria, and Arabia.

As to the contemporary scene it was one where, in the minds and experiences of the masses, gods held influence and power over certain buildings, cities, territories, states, and nations. It was a world governed by deities, by astrology and the occult. Tertullian spares no criticism of temple worship of the many pagan gods. "The principal crime of the human race, the highest guilt charged upon the world, the whole procuring cause of judgment is idolatry" (Tertullian, *On Idolatry*, 2.1; in *ANF*, Vol 3, p. 61).

Tertullian recognizes the existence of some laudable elements in paganism but rather than interpret this due to the constitutionally given *Logos* in the mind of all, as did Justin and Origen, he understood this as due to natural law given first in an unwritten form to Adam and Eve and through them passed down orally to the nations. This corresponds to number two above. This is the theory that what is true in pagan thought is a residual from primeval times. In this, Tertullian, of course, speculates.

He also believed, along with other apologists, that the ancient pagans must have read Hebrew scriptures to have arrived at their truth. In his argument against Marcion he says: "Moses and God existed before all your Lycurguses and Solons. There is not a single later age that does not derive from primitive sources" (Pelikan 1971:35). This, along with the belief in the transmission of a residual truth, takes the view that the earlier is the better. It doesn't matter that neither Tertullian nor the fathers could prove this claim. What mattered was its effect on contemporary pagan thinkers who were inclined to place a high value on antiquity. The older was indeed the truer.

In sum, Tertullian takes a very exclusive position toward paganism in all its manifestations: philosophical and contemporary. Grant summarizes it this way. Though Justin, Irenaeus and Clement were "friendlier to Greek Philosophy than other Christians of their time (e.g. Tatian and Tertullian) they really had no use for Greek, Roman and oriental religions. They identified such religions as idolatry and considered them false" (Grant1988:288).

The Age of Barbarian Christianity: 400-1500 C.E.

Western Christianity in the period from 400 to 1500 now crosses additional cultural and religious boundaries penetrating into the barbarian territories of western and northern Europe which are to be the setting for new states. What is new in western Christianity, says Andrew Wall, is the idea of a Christian nation.

Of apparent significance to our topic in this period is Thomas Aquinas' *Summa Against the Gentiles*. It was written to Christians about "Gentiles," meaning of course pagans. Ironically there were very few living "Gentiles" around, and those there were could not have appreciated the polemic directed against them. Aquinas was writing against a backdrop of many centuries of conflict with classical thought without himself personally having contact with non-Christian thinkers. His work, of great importance for subsequent centuries of Catholic Christians, did not constitute anything new in Christianity's perceptions of and encounters with the larger religious world (See Pelikan 1971:39).

Perhaps the most significant development outside Europe, but profoundly impacting it during this period, is the rise of Islam and its threat to these Christian states. Pelikan says that Islam posed "the most powerful organized alternative to Christianity until the rise of the Comintern in the twentieth century" (Pelikan 1974:27).

But it is not the new religious competition in the form of militant Islam that I want to highlight in this period. Rather I wish to turn to a late medieval occurrence to examine what a rough go Christians had and continued to have for some centuries when dealing with religions in the far east.

When Franciscan friar William of Rubruck arrived in the court of Mongke Khan in Mongolia in 1253 C.E. he was one of ten Dominican and Franciscan monks over a period of 100 years from 1245-1346 who were attempting to win the Mongols to Christ (Moffett 1992:404-420). What he, his brother missionaries and subsequent missionaries to the east in succeeding centuries discovered, was a religious world the likes of which they had never before encountered and which constituted an absolutely new religious challenge in the history of the church.

Richard Fox Young examines William's experience in debating with a Buddhist monk in the year 1255 (Young 1989: 100-137). Besides calling attention to the fact that this debate is the first ever recorded between a Buddhist and a Christian, the value of Young's study is in showing the difficulty which William had in dealing with the religions against which he was competing for acceptance. William's experience symbolizes the immense work that remained to be done to understand the sophisticated Eastern religious thought world Christian missionaries were now encountering. Though there were notable inroads into the mysteries of Indian and Chinese thought by subsequent Catholic missionaries like Robert D'Nobili and Mattheo Ricci, it remained a religious world which was not carefully studied until the modern period.

Prior to their conquests the Mongols had remained undisturbed in their centuries old shamanistic beliefs and practices. Their understanding was that the world was populated with gods and spirits that controlled their lives yet could also be harnessed for good. Similar to the autochthonous religious world of ancient and contemporary cultures, at the top was "Eternal Heaven" *(Mongke Tngri)* or "Father of Heaven" who dwelt in the sky, the image of which was the sun. But there were a host of *tngri* (powers) numbering as many as 100 that were more approachable and intimate with daily life. There were also miscellaneous spirits: familial, territorial and ancestral.

William arrived at the court to find this indigenous Mongol religion in transition since it was being challenged from several directions. Buddhist and Taoist functionaries from China, Central Asia and Tibet were also present in the Khan's court to explain the way of the Buddha and the Tao. These had been invited by previous khans to join the bevy of court counselors on things spiritual, administrative and political. As religious representatives they were in the vanguard of Chinese religionists who sought to introduce a better way to the Mongol barbarians. The presence of these Buddhist and Taoist believers had the potential of usurping the function of the traditional shamans. But from the Khan's perspective they merely offered an opportunity for him to intentionally supplement and improve, though to that degree also alter, the traditional Mongol religion.

William's presence is then somewhat unique. He found himself in dialogue with sophisticated barbarians (Buddhists and

Taoists) who saw themselves as seeking religious change of those whom they too considered barbarians (Mongols and Christians).

According to William's account, the Khan sponsored a quadrilateral debate on Pentecost eve, 1254, between representatives of the indigenous Mongol religion, Buddhists, Taoists and Christians. The court debates were to provide the Khan with the opportunity to hear these representatives interact, debate and argue. The Khan would draw conclusions he felt were appropriate.

There was not much actual camaraderie or tolerance between the Buddhists and Taoists at court. Some decades before this debate Chang-chun the Taoist (1148-1227) had attempted to improve his status at court by placing the Buddhist Yeh-lu Chu-tsai (1189-1243) in a bad light by making statements to the Khan from which it could be inferred that Buddhists were "envious of the ecstatic experiences enjoyed by the Taoists" (Young 1989: 107). Further tension occurred when financial privileges were sought by Taoists and granted by Genghis Khan leading to uncivil relations at the time William came on the scene.

The Buddhist, Yeh-lu Chu-tsai, viewed Taoist grounds for the claim to superiority quite differently. Ever since the Chinese Tang dynasty times Buddhists, Taoists and Confucians had been recognized as three religions (*san chiao*) with a common origin and common goal. The goal, stated in largely Confucian terms, was self-cultivation and each religion brought its own unique helps to that end. The religions were thus co-religions with a common aim.

Yeh-lu Chu-tsai's views show how this traditional conception of mutual tolerance was more an ideal than reflection of fact. His interpretation of the *san chiao* (three religions) theory placed these religions into a hierarchy with Taoists at the bottom, Confucians in the middle and, not surprisingly, Buddhists at the top. Yeh-lu Chu-tsai encouraged his patron Genghis Khan to become a Buddhist sage since it was a better way for him than becoming either a Confucian or Taoist sage. This, then, is the setting for the debate at the Khan's court.

According to William's journal the Khan's summons to debate read as follows: "each of you says that his doctrine is the best, and his writings the truest. So he (the Khan) wishes that you shall meet together, and make a comparison, each one writing down his precepts, so that he himself may be able to know the truth" (Young 1989:111-12).

Christianity and the Religions in History 153

The opening exchange between William and Fu-Yu was whether the debate should be about the origin of the world and the nature of the soul as suggested by Fu-yu or as suggested by William that it be concerning God "about whom you think differently from us." In the exchange that followed Fu-Yu offered that only fools believe God is one while the wise say there are many. Further, he proposed that "though there is one (God) in the sky who is above all others, and of whose origin we are still ignorant, there are ten others under him, and under these latter is another lower one. On the earth they are infinite in number." William asked if this one God was omnipotent to which Fu-fu countered: "If your God is as you say, why does he make the half of things evil?" This did not go anywhere but when William proposed they return to the question "whether....any god is omnipotent" Fu-yu responded that no god is. This was followed by William's response: "Then no one of your gods can save you from every peril, for occasions may arise in which he has no power. Furthermore, no one can serve two masters: how can you serve so many gods in heaven and earth?" (Young 1989:113-115).

The debate between the two abruptly ended here as Fu-Yu appeared to be speechless. That night William confesses in his journal that he felt he had won the debate. That is why he was so surprised when he was summoned to the court the next day and told that he must forthwith leave the kingdom while Fu-Yu could stay.

William records the final exchange between Mongke and himself. Admonishing William not to put down what Mongols held sacred the Khan said: "We believe that there is only one God by whom we live and by whom we die, and for whom we have an upright heart." Given Mongol belief in a large number of deities surrounding them but headed up by *tngri* or "Eternal Heaven" he could only have been thinking of Eternal Heaven as a sort of first among equals.

> When William attributed this to the grace of God, Mongke added a caveat to distinguish the Mongol worship of Eternal Heaven from Christian monotheism: 'God gives you the Scriptures, and you Christians keep them not. You do not find in them that one should find fault with another do you?' (Young 1989:104).

With this the interview was finished and William's only choice was to follow the sovereign's directive.

What went wrong? It was not a matter of tactlessness nor any personal failure. Rather it was that William, though perhaps as knowledgeable as any Christian alive about Buddhist beliefs, did not understand one of the main tenets of Chinese Buddhist thought—*upaya*. For William, if one affirmed that there was only one god, it could not be rationally maintained that there were many. William followed the logical and historic Christian position so nicely expressed by Tertullian in his argument with idolaters of his day. To them he said: "You cannot continue to give preference to one without slighting another, for selection implies rejection" (Tertullian, *Apology*, Ch 13 in *Ancient Nicene Fathers*, Vol. III, pt 1. 29).

But the selection of one religious truth did not imply the rejection of its opposite to Fu-Yu. And ignorance of this not only cost him the debate and resulted in his banishment, but removed him as a contestant for the Khan's conversion. The field was now left to Buddhists and Taoists who as disputants did understand the doctrine of *upaya*.

Upaya was a doctrine proposed by the Chinese Tien-Tai patriarch Zhi-yi (538-597) in the sixth century C.E. to account for conflicting and logically irreconcilable Buddhist texts originating from India while at the same time claiming to be authentic. Which, if any, of these texts were taught by the Buddha, was the question. If one took a strictly logical approach, one would have to select one or some and reject a great many others. They could not all be right (on logical grounds) but how could any be wrong when they came from Indian Buddhist missionaries and enjoyed extensive support?

Into this context Zhi-Yi proposed the interpretation offered in one of those texts, the *Lotus Sutra* (*Saddharmapun-darika*). It states that the Buddha taught all the texts as *upaya* or "skillful means." That is, the Buddha taught his disciples according to their readiness to understand. To the immature, he taught the Tripitaka. To the more mature he taught the *prajna* texts. To the fully mature he taught the *Lotus Sutra* as the highest and most complete statement of the truth. The texts taken together were so diverse in their teaching that some said the Buddha was a man while others said he was a god. Some taught that one could only attain nirvana by strenuous personal effort while others taught that personal effort was insufficient and only the grace of Buddhas and Bodhisattvas would avail. Some refused to comment on what happens to the individual at death, while others (*Sukhavativyuha*) promised a paradise for those who had faith in the Buddha.

Young analyzes Fu-Yu's advantage over William in this way: "Buddhism is purposely pluriform because the Dharma is difficult to grasp. If from the outside it appears contradictory, from the inside it is perfectly consistent, in terms of *purpose* if not of *meaning* and *logic*. Provisional truth is not absolute; lower truth can obscure or even conceal higher truth. Nevertheless, all truth is *valid* as such and should not be condemned, excluded, or withheld from individuals who do not yet recognize its inadequacy" (Young 1989:131).

William did not succeed with Mongke because he took an either/or attitude toward Mongol belief in many gods. In his view there were only two choices: god was one or gods were many. But William lost out to Fu-Yu in the view of the Khan, because Eternal Heaven and the other Mongol *tngri* were accepted by the Buddhists while William's religion made no room for them. Fu-Yu accepted the *tngri* provisionally, not because it was true, but as an expedient means. Due to Mongke's limited karmic development, he "had no capacity at that moment to conceive of anything higher" (Young 1989:134).

This is only a single incident but it was not to be an isolated one. Again and again Christian witnesses in the Far East failed to understand the religious thought forms of those they encountered. Would an understanding of *upaya* by William have enabled him to succeed? Probably not. But at least he would not have failed on that account. He may have found a different way to deal with his opponents and the Khan's religion.

The Age of Revision and Expansion: First Stages of World Christianity: 1500-1800 C.E.

Three significant developments in this period are the success of revisionist Christianity under the leadership of the reformers, expansion of the Christian mission as European nations discovered and aggressively conquered overseas lands within the reach of their maritime technology and the intellectual challenges arising through the "Enlightenment" which provoked defense and accommodation.

There is not a lot to be said about Protestant attitudes toward and relationships with non-Christian religions at the beginning of this period other than with respect to Islam.

> Although the religious leaders of the Age of Reformation were seldom directly concerned with the significance of non-Christian religions, the problem at times claimed their attention in connection, especially, with the threat presented by the Ottoman Turks or with the question of the salvation of virtuous pagans, raised with urgency by both the recovery of classical literature and the discovery of new peoples overseas (Williams 1969: 319).

The Reformers did not have the intimate contact with the non-Christian world which the writers of the Patristic era experienced. But the Patristic writers seem to reflect more on religions of the past, now largely superseded by Christianity, than on the religions current with their times. The Reformers, on the other hand, though much further from living contact, had to deal with a contemporaneous religion directly affecting their lives. They lived under the looming shadow of expansion of the Muslim Ottomans into Europe. Already three patriarchates in the east had come under their rule and religion.

Concerning the issue of classical pagans, Luther did not reflect overly much about this question though he does take a considerably more conservative approach than either Erasmus or Melanchthon. He held the opinion that those elements in the pagan writers which echo divine truth were probably handed down to them from pre-Noachian times. Luther was thus affirming a position taken by Tertullian, which, as we saw above, was itself one of eight taken by the church fathers regarding the pagan philosophers. "This is one of the few instances of Luther's use of a patristic theme in speaking of non-Christian religions" (Williams 1969:351)

Prior to Luther, theologians of the Middle Ages had proposed three theories regarding Islam, at least two of which were affirmed by Luther. 1) Islam was a chastisement of Christians by God for their schisms and moral declensions. 2) Muhammad was either an emissary of Satan or the Anti-Christ since he usurped the finality of Jesus Christ and his revelation. 3) Allah was merely another name for the true and living God and that God might give Muslims salvation by virtue of their obedience to the Quran (Williams 1969:323-324)

Luther took a kinder view of the Muslim philosopher he did know than of the ordinary Muslim he did not. He thought it not likely that a philosopher like Avicenna, devoted as he was to mind and reason, actually believed in the Quran. One pursuing unrevealed truth would not find much of value in something so obviously bogus. But there were the general rank and file Muslim believers whom he referred to in inflammatory terms as "gross filthy sows." Of them Luther says "they do not know why they live or what they believe" (Williams 1969:347). Strong language! But one must be cautioned that Luther, in the same context, referred to Popish Christians as "plain sows."

From the biblical and theological perspective Luther applied to Islam what he applied to the Pope: they were a religion that sought to be accepted with God by good works. By taking this view, Luther contributed something of his own to the menu of Christian interpretations that had been growing since the Patristic era. For Luther, Christianity had become a religion of self-righteous recitation. Recitation of truth without the reality of experience. Recitation of doctrine and creed that had been fatally corrupted by medieval scholasticism. Luther hoped to turn Christianity back from dead religion to a pristine doctrine and experience. He saw Islam like he saw Christian works righteousness. All those who attempt to gain acceptance with God by good works are bound to be excluded by God.

Yet there may have been some admiration for Islam here too, for Luther must have known something of *salat*, the practice of prayer five times a day. He may have favorably contrasted the austere and imageless mosque with the lavish cathedrals of Europe. Indeed, Luther may have complimented Islam when he observed there was a more intense earnestness among pagans (meaning Muslims) than among Christians. He drew on Jesus' words in Luke 16:8: "the sons of this world are wiser than the sons of light." Yet Luther makes no statements that would lead us to believe there could be salvation for Muslims or for pagans.

Luther took limited interest in the Quran. It had been available in Europe as early as 1143 C.E. when it was first translated into Latin by Robertus Ketenensis but apparently he had not read it until late in his career. He had read a 1320 C.E. polemic against the Quran entitled *Confutatio Alcorani* and translated it into German with his own added apologetic. In 1542 he read the Quran and concluded that three-fourths of it was nothing more than a tissue of lies.

A new translation of the Quran was prepared by Theodor Bibliander, a Zurich theologian, which was opposed by the authorities. Luther demurred, however, and in the preface which he was invited to write, he took a very hard line against Islam by indicating that evangelical Christians should separate themselves from "Jews Turks and Gentiles...if they really do consider that it is alone God eternal, creator and sustainer of all things, who hears our prayers and is ready to give us eternal life." To this Williams adds: "Never before had Luther made it so explicit that he regarded his God as utterly different from that not only of Muslims and Jews but also of papists, Anabaptists, and other heretics" (Williams 1969:350).

Luther also viewed Islam from a political perspective. He regarded the menace of the Turks as God's instrument in judging the false and idolatrous ways of the Roman Church. In a context in which Luther opposed the Pope's power of remitting the penalties of sins for the purpose of raising revenues for the crusades, he remarks that the Pope's anti-Turk crusade in fact opposed God's intent to use the Turks as a punishment for the church. The Turks would bring about a judgment which the church was unable to avert through repentance. Leo X's rather accurate summary of Luther's view is this: "To fight against the Turks is to resist God's visitation upon our iniquities" (Williams 1969:339). This did not mean that Luther had a positive view of Islam but only that it was an agent of God for punishment. In Luther's view, the Turks were "God's rod and the Devil's servant" (Williams 1969:341).

Luther's experience with and attitude toward Islam teaches us at least two things. Social and political realities can and often do influence one's attitude toward the religions of others. Secondly, wherever the church is in understanding its own theology will surely affect one's outlook on the religions. This is made abundantly clear in the next period.

World Christianity: Religious Worlds Collide: 1800-2000 C.E.

It was in the nineteenth and twentieth centuries that Christianity significantly penetrated two of the last remaining centers of historic religions. After 1860 India and China receive hundreds and even thousands of Christian witnesses who establish churches in the heartland of Hindu, Buddhist, Taoist and Confucian traditions. It was at about the same time that the academic study of religion with its non-theological interpretations was launched with the effect of removing Christianity from any special status vis-a-vis other religions. These two developments were interrelated.

This vigorous nineteenth-century missionary movement not only assured that Christianity would be truly global, but that the religions encountered would never be the same. Regarding China, John King Fairbank said that the missionaries alone sought to change China not just trade with them (Fairbank 1974:2).

In both China and India, the missionaries won comparatively few converts but their influence in indigenous social and religious matters was significant. That is seen especially in India. William Carey's commitment to translate selected Hindu classics including the *Ramayana* was so that missionaries and young Indian Christians alike could become conversant with the religious views of Hindus and thus avoid appearing to them as "barbarians." According to Carey,

> it is very important that we should gain all the information we can of the snares and delusions in which these heathens are held. By this means we shall be able to converse with them in an intelligible manner. To know their modes of thinking, their habits, their propensities, their antipathies, the way in which they reason about God, sin holiness, the way of salvation, and a future state, to be aware of the bewitching nature of their idolatrous worship, feasts, songs, etc., is of the highest consequence, if we would gain their attention to out discourse, and would avoid being barbarians to them (Speer 1933:147).

It is a matter of history that Carey's mission contributed to significant Hindu reform. Ram Mohun Roy's Brahmo Samaj joined with the missionaries in criticism of widespread practices of infanticide, *devadasi* and *sati*. Roy did not become a Christian but accepted a monotheistic orientation and was opposed to idol worship. While many Bengalis were influenced to think seriously about revising their religious practices if not their beliefs, others such as Dayananda Saraswati took a more defensive stance in launching the Arya Samaj which continues today. The attack on other Hindu institutions including women's social and educational conditions helped to stimulate what has been called the Hindu Consciousness movement, which helped to give Hindus an identity vis-a-vis western Christianity.

Carey's skills as a Sanskritist led to his employment by the East India Company to teach British employees Sanskrit literature at Ft. Williams College. While he was only one contributor to the growing interest in the indigenous religious and philosophical literature of India, by mid-century the foundations had been laid for the modern discipline of *religionswissenschaft*, the science of religion. Other missionaries contributed their part as well. James Legge (1815-1895) sent out by the London Missionary Society in 1839 translated the *I-Ching* and other ancient classics and took the first chair of Chinese literature established by Oxford University. Journals and ethnological materials of missionaries provided academics information about cultures and religions.

In the latter half of the century pioneers in the disciplines of psychology, anthropology and sociology all made religion an important subject of investigation. Edward Burnett Tylor's *Primitive Cultures* (1871) explained the rise of religion and the belief in God based on his speculations about primitive people's mistaken interpretation of deceased relatives they met in their dreams. Durkheim gave a sociological interpretation to the genesis of belief in God and Freud saw religion as rooted in illusion.

While religion was debunked by some, others synthesized and harmonized it into some essential unity. The emphasis was not upon their distinct identities, religious goals and religious means but upon their intuited essences or their phenomenological similarities. Scant or no attention was paid to their differences, their opposites or contradictions.

The study of comparative religions and the science and philosophy of religion tended with many, and in its popular effect, to create the idea that religion is a universal and essentially identical thing always and everywhere, and that each historic religion, Christianity included is only a branch of a common trunk (Speer 1933:170).

Christians were now offered alternative ways to understand the religions. They could choose to continue to evaluate religions as before based on the Bible and theology which, since the Patristics, had been almost uniformly negative as saving entities. Or they could adopt some combination of the traditional and the modern. The impact of *religionsgeschichte* in America along with critical biblical studies and theological liberalism steadily eroded the special nature of Christianity in the un-derstanding of many mainline Christian leaders.

This sea change in the way Christians looked at themselves and religious others has to do with what Lesslie Newbigin calls the prevailing plausibility structure. The prevailing plausi-bility structure is that which tells a culture what is true and what is of value. The reigning plausibility structure places religion, morality and values in the same category as aesthetics. There are no absolutes governing anything nor assisting moderns in distinguishing the true from the false in the religious arena.

If Newbigin and others are right, Christianity with its view of the religions in the broader culture is at a crisis moment on the threshold of the twenty-first century. Throughout the history of Christianity it was seldom questioned that the truth was knowable, subject to rational supports and worthy of pursuit. Christians have honestly believed the gospel message to be finally true. But if John Hick, Paul Knitter and other religious pluralists have their way, all ideological positions (their own excepted!), not just Christian ones, will be set aside as mere cul-tural variations rooted in matters other than claims to ultimacy.

Gordon Kaufman's analysis of Don Richardson's book *Peace Child* is a good example of this trend. The Richardsons went to the Sawi of Irian Jaya to teach them the Christian faith centering on Jesus Christ as God and Savior. Kaufman notes how the presence of the Richardsons resulted in intertribal warfare before the preaching of Christ could occur. When the Richardsons decided to leave, the Sawi villages agreed to make peace by the traditional manner, the exchange of a child between the two sides with each pledging to care for the child of the other tribe. Kaufman comments: "The Richardsons were able to recognize these analogies and see that precisely this sort of actual reconciliation and peacemaking, with resultant human fulfillment, was what Christianity was all about" (Kaufman 1976:120). He goes on to ask "Is the meaning of Christ to be understood as primarily (though of course not exclusively) a matter of subscribing to certain ideas (about God, Christ, humanity, etc.)? Or is the primary significance of Christ fundamentally nonideational, having to do with the basic quality, style, and character of human life? .... Once this proper subordination of the ideational to the existential in Christian faith is recognized, much of the theological difficulty for moderns with traditional christological talk can fall away" (Kaufman 1976:120-121).

Kaufman's abandonment of the "ideational" is only one manifestation of the serious challenges directed at "traditional" Christology. By implication other religions must also give up their ultimate truths as well if the present trend continues.

In conclusion, it may be that in order to respond to this relativist approach, Christianity and the religions will have to form a common front against those who would destroy what is precious to them. Should that unlikely occurrence happen, that too would be a part of the history of Christianity and its relationship with the religions of the world.

Reference List

Aldwincle, Russell
    1982   *Jesus—A Savior or the Savior?* Macon, GA: Mercer University.

Alger, William
    1880   *The Destiny of the Soul.* Boston: Roberts Brothers.

Braaten, Carl E.
    1992   "Christianity Needs a Theology of Religions." In *No Other Gospel: Christianity among the World Religions.* Minneapolis: Fortress.

Chapman, Colin
    1990   "The Challenge of Other Religions." In *World Evangelization* (January):17.

DeCosta, Gavin
    1986   *Theology and Religious Pluralism.* New York: Basil Blackwell.

Dewick, E. E.
    1953   *The Christian Attitude to Other Religions.* London: Cambridge.

Edwards, David, and John R. W. Stott
    1988   *Evangelical Essentials.* Downers Grove, IL: InterVarsity.

Fairbanks, John K., ed.
    1974   *The Missionary Enterprise in China and America.* Cambridge, MA: Harvard.

Grant, Robert M.
    1988   Review of *Divine Pedagogy: A Patristic View of Non-Chrisian Religions* by Chrys Saladanha. *The Journal of Religion* 6:288-289.

Grinfield, Edward
    1827   *Nature and Extent of the Christian Dispensation with Reference to the Salvability of the Heathen.* London: Rivington.

Hodge, Charles
    1940   *Systematic Theology*, Vol. 3. Grand Rapids, MI: William B. Eerdmans Publishing Company.

Kaufman, Gordon
    1976   *Christian Theology: A Case Method Approach.* Robert A. Evans and Thomas D. Parker, eds. 1st edition. New York: Harper and Row.

McDonald, H. D.
    1985   *The Atonement of the Death of Christ*. Grand Rapids, MI: Baker.

Moffett, Samuel Hugh
    1992   *A History of Christianity in Asia*, Vol I. San Francisco: Harper Collins.

Morris, Leon
    1956   *The Apostolic Preaching of the Cross* Grand Rapids, MI: Eerdmans.

Pelikan, Jaroslav
    1971 *The Emergence of the Catholic Tradition (100-600)*. Vol. 1 of *The Christian Tradition*. Chicago: University of Chicago.
    1974 *The Spirit of Eastern Christendom (600-1700)*. Vol. 2 of *The Christian Tradition*. Chicago: University of Chicago.

Plumptre, E. H.
    1898   S*pirits In Prison*. London: Isbister.

Ramm, Bernard
    1985   *An Evangelical Christology*. Nashville: Thomas Nelson.

Roberts, Alexander and Donaldson, James
    1972   *The Ante-Nicene Fathers*. Vols. 3-4. Grand Rapids MI: Eerdmans.

Sanders, John
    1992   *No Other Name*. Grand Rapids, MI: Eerdmans.

Speer, Robert E.
    1933   *The Finality of Jesus Christ*. Westwood, NJ: Fleming H. Revell.

Stott, John R. W.
    1988   *Evangelical Essentials: A Liberal-Evangelical Dialogue*. Downers Grove, IL: InterVarsity.

Tertullian
    1978   "On Idolatry." In *The Ante-Nicene Fathers*. Alexander Roberts and James Donaldson, eds. Vol. 3. P. 61. Grand Rapids, MI: Eerdmans.
    1978   "The Apology." In *The Ante-Nicene Fathers*. Alexander Roberts and James Donaldson, eds. Vol. 3. P. 29. Grand Rapids, MI: Eerdmans.

Wall, Andrew
    1990   "Conversion and Christian Continuity." *Mission Focus* 18(2):17-21.

Warfield, B.B.
    1952   "Are They Few That Be Saved?" In *Biblical and Theological Studies*. Philadelphia: Presbyterian and Reformed.

Williams, George Huntston
    1969   "Erasmus and the Reformers on Non-Christian Religions and *Salus Extra Ecclesiam*." In *Action and Conviction in Early Modern Europe*. Theodore Rabb and Jerrold Seigel, eds. Princeton, NJ: Princeton.

Young, Richard Fox
    1989   "*Deus Unus* or *Dei Plures Sunt?* The Function of Inclusivism in the Buddhist Defense of Mongol Folk Religion Against William of Rubruck (1254)." *Journal of Ecumenical Studies* 26(1):100-137.

9

RELIGIOUS BORROWING AS A TWO-WAY STREET: AN INTRODUCTION TO ANIMISTIC TENDENCIES IN THE EURO-NORTH AMERICAN CONTEXT

A. Scott Moreau

Cultural borrowing is rarely a one-way street, though our focus in general has tended in the direction of our impact on the lives of the other. For example, in discussing world religions we may examine the impact *of* the church on the religion(s) in question without looking at the impact of the religion(s) *on* the church. Alternatively, we may gravitate towards examining the means of communicating Christ more effectively in alternate religious contexts without discussing how they are communicating their messages to us. We can discuss the question of syncretism in "mission" churches outside of the North American context, but not take the time and effort to turn, in metaphorical terms, the telescope around and place missiological focus on syncretism within our own camp. In this chapter, I will examine some general foundations for addressing the reality of the cross-currents in religious encounter, giving some attention to the impact of an ever-increasingly pluralistic and spiritistic context on the Euro-North American evangelical church.

Two primary foci may be used as lenses for examining this important issue. I will first examine worldview and significant ramifications of the recent cultural shift as it appears in selected literature of religious encounter. Then, both because of the intertwining of world view and mythic framework, and because our mythic framework provides a lens through which the motivation of certain approaches may be understood, I will present selected aspects of North American myth and show how it is impacting our approaches to cross-religious encounters.

Worldview

Worldview is the complex and interactive set of assumptions through which we arrange our ideas and images of the world we inhabit. It is essentially pre-theoretical in character; it is the foundation upon which theories and the methods of theorizing are built (Walsh 1992:16). As such, it is a belief system (Dodd, 1991:75; Olthius 1985:155) of the basic assumptions we make about reality (Hiebert 1985:45). Because it is pre-theoretical, it is generally not found at the conscious level, and the as-sumptions which comprise it are not necessarily coherently linked to each other—they may even be contradictory. Rarely do we even recognize its existence—it so informs us as to "what is right" that we rarely (if ever) question its assumptive character. The kinds of issues with which world view is concerned include (see Walsh 1992:19; Redfield 1957:85-86; and Kraft 1989:181-205):

1. Where am I? (What is the nature of reality; what is time and space?)
2. Who am I? (What does it mean to be human; what are "being" and "existence"?)
3. Who is in charge? (What powers control the reality I inhabit?)
4. How do I know? (By what logic is knowledge derived?)

Answers to these questions are found at two levels—the conscious and articulated (usually through the formal philosophies of life seen in the culture) and the unconscious and unstated (seen in the social patterns of a culture, but not thought through consciously).

In developing an understanding of the ways in which animistic ideas have penetrated our culture, we must briefly consider one aspect of how world views are constructed. There are at least five foundational building blocks which provide the boundaries for worldview construction. These include image of God in all people, our genetic parameters, our sinful or transformed nature, our life history (including enculturation), and the language(s) we use. Space permits discussion of only one of these blocks, namely the fact of our creation in the image of God.

Because we are made in his image, we have an built in desire to relate to him as the One we image. If Wink is correct in stating that our images of God create us (Wink 1992:48), then this block is at the very core of who we are and provides the driving direction for worldview. It permeates every aspect of our existence, and drives us to find religious significance in life and to attribute to the powers which govern our world image-significance. This concern has resulted in an almost infinite variety of postulated cosmic powers which serve as image replacements in every culture of the world. The different "geographies" of these powers in various cultural settings may be called powerscapes (e.g., landscapes of the powers)

The outlines of every culturally-derived powerscape will be founded on the culture's identification of the power(s) which dominate that culture's existence. People of every culture postulate a rich variety of power sources which impact their world (Jacobs 1979; Hiebert 1982; Burnett 1990). Their understanding of these powers forms the religious landscape they inhabit, and their assumptions about these powers gives them the range of answers to the questions of life and faith that they ask. The types of powers accepted as real by the culture are deeply embedded in the cultural fabric, and inform life not just in the religious arena, but in every aspect of daily living. Each power within the worldview will have defined lines of authority, responsibility, and accessibility which can be thought of as spheres of operation. In the case of personal powers, the culture may not perceive these powers as being cooperative with each other. Just like people, at times they work together and at times they conflict. This results in a type of religious equation of power interaction, which is reasonably stable in a culture, though it is open to change. It enables a people to know which power to call on for each of the problems or needs in life, and helps them make sense out of the chaos life brings to them.

The ascriptions to the powers are not limited to names and spheres of influence. Corresponding to the vocabulary and sphere of influence will be emotional responses and attachments to each power. This in turn will define the types of scripting developed in the culture by which a person knows what power(s) to call and how to call on them (Jacobs 1979; Nuckolls 1991). Three classes of powers may be identified: impersonal, psychological/social, and personal (disembodied) powers. Of these three, of most importance to this discussion are the personal powers.

In the vast majority of the world's cultures, personal powers which transcend the physical realm are acknowledged. These include spirits of all types. Because such powers are viewed as relational, the relational rules in the culture often carry over in relating to the powers. They may demand the same type of respect, means of initiation, and methods of supplication and petition used in approaching people in positions of social power. The powers will be expected to respond within a context of culturally defined relational rules. Nothing is perceived to take place naturally; everything has a cause framed in personalized spiritual terms and related to the spiritual powers recognized by the culture. This particular powerscape is known as animism. Anthropologists have dropped use of the term because of its evolutionary and pejorative connotations. Nevertheless, the term very effectively describes the powerscape of many people of the world, and therefore is still used by missiologists.

Myth

Worldview is closely connected to our mythic structures. As with worldview, no single accepted definition of myth exists. However, there is general agreement that the common understanding of myth as untrue stories about the past is not what sociologists today mean by the term (O'Flaherty 1988:25). Abstractly, myths are culturally derived instruments which serve as paradigms of behavior (Eliade 1963). Not necessarily tied to any single story, myths convey large, controlling images which give meanings to the events of life (Murray 1960). The primary issue with myth in this sense is not whether any particular story is true, but how it operates in the belief system of the culture. The myths of a culture provide the frames of reference within which thought is formulated, and serve as both the lens and the blinders of that culture (Summerhill 1985). Myth, like worldview, offers ways of ordering experience, informs people about themselves, expresses a saving power in human life, and provides patterns for human actions (Barbour 1974). Among other things, myth is a source for our cognitive categories, the integrating factor in our adaptation to life, the charter to our behavior, and the legitimization of our social institutions (Honko 1984). What are some of the mythic themes and structures in North America?

170   Christianity and the Religions

Here we will briefly focus on four: the joy of the fight, good is obvious, the hero, and millenarian utopianism.

As a culture, we focus on the actual *fight* as opposed to the outcome of the fight (Hiebert 1992). Our myth structure glorifies violence to the extent that the "action" is all we want in action movies (and books and cartoons and ...). We never give as much space to the "happily ever after" phase as we do to the violent struggle that precedes the peaceful ending. Further, our mythic value of violence demands that the hero fight the villain. Compromise is never possible, surrender unthinkable. The hero and the villain never learn; they are doomed to fight again and again eternally (Wink 1992:18).

The second mythic theme is that right and wrong will always be clearly seen and easily judged (good guys wear white, bad guys wear black). We do not want to have to ask who is good or who is bad. We prefer it to look obvious and rarely question beneath the surface. The enemy is easy to spot and his or her motivations and emotions are easily seen as evil. Further, we rarely are willing to explore in depth the possibility that the hero might be the one who is fundamentally wrong.

A third mythic theme that of the hero as seen through Euro-North American eyes (see Wink 1992:18-20). This hero, though tempted, *always* makes the right choice in the end. He (only rarely she) *always* snatches victory from the very jaws of defeat so that chaos will not overcome the world. Even though the enemy cheats, the hero never stoops to that level. Instead, the hero always discovers hidden inner resources by which he overcomes the villain. Our mythic heroes are often loners motivated by individual commitment to ideals (Superman, Lone Ranger) or revenge (Spiderman and Batman). They rarely question their own motivation; they always know that are doing right. The means by which they overcome the enemies are violent ones—they never seek to redeem the enemy, only to destroy him (Wink 1992:19). Linked to theme of good and evil being easy to distinguish, the violence of the hero is "good," while that of the villain is "bad."

A fourth mythic theme is that of the idea of a millenarian utopia. While we may not describe what it means to live happily ever after, and suspect that it may be boring, we certainly strive for that type of life. This particular mythic theme incorporates the others already described. The consummation of history is one we must fight for (theme one); it is easy to tell right from wrong in light of our utopian vision (theme two); and our heroes are responsible for bringing it into being (theme three). One historian has gone so far as to note:

> Our history has been essentially the history of one long millenarian movement. Americans, in their cultural mythology, are God"s chosen, leading the world to perfection. Every awakening has revived, revitalized, and redefined that culture core (McGloughlin 1978:19).

Worldview Shift and Myth in North America

How does a worldview shift, and what is the result? Worldviews can shift when changes in the circumstances of life demand such a shift before the world will make sense to the culture again. This can be seen when a technologically more-advanced culture imposes itself on a technologically less-advanced culture. It can also be seen when a people of an absolutist religion encounter a people of a relativist religion, in which case both worldviews may shift towards each other. However, worldview shifts do not always affect every component of world view. Due to shifting in perceptions of stresses and strains, some aspects of worldview will shift more radically than others. Myth may remain unaffected, if the cognitive categories supported by myth are flexible enough to adapt to the new world view. Alternately, core myths may change drastically or be abandoned altogether, especially with religious conversion. Even so, the values associated with the previous myths do not automatically change, and may even continue to provide an interpretive grid for any new myths that arise. Further, our worldview is constantly changing as the circumstances around us change. For example, in the 1950s the chief complaints of conduct in schools centered on issues such as speaking out of turn and horseplay in the halls. Today they focus on student violence, drugs, and disdain for authority. The worldview of school and the myth of the ideal school in Euro-North American thinking has been shaken, and a new myth of what actually takes place in the halls of the schools (especially innercity schools) has dramatically changed our understanding of the educational process.

172 Christianity and the Religions

In relationship to this chapter, more germane is the evidence of a recent world view shift in Euro-North American culture from scientific materialism towards an eclectic spiritism (Pattison 1977; Wright 1990:6-7). Evidence for this shift includes the rise in popularity of magic and New Age thinking (Melton 1990; Melton and Poggi 1992:5-27); the revival of occult (Cohen 1990:346), pagan, and wiccan traditions (Bass 1991; Adler 1986:41-93); and a heightened interest in angels (Gibbs 1993). Religion in North America has become a consumer item (Walker 1987:136-41) with ever more new and experimental forms being introduced. Following the myth of right and wrong being easy to distinguish, this spiritism borrows from any source, looking for things that work rather than well-grounded theological or philosophical roots.

This shift has not been limited to the larger culture. The broad popularity of Frank Peretti's spiritual warfare novels (1986 and 1989) and other similar fictional literature, the spate of new spiritual warfare titles from Christian publishing houses, and the wealth of conferences and course offerings in evangelical institutions addressing the issue demonstrate how pervasively the church has been impacted. The culture, and together with it the evangelical church, has moved in a spiritual direction in the sense that personal spiritual powers, once out of sight in our worldview, have now come into prominence. In one respect we can rejoice—a spiritual approach to the world is more in tune with the biblical worldview than an agnostic (or atheistic) scientific materialism. In another respect, however, we must be aware of the danger of shifting too far (Hesselgrave 1988:151-2) into what may termed a functional evangelical animism (see Burnett 1988 and Steyne 1989:48-53) and a corresponding set of "Christian magical" practices.

In the recent corresponding rise of evangelical interest in spirits as viable powers in our worldview, the church faces a situation not dissimilar to that of missionaries working among animistic peoples. Cohen notes the central issue:

> While the missionaries' success depends to no small measure on their thorough cognitive understanding of the native world view, their own religion, and the very purpose of their sojourn among the natives, precludes their normative

identification with that world view (Cohen 1990:347).

In other words, missionaries are expected to develop an empathetic understanding of the animistic worldview without becoming spiritists in the process (Cohen 1991:116). The challenge of the twentieth-century North American evangelical church is increasingly similar to that of the missionary. With the heightened interest in the work of spirits, we have been moving towards a more biblical worldview. At the same time, however, there are signs that we are in danger of moving beyond it. For example, I see a sharp increase in what might be called a Peretti approach to powerscapes. Frank Peretti's broadly popular books did not so much chart a new worldview in the evangelical community towards the powers as capture and crystalize the changes that had already taken place (Wink 1992:7-9; see also Seel 1993:43-46). In both of his warfare novels (*This Present Darkness*, 1987, and *Piercing the Darkness*, 1989) the Euro-North American mythic themes described above are interwoven together with an animistic assumption that demonic and angelic entities are directly involved in every human action. Battles, both human and spiritual, pervade the books. Good and evil are always clearly seen. The heroes of the books always make the right choices in the end. The question is not "Who is right?" but rather "Will the right one win?" Finally, the books certainly portray the millenarian vision towards which we strive. In both cases, breaking the satanic counterfeit kingdom is the focus, with the goal of mind of the coming of God's true kingdom. The themes are not evil, but the encroachment of animistic values in the development of the themes and the resulting popularity of these books should force us to stop and consider the possible consequences of this type of thinking. The broad popularity of his books together with a corresponding ignorance of other spiritual warfare authors in the church shows at the very least a fascination with the concepts, and at worst the movement towards a worldview which is an amalgamation of Christianity and spiritism.

Closely tied to Peretti powerscapes are evidences of what Lewis called an unhealthy interest in the demonic (Lewis 1961:9). The essence of "demonomania" (coined by J. E. D. Esquirol 1845) is "an over-inclination to explain things in terms of the demonic" (Wright 1990:114). Demons are seen as the cause of a multitude of problems ranging from reinforcing compulsions (Kraft 1992:

109), being the driving force behind all rock music (Brown 1986: 63), to the demonization of whole cultures (Bubeck 1991:45-46). Again, evil is clearly seen (mythic theme two), and it is up to the deliverance counselors to save individuals (or whole cultures) from demonic take-overs (mythic themes one and three). We have no argument with the clear presentation in Scripture about Satan's desires, demonic followers, and temporary domination of this world. However, we cannot focus on these issues apart from the lens of the love, sovereignty, mercy, and grace of God.

Another trend evidenced is a sort of functional dualism (see Warner 1991:28 and Anderson 1993:249) in which Satan is controlling every event and organization that exists on earth (displayed in authors such as Hammond and Hammond 1973 and Brown 1986). He is ascribed an almost omnipotent capability, seen especially when those who have been involved in Satanism come to Christ and have their testimony published (Warnke 1972; Stratford 1986; Brown 1986). This fits the myth of evil being clearly recognized (myth two) as well as the myth of the hero (who faces a villain larger than life, myth three). Recent exposes have demonstrated the problem with giving too much credence to published stories (e.g., Lauren Stratford's testimony discredited by Pasantino and Pasantino 1990; Mike Warnke exposed by Trott and Hertenstein 1993; see also Wright 1991:99-123). As Schlier noted, Christ has left the devil only whatever power unbelief allows him (Schlier 1961:58). Our goal is to *dis*believe in Satan (Wright 1990:25); to believe *against* him rather than to believe *in* him (Weber 1981:489).

A final area in which animistic tendencies have made inroads in the Euro-North American evangelical church is the recent advocacy of warfare prayer against territorial spirits *as the single most important strategy* we can utilize in reaching the unreached (Otis 1991 and 1993; Dawson 1989; Jacobs 1991; Lea 1989; Wagner 1993). At stake is not the existence of such spirits; that seems clear from biblical data (especially Daniel 10:4-11:1). The question is whether God calls us to engage in direct prayer against these spirits as a key strategy in reaching the world for Christ. Such a strategy is nowhere taught in the Bible and cannot be substantiated in church history (Arnold, 1994). Those who envision themselves as heroes (myth three) who are needed to bring in God's kingdom (myth four) and who love the battle (myth one) are particularly susceptible to this approach. At the very least we ought to be extremely cautious about emphasizing such a strategy as the key to reaching the world for Christ (White 1992 and 1994).

What can we do to facilitate a better understanding of the impact of religious encounter within our own camp? As a church, we need to uncover (or recover?) a more balanced biblical Christian metaphoric structure. The issue is not developing some new Christian framework as much as it is discovering the biblical framework God has already given us in his Word. What are the biblical images from which we derive a fully Christian picture? The core metaphor for engaging the powers of this world should not be that of conflict, but that of God's rule and our resulting ethos of *shalom* built on the foundation of Kingdom ethics (Hiebert 1992). In relating to God, several other important metaphors need deeper biblical exploration and incorporation into our worldview. These include metaphors of transformation (our minds being renewed, the new man/old man image), metaphors of identity (we are citizens of heaven, members of God's house, and children of God), metaphors of growth (walking in the light, bearing fruit) and metaphors of engagement (standing before the enemy, struggling, using kingdom weapons and ethics).

Additionally, we need to rebalance our focus on both the psychosocial and the spiritual. In applying the theology of identity in Christ to the Ephesians, Paul exhorted them to live in light of the kingdom ethics of humility, patient endurance, forgiveness, lovingly speaking the truth, and mutual submission in a variety of social contexts. Without using the terminology, he called them to recognize both Satan's activities and their responsibilities in the psychosocial sphere. One of the dangers in any movement towards animism is a reductionism which denies the reality of personal psychology and social context as significant factors in dealing with the spiritual problems people face. I am often asked whether a problem is psychological or spiritual, and the answer is that the question itself is flawed. We are whole creatures, integrated throughout. Psychological issues have spiritual consequences, just as spiritual issues have psychological consequences. Though in the anthropological literature the tendency is to assume the demonic has no ontological basis, some anthropologists do take the phenomena of demonization seriously and worthy of scholarly research. However, their analyses are generally limited to the psychosocial side (see, for example Walker 1972; Goodman 1988, and the case studies in Middleton and Winter 1963; Beattie and Middleton 1969; and Crapanzano

1976). In contrast to secular anthropological literature, the evangelical literature tends to focus so intensively on the demonic that the psychosocial is often not given sufficient attention. I found this true in both Burnett (1988) and Van Rheenen (1991), though there are several notable exceptions (e.g., Augsburger 1986; Schuster 1987; Bufford 1988; Payne 1991). This has been carried over to evangelism, in which the more recent literature on territorial spirits implies that we need to discover the name of the spirit(s) in control of a territory, pray it (or them) into submission, and only then we will reap a great harvest for Christ (e.g., see Wagner 1990, 1991, 1992, 1993). This overlooks the reality of dehumanizing social structures, disposes the dynamics of human choice to sin, and reduces social factors to personal ones (discussed in Wink 1992:74-77). One mark of competency in intercultural communication is the ability to recognize the complexities of life issues and avoid simple dichotomies (called cognitive complexity, Gudykunst and Kim 1992:147). The more competent communicator is less likely to be ethnocentric and more likely to recognize inconsistencies in his or her belief system than the less competent communicator is. The same should also serve as a mark of competency in developing models of spiritual warfare. Rather than going the more animistic direction by simply externalizing an enemy (e.g., a demon) on which we place all blame for our wrong choices or denying that the enemy exists, we must develop integrated models which acknowledge the truth of *both* the spiritual and the psychosocial dynamics in spiritual conflict.

Conclusion

I have been greatly encouraged by the recent heightening of interest in spiritual realities within evangelicalism as evidenced by the explosion of literature, conferences, and courses. I affirm that there are "jokers" in the deck; that Satan and demons are real, ontological beings (and not just the interiority of structures, *contra* Wink 1992) who seek to wage war against the Creator by influencing his created order in any way they can. I affirm the biblical truth that every believer, whether acknowledged or not, is called to participate in this warfare and stand against Satan's attacks (Eph 6:10-18). At the same time, however, I am concerned about the potential dangers in the recent development of a kind of spiritual warfare industry. We must avoid the sensationalism that wins audiences at the expense of biblical integrity. We must also avoid the entrapment of delighting in power for power's sake, and keep our eyes firmly fixed on the issues Jesus said were of higher priority (e.g., our salvation; Lk 10:20). We must not allow our worldview to move into an unbiblical animism, and we must exercise caution in advocating techniques and strategies that resemble magic more than biblically responsible ministry. God *has* given Christians a significant role to play in spiritual warfare, but he calls us to wage this warfare on his terms, not ours. May he enable us to maintain our integrity and sensitivity as we seek to engage in the works he prepared in ad-vance for us to do (Eph 2:10).

Reference List

Adler, Margot
    1986   *Drawing Down the Moon: Witches, Druids, Goddess-Worshippers, and Other Pagans in America Today.* Boston: Beacon.

Anderson, Neil
    1993   *Living Free in Christ.* Ventura, CA: Regal.

Arnold, Clinton
    1994   "What About Territorial Spirits?" *Discipleship Journal* May/June, p. 81.

Augsburger, David W.
    1986   *Pastoral Counseling across Cultures.* Philadelphia: Westminster.

Barbour, Ian G.
    1974   *Myths, Models and Paradigms: A Comparative Study in Science and Religion.* New York: Harper and Row.

Bass, Dave
    1991   "Drawing Down the Moon." *Christianity Today.* April 29:14-19.

Beattie, John, and John Middleton, eds.
    1969   *Spirit Mediumship and Society in Africa.* London: Routledge & Kegan Paul.

Brown, Rebecca
    1986   *He Came to Set the Captives Free*. Chino, CA: Chick.

Bubeck, Mark I.
    1991   *The Satanic Revival*. San Bernardino, CA: Here's Life.

Bufford, Rodger K.
    1988   *Counseling and the Demonic. Resources for Christian Counseling.* Vol. 17. Gary R. Collins, gen. ed. Dallas: Word.

Burnett, David
    1990   *Clash of Worlds*. Eastbourne, E. Sussex: MARC Europe.

Cohen, Eric
    1990   "The Missionary as Stranger: A Phenomenological Analysis of Christian Missionaries' Encounter with Fold Religions." *Review of Religious Research* 31(4): 337-350.
    1991   "Christianity and Buddhism in Thailand: The 'Battle of the Axes' and the 'Contest of Power.'" *Social Compass* 38(2):115-140.

Crapanzano, Vincent
    1977   *Case Studies in Spirit Possession*. New York: Wiley.

Dawson, John
    1989   *Taking Our Cities for God: How to Break Spiritual Strongholds*. Lake Mary, FL: Creation House.

Dodd, Carley H.
    1991   *Dynamics of Intercultural Communication*. 3rd edition. Dubuque, IA: Wm. C. Brown.

Eliade, Mircea
    1963   *Myth and Reality*. New York: Harper and Row.

Esquirol, J. E. D.
    1845   "Demonomania." In *Vampires, Werewolves and Demons: Twentieth Century Reports in the Psychiatric Literature*. Richard Noll, ed. New York: Brunner/Mazel. Reprinted from *Mental Maladies: A Treatise on Insanity*. E. K. Hunt, trans. Philadelphia: Lea and Blanchard.

Gibbs, Nancy
    1993   "Angels Among Us." *Time*, December 27:56-65.

Goodman, Felicitas
    1988   *How about Demons? Possession and Exorcism in the Modern World*. Bloomington: Indiana University.

Gudykunst, William B., and Young Yun Kim
    1992   *Communicating with Strangers: An Approach to Intercultural Communication*, 2nd edition. New York: McGraw-Hill.

Hammond, Frank, and Ida Hammond
    1973   *Pigs in the Parlor: A Practical Guide to Deliverance*. Kirkwood, MO: Impact.

Hesselgrave, David J.
    1988   *Today's Choice for Tomorrow's Mission: An Evangelical Perspective on Trends and Issues in Missions*. Grand Rapids, MI: Zondervan.

Hiebert, Paul
    1982   "The Flaw of the Excluded Middle." *Missiology: An International Review* 10: 35-48.
    1985   *Anthropological Insights for Missionaries*. Grand Rapids, MI: Baker.
    1992   "Spiritual Warfare: Biblical Perspectives." *Mission Focus* 20(3):41-46.

Honko, Lauri
    1984   "The Problem of Defining Myth." In *Sacred Narrative: Readings in the Theory of Myth*. Alan Dundes, ed. Pp. 51-52. Berkeley: University of California.

Jacobs, Cindy
    1991   *Possessing the Gates of the Enemy*. Grand Rapids, MI: Chosen.

Jacobs, Donald R.
    1979   "Conversion and Culture—an Anthropological Perspective with Reference to East Africa." In *Gospel and Culture: The Papers of a Consultation on the Gospel and Culture, Convened by the Lausanne Committee's Theology and Education Group*. John Stott and Robert T. Coote, eds. Pp. 175-94. Pasadena, CA: William Carey Library.

Kraft, Charles H.
    1989   *Christianity with Power: Your Worldview and Your Experience of the Supernatural*. Ann Arbor, MI: Vine.

1992   *Defeating Dark Angels: Breaking Demonic Oppression in the Believer's Life.* Ann Arbor, MI: Vine.

Lea, Larry
1989   *The Weapons of Your Warfare: Equipping Yourself to Defeat the Enemy.* Altamonte Springs, FL: Creation House.

Lewis, Clive S.
1961   *The Screwtape Letters.* New York: MacMillan.

McGloughlin, W.
1978   *Revivals, Awakenings and Reform.* Chicago: University of Chicago.

Melton, J. Gordon.
1990   "Introductory Essay: An Overview of the New Age Movement." In *New Age Encyclopedia.* J. Gordon Melton, ed. Pp. xiii-xxxii. Detroit: Gale Research.

Melton, J. Gordon, and Isotta Poggi
1992   *Magic, Witchcraft, and Paganism in America: A Bibliography.* New York: Garland.

Moreau, A. Scott
1990   *The World of the Spirits: A Biblical Study in the African Context.* Nairobi, Kenya: Evangel.

Murray, Henry Alexander
1960   *Myth and Mythmaking.* New York: George Braziller.

Nuckolls, Charles W.
1991   "Culture and Causal Thinking: Diagnosis and Prediction in a South Indian Fishing Village." *Ethos* 19:1-51.

O'Flaherty, Wendy Doniger
1988   *Other People's Myths: The Cave of Echoes.* New York: MacMillan.

Otis, George
1993   "An Overview of Spiritual Mapping." In *Breaking Strongholds in Your City: How to Use Spiritual Mapping to Make Your Prayers More Strategic, Effective and Targeted.* C. Peter Wagner, ed. Pp. 29-47.

Passantino, Bob, and Gretchen Passantino
1990   "Satan's Sideshow: The True Lauren Stratford Story." *Cornerstone* 18:24-28.

Pattison, E. Mansell
    1977   "Psychosocial Interpretations of Exorcism."
                Journal of Operational Psychiatry 8:5-19.
Payne, Leanne
    1991   *Restoring the Christian Soul through Healing Prayer*. Wheaton, IL: Crossway Books.
Peretti, Frank
    1986   *This Present Darkness*. Westchester: Crossway Books.
    1989   *Piercing the Darkness*. Westchester: Crossway Books.
Redfield, Robert
    1957   *The Primitive World and Its Transformations*. Ithaca, NY: Cornell.
Schlier, Heinrich
    1961   *Principalities and Powers in the New Testament*. New York: Herder and Herder.
Schuster, Marguerite
    1987   *Power, Pathology, and Paradox*. Grand Rapids, MI: Zondervan.
Seel, John
    1993   *The Evangelical Forfeit: Can We Recover?* Grand Rapids, MI: Baker.
Steyne, Philip M.
    1989   *Gods of Power: A Study of the Beliefs and Practices of Animists*. Houston, TX: Touch Publications.
Stratford, Lauren
    1988   *Satan's Underground: The Extraordinary Story of One Woman's Escape*. Eugene, OR: Harvest House.
Summerhill, William Roy, Jr.
    1985   *Holy War within the Mythic Horizon of American Christian Biblical Fundamentalism*. Ph.D. dissertation, The Catholic University of America.
Trott, Jon. and Mike Hertenstein
    1993   *Selling Satan: Mike Warnke and His Ministry of Deception*. Chicago: Cornerstone Library.
Van Rheenen, Gailyn
    1991   *Communicating Christ in Animistic Contexts*. Grand Rapids, MI: Baker.

Wagner, C. Peter, ed.
    1990   *Wrestling with Dark Angels: Toward a Deeper Understanding of the Supernatural Forces in Spiritual Warfare.* Ventura, CA: Regal.
    1991   *Engaging the Enemy: How to Fight and Defeat Territorial Spirits.* Ventura, CA: Regal.
    1992   *Warfare Prayer.* Ventura, CA: Regal.
    1993   *Breaking Strongholds in Your City: How to Use Spiritual Mapping to Make Your Prayers More Strategic, Effective, and Targeted.* Ventura, CA: Regal.

Walker, Andrew
    1987   *Enemy Territory: The Christian Struggle for the Modern World.* Grand Rapids, MI: Zondervan.

Walker, Sheila S.
    1972   *Ceremonial Spirit Possession in Africa and Afro-America: Forms, Meanings, and Functional Significance for Individuals and Social Groups.* Leiden: E. J. Brill.

Walsh, Brian J.
    1992   "Worldviews, Modernity and the Task of Christian College Education." *Faculty Dialogue* 18:13-30.

Warner, Timothy
    1991   *Spiritual Warfare: Victory over the Powers of This Dark World.* Wheaton, IL: Crossway.

Warnke, Mike
    1972   *The Satan Seller.* Plainfield, NJ: Logos International.

Weber, Otto
    1981   *Foundations of Dogmatics.* Vol. 1. Darryl L. Guder, trans. and ann. Grand Rapids, MI: Eerdmans.

White, Thomas B.
    1992   *Breaking Strongholds: How Spiritual Warfare Sets Captives Free.* Ann Arbor: Vine Books.
    1994   "Handling Spiritual Warfare." Presentation at North American Conference for Itinerant Evangelists.

Wink, Walter
    1992   *Engaging the Powers: Discernment and Resistance in a World of Domination*. Philadelphia: Fortress.

Wright, Nigel
    1990   *The Satan Syndrome: Putting the Power* of *Darkness in Its Place*. Grand Rapids, MI: Zondervan.

10

THE UNIQUENESS OF CHRIST IN MISSION THEOLOGY

Charles VanEngen

My thesis is the following. "Jesus Christ is Lord" is a foundational biblical, personal faith-confession that corrects the traditional pluralist, inclusivist, and exclusivist positions held by Christians concerning other religions and calls God's missionary people to be mobilized by the Holy Spirit to participate in Christ's mission which is culturally pluralist, ecclesiologically inclusivist, and faith particularist.

Introduction

Many of us would agree with Clark Pinnock when he says, "By all accounts the meaning of Christ's lordship in a religiously plural world is one of the hottest topics on the agenda of theology in the nineties."[1]

The topic has been a matter of the church's reflection since the first century. Since the late 1400s, the missionary expansion of the churches (both Roman Catholic and Protestant) has tried conquest, accommodation, adaptation, indigenization, acculturation, contextualization and inculturation in its relationship to other religious traditions. At the International Missionary Council's meeting in Tambaram, Madras, India, in 1938,[2] Hendrik Kraemer replied to William Hocking's earlier criticisms that led to the "Laymen's Foreign Mission Inquiry," by presenting *The Christian Message in a Non-Christian World*, based on his missiological interpretation of Karl Barth.[3]

The matter has received increasing attention, particularly from the Roman Catholics after the Second Vatican Council,[4] and from the World Council of Churches since the Second World War.[5] Four years ago Gerald Anderson documented 175 books published in English between 1970-1990 that dealt with the subject of "Christian Mission and Religious Pluralism" (Anderson 1990). Three years later Anderson wrote, "No issue in missiology is more important, more difficult, more controversial, or more divisive for the days ahead than the theology of religions" (Anderson 1993:200).

Evangelicals have only recently begun to give attention to this matter (Covell 1993:162-163). At the 1979 Evangelical Consultation on Theology and Mission, held at Trinity Evangelical Divinity School, and in spite of the fact that the title of the published papers was *New Horizons in World Mission*, no major presentation dealt with the topic of other religions. (See David Hesselgrave: 1979.) Fortunately, during the 1980s a number of evangelicals have made significant contributions to the conversation.[6]

In this chapter, I will present my understanding of three generally-accepted positions or paradigms, suggest a fourth, examine two foundational assumptions that impact all four, and draw three major missiological implications from the fourth paradigm.

Three Well-known Paradigms of Christian Attitudes to Other Religions

It is now common to subdivide the subject into three broad perspectives: pluralist, inclusivist, and exclusivist (or restrictivist). But the use of these terms is a rather recent phenomenon, and we need to examine their use.[7]

One of the earliest uses I have found of the three-part typology appeared in 1989 in *Religious Studies Review* articles by Paul Knitter and Francis Clooney.[8] By 1991 and 1992, the three-part typology had become common currency, at least among evangelicals.[9]

Harold Netland (1991:8-35) follows this structure, but qualifies his acceptance of it. "The use of the term 'exclusivism,'" says Netland, "is somewhat unfortunate since it has for many people undesirable connotations of narrow-mindedness, arrogance, insensitivity to others, self-righteousness, bigotry, and so on. In the context of the current debate, however, the term is unavoidable, because of the widespread use today to refer to the position represented by the Lausanne Covenant" (1991:34-35).[10]

Have we evangelicals given away too much by too easily accepting these terms? First, notice that "pluralist" is positive in terms of a multi-cultural and multi-religious world of which we are all increasingly conscious. The word "inclusivist" is positive in terms of wanting to open our arms to receive all those who are loved by God. But "exclusivist" is a negative word. Is this by accident, or by design? Few of us would like to be accused of being individually, institutionally, culturally, economically, politically, or socially "exclusive."

Secondly, what is the basis on which these words are being compared? If the basis is tolerance, the pluralist and inclusivist would seem to espouse tolerance, the exclusivist intolerance. If the basis is love? The pluralist loves everyone, as does the inclusivist, for they "(refuse) to limit the grace of God to the confines of the church," says Pinnock (1992:15). It is the so-called exclusivist, or restrictivist who, as Pinnock says, "restricts hope..." and therefore relegates people of other religions to "zones of darkness," refusing to love all peoples enough to offer them a "wider hope" (1992:14). If the basis of comparison is global openness vs parochialism, the exclusivist position looks ancient, out-of-date, and narrow.

Thirdly, if the basis of comparison is optimism vs pessimism, the inclusivist position is, in Pinnock's words, "optimistic of salvation "(e.g. 1992:153), while the so-called "restrictivists" demonstrate a "negative attitude toward the rest of the world" (1992: 13), a "pessimism of salvation, or darkly negative thinking about people's spiritual journeys" (1992, 182). Thus Pinnock is forced to assess the exclusivist view of judgment in rather harsh terms.

> We have to confront the niggardly tradition of certain varieties of conservative theology that present God as miserly, and that exclude large numbers of people without a second thought. This dark pessimism is contrary to Scripture and right reason (Pinnock 1992:153-154)

John Hick describes the exclusivists in equally strong terms.

[The exclusivist's] entirely negative attitude to other faiths is strongly correlated with ignorance of them....Today, however, the extreme evangelical Protestant who believes that all Muslims go to hell is probably not so much ignorant...as blinded by dark dogmatic spectacles through which he can see no good in religious devotion outside his own group.[11]

As evangelicals, we need to gain a better understanding of the basis for this caricature of the exclusivist position by both inclusivists like Pinnock and pluralists like Hick. In order to do this, we need to lay the three paradigms side-by-side. To do this in a short space, and at the risk of severe over-simplification, I will represent each paradigm graphically and briefly describe my own summarized interpretation of its over-all theological and missiological contours. The reader may wish to examine these summarizations to see if their description is close to the reader's perception of these paradigms.

A Fourth Possibility: An "Evangelistic Paradigm"

Let me suggest a fourth paradigm: the "Evangelist." I have chosen this name because I want to present a paradigm whose starting point and center is the EVANGEL, the confession by his disciples that *"Jesus is Lord."*[12] The "Evangelist" paradigm may be presented on page 191.

However, before we look at the missiological implications of this fourth paradigm, we need to clarify two foundational presuppositions that influence all four options: (1) our understanding of the relation of faith and culture and (2) the relation of Christology and soteriology.

Christianity and the Religions

Pluralist — A Creation Paradigm

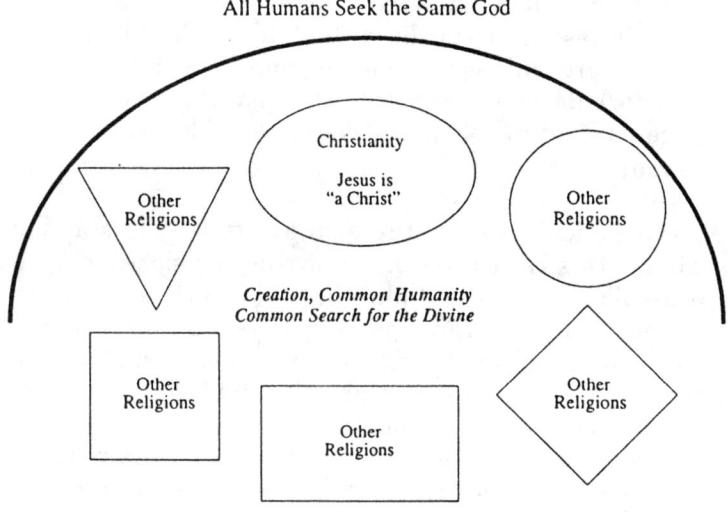

Figure 27
Pluralist—A Creation Paradigm

- Begins with creation, and the **fact** of religious pluralism
- Relativist as to both culture and faith
- **Prior choice**: common humanity
- Concerned about peoples of various faiths co-existing together
- *"As in Adam"*: all were created good[13]
- Predominantly horizontalist
- Religion is expression of individual subjectivity or culture
- Weak theology of the Fall or sin[14]
- Optimistic about culture/faith
- Bible is only the Christian's book, among other holy books
- No conversion, no transformation—actually supports status quo
- No necessity for personal faith-relationship with Jesus Christ
- Holy Spirit works everywhere in world with no relation to Christ or to the church
- Pessimistic about the Church
- No kingdom of darkness or recognition of the demonic
- Newbigin and Netland are right: ultimately relative pluralism is illogical
- Ultimately pluralists cannot dialogue—conversation stops
- Unrelated to issues of folk-religions
- Related especially to "academic" views of world religions
- Mission is irrelevant, unnecessary, demeaning, disrespectful

Inclusivist—
A Paradigm of Universal Soteriology

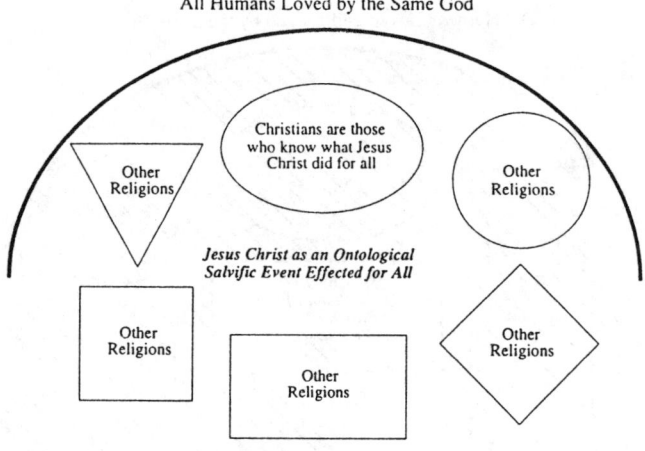

Figure 28
Inclusivist—A Paradigm
of Universal Soteriology

- Begins with the unique Christ-event ontologically for all people
- Not relativist about Jesus Christ, but weak in personal relationship to the living Jesus Christ
- Relativist about the form of universal christological soteriology
- **Prior choice**: All will ultimately be saved by a loving God (John Hick 1980)
- Concerned about peoples of various faiths co-existing together
- "As in Adam...So in Christ, *all are saved*" is emphasized
- Rather strongly verticalist soteriology, weakly horizontalist
- Many religious forms ultimately are based on Christ-event
- Weak theology of the Fall or sin
- Generally optimistic about culture/faith
- Bible as God's inspired revelation for all
- Strongly concerned about the uniqueness of Christ ontologically
- Personal relationship to Jesus Christ is desirable, not normative
- Conversion is good, but not necessary, weak in transformation
- Holy Spirit separated from Christology [15]
- Pessimistic about the institutional church
- No kingdom of darkness or recognition of the demonic
- Ultimately inclusivism is patronizing—everyone gets saved in the Christ-event whether they know or want it or not—cannot say NO to God
- Mostly unrelated to issues in folk-religions
- Related especially to "academic" views of world religions
- Mission is telling people they are already saved in Jesus Christ

Exclusivist—
An Ecclesiocentric Paradigm

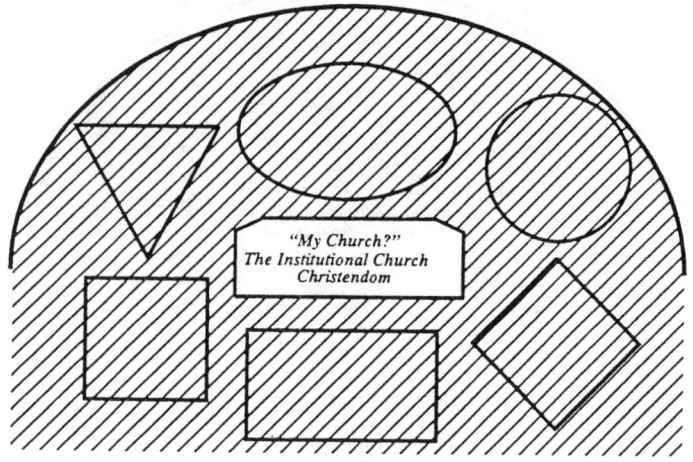

Figure 29
Exclusivist—An Ecclesiocentric Paradigm

- Begins with church as the "ark of salvation"
- Absolutist re: personal allegiance to Jesus Christ *in the Church*
- Assumes a rather medieval, institutional understanding of "extra ecclesiam nulla salus"
- **Prior choice**: salvation only in (my) institutional church
- Concerned that all non-Christians become Christians in the church
- "As in Adam... *all sinned*" is emphasized
- Strongly verticalist
- Religious systems/cultures outside the church are all sinful
- Religious co-existence is possible only as people become Christians and part of the institutional church
- Heavy emphasis on theology of the Fall and sin
- Pessimistic about culture/faith
- Bible is God's inspired revelation proclaimed through the church
- Strongly concerned about uniqueness of Christ
- Strong emphasis on conversion in Jesus Christ, in and through the church
- Holy Spirit is predominantly mediated in word, worship, sacrament
- Very optimistic about the church—ecclesiocentric [16]
- Over-emphasis on kingdom of darkness, not much about demonic
- Ultimately triumphalistic, dominating, self-serving
- Has done well among folk-religions, poorly among world religions
- Mission is rescuing people out of sinful cultures into the church

The Uniqueness of Christ 191

Evangelist—A Fourth Paradigm?

All Humans Loved and Judged by God

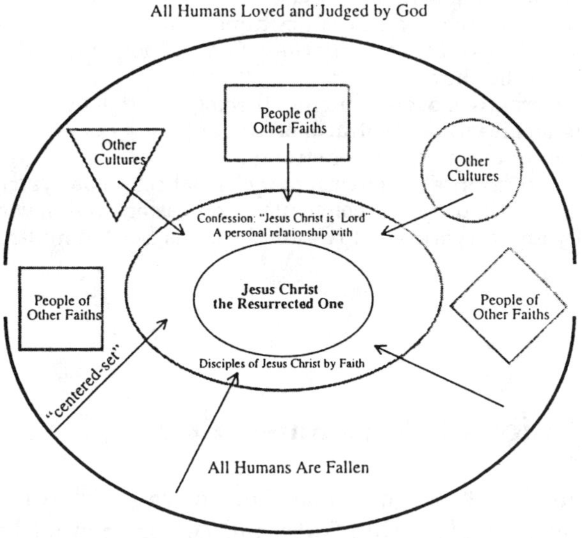

Figure 30
Evangelist—A Fourth Paradigm

- Begins with the confession "Jesus Christ is Lord"[17]
- Absolutist about a personal faith relationship with the risen Jesus Christ is Lord, relativist in terms of the shape this takes in church and culture
- **Prior choice**: personal faith-relationship with Jesus Christ: born, lived, ministered, died, rose, ascended, coming again—by grace, through faith, in the power of the Holy Spirit
- Does not accept complete symmetry of "As in Adam...so in Christ"
- Equally verticalist and horizontalist
- All cultures (including my own) are fallen, all cultures can teach us something new about how "Jesus Christ is Lord"[18]
- Concerned about human co-existence amidst multiple cultures and religions
- Takes seriously the consequences of the Fall and of sin
- Somewhat optimistic about cultures, culture-affirming yet pessimistic about human sinfulness
- Bible, salvation and faith all call the institutional church to repentance and renewal—to confessing anew in word and life, "Jesus is Lord"
- Bible is God's inspired revelation for all humanity and has new things to say to each new culture where the gospel takes root
- Strongly conversionist, can be strongly transformational
- The same Holy Spirit works simultaneously but differently in the world, in and through the church, in the believer for mission in the world

- Softly optimistic about the institutional church, but more intentionally oriented toward the Kingdom of God
- Strong in the church's call to self-critique
- Conscious of the kingdom of darkness and the demonic both in the world and in the church
- Ultimately creative, ever-changing, theology-on-the-way that calls for new christologies in new cultural settings
- Can do well in folk-religious environment
- Tends to be confrontational with other global religious systems
- Mission is calling people to conversion, confession, and new allegiance, personally and corporately, to Jesus Christ as Lord in multiple cultures

The Relation of Faith and Culture

As the church becomes more and more a global community, it is increasingly clear that faith and culture cannot be entirely separated from each other. The gospel does not take place in a cultural vacuum, but is always incarnated in a specific cultural context. That is, it is infinitely "translatable," as Lamin Sanneh has said (1989:50-51). Yet we must affirm also that culture and faith are not identical. As Charles Kraft says, "We deduce then, that the relationship between God and culture is the same as that of one who uses a vehicle to the vehicle that he uses.... Any limitation of God is only that which he imposes upon himself—he chooses to use culture, he is not bound by it in the same way human beings are" (1979:115).

Not only must we distinguish God from culture, but we must also separate the faith of the individual from his or her culture.[19] We need to affirm approaches to other faiths that take seriously the culturally appropriate shape given the gospel in each time and place. But that is a far cry from equating culture and faith. Thus Paul Hiebert affirms,

> The gospel must be distinguished from all human cultures. It is divine revelation, not human speculation. Since it belongs to no one culture, it can be adequately expressed in all of them. The failure to differentiate between the gospel and human cultures has been one of the

great weaknesses of modern Christian missions (1985:53).

The difference between faith and culture is not only anthropologically accurate, it is also supported historically and biblically. Historically, one needs only review the history of the church to realize that the gospel of faith in the lordship of Jesus Christ has always tended to break out of the cultural molds that would imprison it. Originally the gospel was not Western at all—it was Middle-Eastern. It began among Aramaic-speaking Jews. Then it took shape in Greek culture, Roman culture, North African cultures, and on to Ethiopia, India, the Near-East, the Arabian peninsula, then on to Europe, and so forth. To associate any culture too closely with biblical faith is to ignore the historical expansion of the church.

But more profoundly, the distinction between faith and culture is biblically essential. This issue is at the heart of Acts and Romans.[20] In Acts and Romans the issue is precisely how the same faith in Christ's lordship can take shape in a variety of cultures. The difference between faith and culture is also essential for our understanding of Galatians, Ephesians and Colossians, for example. "The mystery," says Paul, "is that through the gospel the Gentiles (the ethne, comprising a multiplicity of cultures) are heirs together with Israel, members together of one body, and sharers together in the promise of Christ Jesus" (Eph 3:6, 15). 1 Peter and Revelation would not make much sense either, without a distinction between faith and culture. We now know that people of many cultures can have the same faith, and people of the same culture can have many faiths—or, in the case of the secularized post-Christian West, no faith at all.

Now this issue is more important than it may seem. One of the most disturbing aspects of the literature relevant to our topic is the close, nearly synonymous, relationship that is assumed to exist between faith and culture (see, for example, Ernst Troeltsch 1980:27). Whether we are speaking of Wilfred Cantwell Smith, Karl Rahner, Paul Knitter, John Hick, John Cobb, or Wesley Ariarajah, there is a disturbingly close relationship between faith and culture in their writings.[21] Interestingly, a close examination of the writings of inclusivists like Clark Pinnock, John Sanders and David Lowes Watson reveals the same almost total identification of culture with faith. However, the so-called "exclusivists" also tend to closely equate culture and faith—and in that case, conversion to Jesus Christ sometimes too easily becomes conversion to a particular version of culture-christianity.

The distinction between faith and culture is important theologically and missiologically because the increasing cultural pluralism of our world seems to create the assumption that cultural pluralism should lead naturally to religious relativity. In today's world, Christians and non-Christians, pluralists, inclusivists, and exclusivists are beginning to share one thing in common. We are all being radically impacted by the largest redistribution of people the globe has ever seen. In this new reality, all of us are seeking ways to affirm *cultural relativity*: tolerance, understanding, justice, equality, and co-existence of a new multi-cultural reality. The cities of our world are especially impacted by this.

But cultural relativity can impact our theology and missiology in strange ways, particularly if we hold faith and culture too close to each other. If one views faith and culture as nearly synonymous and one also begins to be open to *cultural* relativism, the next, seemingly obvious step is some form of *religious pluralism*. If one goes all the way with this process, one arrives at the pluralist position.[22] If one cannot go that far and feels strongly constrained to hold tightly to the uniqueness of the cosmic Christ-event, one arrives at the inclusivist position. If one refuses to accept *cultural* relativism, but holds faith and culture to be synonymous, one arrives at an exclusivist position reminiscent of a cultural Protestantism like that of the nineteenth century: conversion is adoption of certain cultural practices, rather than a matter of faith-relation to Jesus Christ. As the evangelical community has become more culture-affirming, the distinction between faith and culture has become harder to maintain, and its impact on our missiology more pervasive.

The Relation of Christology and Soteriology

Secondly, we need to be conscious of the radically different forms the soteriological question takes among pluralists and inclusivists on the one hand, and the exclusivists and "evangelists" on the other. The bottom-line question of the pluralist and inclusivist positions is, "Given the fact that humanity is basically good, and God is a God of love, how is it possible that God could condemn so much of humanity to eternal punishment?"

The exclusivists and evangelists would ask the question differently. We would ask, "Given the fact of the fall, and that 'all have sinned and fall short of the glory of God' (Ro 3:23), how is it possible that so much of humanity may be saved?"

I believe that our theological work concerning Christology in relation to non-Christian faiths must expand beyond the soteriological questions to questions of creation, fall, the nature of humanity, and the nature of sin and holiness. Without examining these, we cannot fully clarify the issues at hand. This is where I believe Pinnock and Sanders are both quite unrealistic about their Christological re-thinking. One cannot make such a substantive change in one's Christology without it being either the beginning of a change in all the other loci of one's theology—or the result of changes already made or assumed.[23]

Missiological Implications

Let me emphasize that I am making a conscious choice here to highlight the Christian's personal relationship with the living Jesus Christ who was born, lived in Palestine during a specific historical time, ministered, died, rose, ascended, and is coming again. The absolutely radical claim of the canonical text of the Bible is that this Jesus lives today, and is the one with whom the Christian disciple relates personally by faith. John Hick recognized in 1980 both the validity and the implications of this perspective (1980:19). As Hick admitted, "If Jesus was literally God incarnate, the second Person of the holy Trinity living in human life, so that the Christian religion was founded by God-on-earth in person, it is then very hard to escape from the traditional view that all [sic] mankind must be converted to the Christian faith" (1980:19).

Of course, this is the crucial point, and sadly John Hick opted to understand the narrative about Jesus Christ in what he called a "metaphorical" manner, rather than a literal description of a verifiable historical person (1980:19). That decision was coupled, in Hick's view, with his prior commitment that "any viable Christian theodicy must affirm the ultimate salvation of all God's creatures" (1980:17). The combination of these two prior commitments is not a neutral position, but rather involves an initial faith-choice that leads logically to a "pluralist" position.

Although there are many missiological implications that flow from the "Evangelist" paradigm, I will limit myself to three basic ones. An "Evangelist" paradigm of Christian attitude to other religions offers a perspective that is (1) faith particularist, (2) culturally pluralist, and (3) ecclesiologically inclusivist.[24]

The "Evangelist" paradigm recognizes the need to integrate both the particularity and the universality of Jesus Christ. The particularity of Jesus Christ's incarnation, ministry, death and resurrection in history continues to stand in dialectical tension with the universality of Jesus Christ's claims to be the Savior of the world. In the midst of this universal-particularism, the disciples of Jesus confess that "Jesus Christ is Lord."

Jesus Christ is Lord: Faith Particularist

The first element of this new paradigm that we need to stress is that it is *personal*. It deals not with religious systems, or theoretical religions as such, but with matters of people and of personal faith (Taber and Taber 1992). Thus we need to be able to deal with these matters in terms of "fuzzy sets," as Paul Hiebert has called them (1983:427), for they have to do with personal faith allegiance to Jesus who lived and ministered in Palestine at a specific time in history.[25] As Gnanakan says, "God's revelation has a historicality and a universality that will need to be reconciled" (1992:19). And such reconciliation is to be found, first of all, in a personal relationship of the Christian with the resurrected and ascended Jesus Christ of history. As Mark Heim (along with many others) has noted, the only truly unique, truly distinctive aspect of Christian faith is "a personal relationship between the Christian and the living Christ" (Heim 1985:135).

Thus in the diagram of the "Evangelistic" paradigm, all the figures are drawn with dotted lines. Confession in *Jesus* as Lord involves a personal faith-relationship that breaks the bonds of all religious systems. This relationship involves all of life with all its contradictions. It is not neat, logical, coherent. Sometimes it may involve what Hiebert has called "the excluded middle" (1982). This relationship is not exclusive, nor arrogant, nor triumphalistic. Rather, it is humble confession, repentance, and obedience. Thus the major question is not in what box or religious system does a person belong. Rather, we are dealing here with a relational "centered set," where the ultimate question is one of discipleship, one of proximity to, or distance from, Jesus the Lord.

This perspective calls into question the institutional structures of all churches, and especially of "Christianity" as a religious system, for the churches are now seen to be the fellowship of disciples of Jesus, whose allegiance is to Jesus more than to a particular institution (contra the "exclusivist" perspective). This also calls into question the inclusivist perspective in its cosmic Christ-event that is salvific for all persons regardless of their personal relationship with Jesus Christ. And it questions the "pluralist" perspective in its relativistic reduction of the confession to Jesus being only "a" christ among many.

The confession of Jesus as Lord calls for stripping away all the layers of the artichoke[26] of cultural accretions that Christians have added to the basic confession. As Paul demonstrates in Romans, and as one sees modeled in Acts, to confess with one's mouth and believe in one's heart that Jesus is Lord—that is all there is. Nothing else really matters.

Thus when I call people of other cultures and faiths to confess "Jesus is Lord," it is not **my** Jesus (exclusivist), nor is it a or any Jesus (pluralist), nor is it the cosmic amorphous idea of Jesus Christ (inclusivist). Rather, it is Jesus *the* Lord, who calls for conversion and transformation of *all* who confess his name. Only in humility, in personal repentance and prayer, and expectation of great cultural diversity may I invite others to join me in confessing JESUS as Lord. Many evangelical theologians and missiologists have affirmed this perspective. Such broad agreement does not minimize the radicalness of the affirmation.[27]

Jesus *Christ* is Lord: Culturally Pluralist

Along with the historicity and relationality of Jesus Christ, we must also affirm the universality of Christ's messianic lordship. As John 1, Ephesians 1, and Colossians 1 state, Jesus the Christ is the creator and sustainer of all the created order. Here we listen carefully to the so-called pluralist concerns. For we ARE concerned about the whole of humanity, and about the care of God's creation. We are concerned about how humans can live together in peace and justice, especially in the midst of increasingly difficult clashes between conflicting religious allegiances.

We need a trinitarian missiology that is Kingdom-oriented, as Johannes Verkuyl has so masterfully pointed out (1993). We need to remember that Christ's lordship is not only over the church (contra the "exclusivist"), but also over all the world. The pluralist and inclusivist perspectives confuse the manner, scope, and nature of Christ's kingly rule in relation to the church (the willing subjects), Christ's rule over all humanity in the world (many unwilling subjects), and over the unseen world. These need to be differentiated.[28]

However, this does not warrant our ignoring matters that deal with all peoples. Rather, Christ's lordship will radically question the "exclusivist" position in terms of other cultures and religions, and will instead open up a much greater breadth for contextualized encounter of Christians with their multiple cultures. Not all so-called non-Christian culture is sinful (contra the exclusivist). But neither is it all relative (contra the pluralist). For all is brought together under the lordship of Christ. Neither all creation, nor every human is ontologically determined to be included in Christ's salvation against their will (contra the inclusivist). Rather, we are called to "test the spirits" (1Jn 4:1-3). Those who confess "that Jesus Christ has come in the flesh" are to be recognized as related to God.

This broad, all-encompassing Christology means that we need to continue to listen carefully to the new Christologies that are arising in Asia, Africa and Latin America. Maximally, all that which does not contradict the biblical revelation concerning the historical Jesus Christ our Lord is open for consideration. Even in the New Testament, we are becoming aware of a multiplicity of Christologies that draw from the greatness of Jesus Christ and shape themselves for specific cultural and historical contexts, as Robert Gundry recently pointed out in a paper entitled, "Diversity and Multiculturalism in New Testament Christology" (1994).

Thus John Levison and Priscilla Pope-Levison (1994) have called us to join them in a search for "an Ecumenical Christology for Asia" that is neither the cosmic Christ who loses touch with real life, nor the suffering Jesus who has is no power to transform. In Latin America we inherited either the impotent Jesus hanging on the cross as a symbol of domination, or the distant Christ who is irrelevant to today's issues.[29]

Clearly, we need to be very careful here (H. Berkhof 1979:48) and must follow a very sensitive process that Paul Hiebert has called "critical contextualization" (1987). As David Hesselgrave has warned, we are constantly faced here with twin dangers: "the risk of going too far," and "the risk of not going far enough" (1988:152).[30]

Jesus Christ is *Lord*: Ecclesiologically Inclusivist

Any discussion of the Lordship of Jesus Christ must begin with a recognition of the Kingdom of God, Jesus Christ's kingly rule in the lives of people and in the church. J. Verkuyl said it well.

> A theology and missiology informed by the biblical notion of the rule of Christ will never fail to identify personal conversion as one of the inclusive goals of God's kingdom...The good news of the Kingdom also has to do with the formation and in-depth growth of the Body of Christ throughout the world and to the end of time...The Kingdom is, of course, far broader than the Church alone. God's Kingdom is all-embracing in respect of both point of view and purpose; it signifies the consummation of the whole of history; it has cosmic proportions and fulfills time and eternity. Meanwhile, the Church, the believing and active community of Christ, is raised up by God among all nations to share in the salvation and suffering service of the Kingdom. The Church consists of those whom God has called to stand at His side to act out with Him the drama of the revelation of the Kingdom come and coming (1993:73)

The Kingdom leads to the church, the disciples of Jesus Christ the Lord. For the church is not only a gathering of individuals, it is much more. "Though faith may be intensely personal," comment Charles and Betty Taber, "religion is irreducibly social" (1992:76). Jesus Christ is Lord not only of creation, he is also head of the Church (Col 1). Thus Jesus Christ sent his Spirit (contra Pinnock's *Logos* christology) at Pentecost to constitute the church. Because Jesus Christ is head of the church, no one else is. The church belongs to no human person, and church growth must be growth in the numbers of disciples of Jesus, as Donald McGavran always affirmed—not proselytism with a view to expanding someone's little ecclesiastical kingdom. The "Evangelistic" paradigm seeks to correct the triumphalism and arrogance of which the "exclusivists" have sometimes been accused.[31]

Because Jesus Christ the Lord is the head of the church, the church's mission is therefore to participate in the mission of Jesus the Christ. This means that the church's mission is *no less* than that which Jesus declares in Luke 4. And it is *as much as* what Paul says in Acts 13: the church is to be a "light to the nations." The church is therefore to focus itself on the whole of humanity. There is always room for one more forgiven sinner. But this also means (contra the inclusivists) that it is the church as church, and not some cosmic idea that gathers disciples. This also signifies (contra the pluralists) that the church of whom Christ is head is called to proclaim that Jesus is *the* Lord of all humanity, not just a christ (see Van Engen 1991:93-94).

This world-encountering church is as broad as all humanity, as accepting as Christ's cosmic lordship and as incorporating and gathering as Christ's disciples. The church is always the same: it is the disciples of Jesus Christ the Lord of creation, of all peoples, and of the church.[32]

CONCLUSION

Ultimately our conviction, reflection, and proclamation involves a restatement of the mystery of the gospel for all peoples. In Paul's words, it involves a mystery that, "for ages past was kept hidden in God, who created all things. His intent was that now, through the church, the manifold wisdom of God should be known...according to his eternal purpose which he accomplished in Christ Jesus our Lord. In him and through faith in him we may approach God with freedom and confidence" (Eph 3:9b-12 NIV). If Paul and the early church could say that in the midst of their cultural and religious diversity, we can feel confident in doing so as well. ***"Jesus Christ is Lord."*** In the midst of many cultures and peoples of many faiths, let's learn to be bold evangelists: faith particularist, culturally pluralist, and ecclesiologically inclusivist.

Notes

[1] Pinnock 1992:7. Chapman quotes Max Warren as saying, "The challenge of agnostic science will turn out to have been child's play compared with the challenge to Christian theology of the faith of other (people)" (Chapman 1990:16). See also Coote 1990:15; Covell 1993:162). Harold Netland quotes Gerald Anderson as saying, "The most critical aspect of the task of forging a viable theology of mission today 'deals with the Christian attitude toward religious pluralism and the approach to people of other faiths'" (Netland 1991:9; quoting from G. H. Anderson 1988:114).

[2] See International Missionary Council, *The World Mission of the Church: Findings and Recommendations of the Meeting of the International Missionary Council*, London: International Mission Council, 1938. An excellent series of articles on Tambaram 1938, appeared in *IRM* 78 (July):307. See also Carl Hallencreutz 1969.

[3] Cf. "The Revelation of God as the Abolition of Religion," in Hick and Hebblethwaite, eds., 1980:32-51.

[4] See *International Bulletin of Missionary Research* 14(2):56-63. See Mikka Roukanen 1990.

[5] See, e.g., Stanley Samartha 1977, 1981; Wesley Ariarajah 1988; Wilfred Cantwell Smith 1980; Kenneth Cragg 1986; Charles Forman 1993; C.S. Song 1975, 1987; Jerald Gort 1992; D.C. Mulder 1985; Anton Wessels 1992; Paul Tillich 1980; David Lowes Watson 1990; and the writings of M.M. Thomas and Paul D. Devanandan.

[6] An excellent survey is given by David Bosch 1988. See also David Hesselgrave 1990; and Richard Bauckham 1979. Folks like Clark Pinnock 1992 and John Sanders 1992; along with others like John Stott 1975, 1981, 1989; Harold Netland 1991; David Hesselgrave 1981, 1988; Michael Green 1977; Carl Braaten 1981; Ajith Fernando 1987; Ken Gnanakan 1992; Andrew Kirk 1992; Mark Heim 1985; William Crockett and James Sigountos 1991; together with J.I. Packer, Carl Henry, Kenneth Kantzer and others have begun to offer us some very substantial food for

thought. David Bosch, Gerald Anderson and Lesslie Newbigin, along with John V. Taylor, Max Warren, Johannes Verkuyl and Arthur Glasser, are among those who have consistently kept before all missiologists, including us evangelicals, the importance of continued and careful reflection on the subject. See also Jack Cottrell and Steve Burris 1993.

[7] In 1985, when Paul Knitter published *No Other Name?* he spoke of "models" of Christian attitudes to other religions: The Conservative Evangelical, the Mainline Protestant, the Catholic, and the Theocentric. In doing so, he downplayed the "pluralist, inclusivist and exclusivist" typology. In 1980, in *God Has Many Names*, John Hick refers to the three major types of approaches, but the words themselves as typological categories are not strongly emphasized. Harold Netland pointed this out in his response to the original reading of this chapter as a paper at the Spring 1994, ETS/EMS Midwestern Conference. In a good reader on *Christianity and Other Religions* (1980), John Hick and Brian Hebblethwaite mention "religious pluralism" and "Christian absolutism," but do not use the three-part typology either. On the evangelical side, Mark Heim (1985) and Ajith Fernand (1987) do not structure their work around these three perspectives.

[8] 15(3):198-207. Carl Braaten seemed to accept the threefold typology in 1987, mentioning Gavin D'Costa and Alan Race as utilizing it—but he does not indicate where it came from. (Braaten 1987:17.)

[9] Clark Pinnock (1992:14-15); John Sanders (1992:1-7); Millard Erickson (in his introductory chapter to William Crockett and James Sigountos 1991:27-33); J. Andrew Kirk (1992:9-15); and Ken Gnanakan (1992) all follow this organization. David Bosch follows a similar typology, but uses the words relativism, fulfillment, and exclusivism (Bosch 1991:478-483) to describe the three major perspectives.

[10] In his response to this paper, mentioned above in footnote 1, Harold Netland commented, "It is probably safe to assume that the term 'exclusivism' was not first introduced into the discussion by adherents of that perspective, but rather is a pejorative term first introduced by those who did not accept that view, who wished to cast it in a particularly unappetizing light. Unfortunately, by default, we evangelicals have allowed others involved

in the debate over religious pluralism to define the category of 'exclusivism', and to do so in unacceptable terms..." (Netland 1994:1)

[11] For similar sentiments, see, e.g., Eugene Hillman 1968:25-27. Hick's sentiment echoes that of Ernst Troeltsch, expressed in a lecture at the University of Oxford in 1923; see Troeltsch 1980:26-28; and Smith 1980:96-98.

[12] The question of what Paul meant in Romans 5:12-19 as to the extent and nature of the symmetry between Adam and Jesus is beyond the scope of this paper. Yet the implications of one's hermeneutic of that passage are profound and deep for our subject.

[13] See, e.g. Griffiths 1980:128-130.

[14] Bradley 1993.

[15] W. Cantwell Smith has felt that "traditional missions are the exact extrapolation of the traditional theology of the church" (1980:90).

[16] See Van Engen 1991:92-94.

[17] See Van Engen 1989:74-100.

[18] See Newbigin 1978:190-191. I have been helped here by an article by John Howard Yoder, "'But We Do See Jesus': The Particularity of Incarnation and the Universality of Truth" (Yoder 1983:66-67)

[19] What I mean by "faith" here is not the same thing as "revelation," which is primarily the action of God, by God's initiative, in God's way. Neither do I mean "faith" in terms of an existential or subjective experience of the numinous, of the "Wholly Other," or of the "Real." Nor do I mean "faith" in terms of an assent to a number of propositions (and concomitant participation in a number of rituals) which allow for the person to be accepted in a specific religious context. Of course, I recognize the validity of all of these as part of a much larger picture. However, at the risk of over-simplification, I believe I am on firm scriptural grounds to define "faith" in this context as including at its most foundational meaning a personal allegiance that derives from a covenantal RELATIONSHIP, an "assurance of things hoped for" (Heb 11:1) that flows from a personal encounter with Jesus Christ by grace, through faith, in the power of the Holy Spirit.

Charles Kraft is developing a fascinating approach to this in his investigation of three encounters: "allegiance, truth and power" that go on in Christian witness. (Kraft1991:258-265; 1992: 215-230.)

[20] See Van Engen 1991:191-193.

[21] For some references to this, see Van Engen 1991:189, footnote 16.

[22] W.A. Visser 't Hooft emphasized the importance of this faith/culture distinction. "To transform the struggle between the religions concerning the ultimate truth of God into an intercultural debate concerning values is to leave out the central issue at stake...ignoring the central affirmation of the faith, that God revealed himself once for all in Jesus Christ" (1963:85).

[23] James Bradley pointed this out in relation to the *Logos* christology that forms the basis of Pinnock's inclusivist position (Bradley 1993:20-22).

[24] I am following Paul Hiebert's lead here in calling missiology to move "Beyond Anti-Colonialism to Globalism" (1991).

[25] See also Hiebert 1979.

[26] I used to say "layers of the onion." But onions have no center, artichokes do.

[27] The reader may consult, e.g., Verkuyl 1989; Glasser 1989; Thomsen 1990; Green 1977; Braaten 1981; Taylor 1981; Scott 1981; Anderson 1950:228-237; Heim 1985:135; Yoder 1983; Neill 1970; Pickard 1991; and Gnanakan 1992.

[28] I have sought to make just such a distinction in Van Engen 1981:277-305 and Van Engen 1991:108-117.

[29] The development of new christologies in Latin America has been extensive and creative. For evangelical perspectives on this, see, e.g. Escobar 1991; Padilla 1986; and Mackay 1933.

[30] See also Kirk 1992:171-187; Fernando 1987:69ff; Nicholls 1979:1984; Newbigin 1978; and Henry 1991:253.

[31] See Gnanakan 1992:154.

[32] See, e.g., Verkuyl 1978:354-368, 1993; Bosch 1991:474-489; Nicholls 1984:131-135; and Kirk 1992.

Reference List

Anderson, Gerald H.
    1988   "American Protestants in Pursuit of Mission: 1886-1986." *International Bulletin of Mission Research* 12(3):98-118.
    1989   "The Truth of Christian Uniqueness." *International Bulletin of Mission Research* 13(2):49.
    1990   "Christian Mission and Religious Pluralism: A Selected Bibliography of 175 Books in English, 1970-1990." *International Bulletin of Mission Research* 14(4):172-176.
    1993   "Theology of Religions and Missiology: A Time of Testing." In *The Good News of the Kingdom*. Charles Van Engen, Dean Gilliland, and Paul Pierson, eds. Pp. 200-210. Maryknoll, NY: Orbis.

Anderson, G.H., and T.F. Stransky, eds.
    1981a   *Christ's Lordship and Religious Pluralism*, Maryknoll, NY: Orbis Books.
    1981b   *Mission Trends No. 5: Faith Meets Faith*, Grand Rapids, MI: Eerdmans; New York: Paulist.

Anderson, Norman, ed.
    1950   *The World Religions*. Grand Rapids, MI: Eerdmans.

Ariarajah, S. Wesley
    1988   "Religious Pluralism and Its Challenge to Christian Theology." *World Faiths Insight* 19 NS:2-15.

Barth, Karl
    1962   *Theology and Church: Shorter Writings, 1920-1928*. New York: Harper and Row, Publishers.
    1962   "Church and Cultures." In *Theology and Church: Shorter Writings, 1920-1928*. Pp. 334-354. New York: Harper and Row.
    1980   "The Revelation of God as the Abolition of Religion." In *Christianity and Other Religions: Selected Readings*. John Hick and Brian Hebblethwaite, eds. Pp. 32-51. Glasgow: Fount Paperbacks.

Bakker, R., R. Fernhout, J.D. Gort, and A. Wessels, eds.
    1985   *Religies in Nieuw Perspective*. Kampen: Kok.
Bauckham, Richard
    1979   "Universalism—A Historical Survey." *Themelios* 4(2): 48-53.
Berkhof, Hendrikus
    1979   *Christian Faith*. Grand Rapids, MI: Eerdmans.
    1988   "The Double Image of the Future." *Perspectives* 3(1): 8-9.
Blum, E. A.
    1979   "Shall You Not Surely Die?" *Themelios* 4(2):58-61.
Boff, Leonardo
    1984   *Jesus Christ Liberator: A Critical Christology for Our Time*. Maryknoll, NY: Orbis.
Bosch, David
    1980   *Witness to the World: Mission in Theological Perspective*. Atlanta: John Knox.
    1983   "An Emerging Paradigm for Mission." *Missiology* 11(4):485-510.
    1988   "The Church in Dialogue: From Self-Delusion to Vulnerability." *Missiology* 16:131-147.
    1991   *Transforming Mission: Paradigm Shifts in Theology of Mission*. Maryknoll, NY: Orbis.
Braaten, Carl
    1981   "The Uniqueness and Universality of Jesus Christ." In *Mission Trends No. 5*. Gerald Anderson and Thomas Stransky, eds. Pp. 69-92. Grand Rapids, MI: Eerdmans. (Originally published in the January, 1980, issue of *Occasional Bulletin of Missionary Research*.)
    1987   "Christocentric Trinitarianism vs. Unitarian Theocentrism: A Response to Mark Heim." *Journal of Ecumenical Studies* 24(1):17-21.
    1990   "The Triune God: The Source and Model of Christian Unity and Mission." *Missiology* 18(4):415-428.
Bradley, James E.
    1993   "Logos Christology and Religious Pluralism: a New Evangelical Proposal." Unpublished paper, presented at Fuller Theological Seminary, Pasadena, CA.

Cantwell Smith, Wilfred
> 1980 "The Christian in a Religiously Plural World." In *Christianity and Other Religions: Selected Readings*. John Hick and Brian Hebblethwaite, eds. Pp. 87-107. Glasgow: Fount Paperbacks.

Chapman, Colin
> 1990 "The Riddle of Religions." *Christianity Today* 34(8):16-22.

Cobb, John
> 1975 *Christ in a Pluralistic Age*. Philadelphia: Westminster.

Congregation for the Evangelization of Peoples and the Pontifical Council for Interreligious Dialogue
> 1992 "Dialogue and Proclamation (Excerpts)." *International Bulletin of Mission Research* 16(3):82-86.

Conn, Harvie, edit.
> 1990 *Practical Theology and the Ministry of the Church 1952-1984: Essays in Honor of Edmund P. Clowney*. Phillipsburg: Presbyterian & Reformed.

Coote, Robert T.
> 1990 "Lausanne II and World Evangelization." *International Bulletin of Mission Research* 14(1):10-17.

Cottrell, Jack, and Stephen Burris
> 1993 "The Fate of the Unreached: Implications for Frontier Missions." *International Journal of Frontier Missions* 10(2):1-6.

Covell, Ralph
> 1993 "Jesus Christ and World Religions: Current Evangelical Viewpoints." In *The Good News of the Kingdom: Mission Theology for the Third Millennium*. Charles Van Engen, Dean Gilliland, and Paul Pierson, eds. Pp. 162-180. Maryknoll, NY: Orbis.

Cragg, Kenneth
> 1986 *The Christ and the Faiths*, Philadelphia: Westminster Press.

Crockett, William V., and James G. Sigountos, eds.
> 1991 *Through No Fault of Their Own? The Fate of Those Who Have Never Heard* Grand Rapids, MI: Baker.

Dawe, Donald, and John Carman, eds.
    1978   *Christian Faith in a Religiously Plural World.* Maryknoll, NY: Orbis.

Dunn, James D.G.
    1980   *Christology in the Making: A New Testament Inquiry Into the Origins of the Doctrines of the Incarnation.* Philadelphia: Westminster.

Erickson, Millard
    1991   "The State of the Question." In *Through No Fault of Their Own? The Fate of Those Who Have Never Heard.* William Crockett and James Sigountos, eds. Pp. 23-34. Grand Rapids, MI: Baker.

Escobar, Samuel
    1991   "Evangelical Theology in Latin America: The Development of a Missiological Christology." *Missiology* 19(3):315-332.

Fernando, Ajith
    1987   *The Christian's Attitude Toward World Religions.* Wheaton, IL: Tyndale.

Forman, Charles
    1993   "Christian Dialogues with Other Faiths." In *Toward the 21st Century in Christian Mission.* James Phillips and Robert Coote, eds. Pp. 338-347. Grand Rapids, MI: Eerdmans.

Gilliland, Dean, ed.
    1989   *The Word Among Us: Contextualizing Theology for Mission Today.* Waco, TX: Word.

Glasser, Arthur F.
    1989   "Mission in the 1990s: Two Views." *International Bulletin of Mission Research* 13(1):2-8.

Gnanakan, Ken
    1992   *The Pluralist Predicament*, Bangalore: Theological Book Trust.

Gort, Jerald D, Hendrik M. Vroom, Rein Fernhout, and Anton Wessels, eds.
    1992   *On Sharing Religious Experience: Possibilities of Interfaith Mutuality.* Grand Rapids, MI: Eerdmans.

Green, Michael, ed.
    1977   *The Truth of God Incarnate.* London: Hodder & Stoughton.

Green, Michael
    1977   "Jesus in the New Testament." In *The Truth of God Incarnate*. Michael Green, ed. Pp. 18-50. London: Hodder & Stoughton.

Griffiths, Michael
    1980   *The Confusion of the Church and the World*. Chicago: InterVarsity.

Guelich, Robert A.
    1989   "What is the Gospel?" Unpublished inaugural lecture as Professor of New Testament, Fuller Theological Seminary, Pasadena, CA.

Gundry, Robert H.
    1994   "Diversity and Multiculturalism in New Testament Christology." Unpublished paper presented at Westmont College, Santa Barbara, CA.

Hallencreutz, Carl
    1969   *New Approaches to Men of Other Faiths*. Geneva: World Council of Churches.

Heim, Mark
    1985   *Is Christ the Only Way?: Christian Faith in a Pluralistic World*. Valley Forge, PA: Judson.
    1987   "Thinking About Theocentric Christology." *Journal of Ecumenical Studies* 24(1):1-16.

Henry, Carl
    1991   "Is It Fair?" In *Through No Fault of Their Own? The Fate of Those Who Have Never Heard*. William V. Crocket and James G. Sigoutos, eds. Pp. 245-256. Grand Rapids, MI: Baker.

Hesselgrave, David
    1981   "Evangelicals and Interrelegious Dialogue." In *Mission Trends No. 5: Faith Neets Faith*. Gerald Anderson and Thomas Stransky, eds. Pp. 123-127. Grand Rapids, MI: Eerdmans; New York: Paulist.
    1988   *Today's Choices for Tomorrow's Mission: An Evangelical Perspective on Trends and Issues in Missions*. Grand Rapids, MI: Zondervan.
    1990   "Christian Communication and Religious Pluralism: Capitalizing on Differences." *Missiology* 18(2):131-138.

Hesselgrave, David, ed.
    1979   *New Horizons in World Mission: Evangelicals and the Christian Mission in the 1980's, Papers and Responses Prepared for the Consultation on Theology and Mission, Trinity Evangelical Divinity School, March 19-22, 1979*. Grand Rapids, MI: Baker.

Hick, John
    1980   *God Has Many Names*. Philadelphia: Westminster.

Hick, John, and Brian Hebblethwaite, eds.
    1980   *Christianity and Other Religions: Selected Readings*. Glasgow: Fount Paperbacks.

Hick, John, and Paul Knitter, eds.
    1988   *The Myth of Christian Uniqueness*. Maryknoll, NY: Orbis.

Hiebert, Paul
    1978   "Conversion, Culture and Cognitive Categories." *Gospel in Context* 1(3):24-29.
    1979   "Sets and Structures: A Study of Church Patterns." In *New Horizons in World Mission: Evangelicals and the Christian Mission in the 1980's, Papers and Responses Prepared for the Consulation on Theology and Mission, Trinity Evangelical Divinity School, March 19-22, 1979*. David Hesselgrave, ed. Pp. 217-227. Grand Rapids, MI: Baker.
    1982   "The Flaw of the Excluded Middle." *Missiology* 10(1):35-47.
    1983   "The Category 'Christian' in the Mission Task." *International Review of Mission* 72(287):421-427.
    1985   *Anthropological Insights for Missionaries*. Grand Rapids, MI: Baker.
    1987   "Critical Contextualization." *International Bulletin of Mission Research* 11(3):104-111.
    1991   "Beyond Anti-Colonialism to Globalism." *Missiology* 19(3):263-282.

Hillman, Eugene
    1968   *The Wider Ecumenism: Anonymous Christianity and the Church*. London: Burns & Oates.

Hocking, William
    1932   *Rethinking Missions: A Layman's Inquiry After One Hundred Years*. New York: Harper and Row.
International Missionary Council
    1938   *The World Mission of the Church*. London: International Missionary Council.
Jongeneel, Jan A.B., ed.
    1992   *Pentecost, Mission and Ecumenism: Essays in Intercultural Theology*. Berlin: Peter Lang.
Kantzer, Kenneth
    1991   "Preface." In *Through No Fault of Their Own? The Fate of Those Who Have Never Heard*. William Crockett and James Sigountos, eds. Pp. 11-15. Grand Rapids, MI: Baker.
Kirk, Andrew J.
    1992   *Loosing the Chains: Religion as Opium and Liberation*. London: Hodder & Stoughton.
Knitter, Paul
    1974   *Towards a Protestant Theology of Religions: A Case Study of Paul Althaus and Contemporary Attitudes*. Marburg: N.G. Etwert Verlag.
    1985   *No Other Name? A Critical Survey of Christian Attitudes Toward the World Religions*. Maryknoll, NY: Orbis.
Kraemer, Hendrik
    1938   *The Christian Message in a Non-Christian World*. London: Edinburgh House; repr. Grand Rapids, MI: Kregel, 1969.
Kraft, Charles
    1979   *Christianity in Culture: A Study in Dynamic Biblical Theologizing in Cross-Cultural Perspective*. Maryknoll, NY: Orbis.
    1991   "Allegiance, Truth and Power Encounters in Christian Witness." *Evangelical Missions Quarterly* 27:258-265.
    1992   "Allegiance, Truth and Power Encounters in Christian Witness." In *Pentecost, Mission and Ecumenism: Essays in Intercultural Theology*. Jan A.V. Jongeneel, ed. Pp. 215-230. Berlin: Peter Lang.
Küng, Hans
    1987   *The Incarnation of God*. New York: Crossroad.

Levison, John R., and Priscilla Pope-Levison
    1994   "Toward and Ecumenical Christology for Asia." *Missiology* 22(1):3-18.

Mackay, John A.
    1933   *The Other Spanish Christ: A Study in The Spiritual History of Spain and South America*. New York: Macmillan.

Moltmann, Jürgen
    1990   *The Way of Jesus Christ: Christology in Messianci Dimensions*. San Francisco: Harper.

Mulder, Dirk C.
    1985   "Alle geloven op éen kussen?" In *Religies in Nieuw Perspective*. R. Bakker, R. Fernhout, J. D. Gort, and A. Wessels, eds. Pp. 137-151. Kampen: Kok.

Neill, Stephen
    1957   *The Unfinished Task*. London: Edinburgh House.
    1970   *Christian Faith and Other Faiths*. New York: Oxford University.

Netland, Harold
    1988   "Toward Contextualized Apologetics." *Missiology* 16(3):289-303.
    1991   *Dissonant Voices: Religious Pluralism and the Question of Truth*. Grand Rapids, MI: Eerdmans.
    1994   "Response to 'The Uniqueness of Christ: Shaping Faith and Mission' by Charles Van Engen." Unpublished paper presented at the ETS/EMS Midwestern Conference, March 17-19, Chicago, IL.

Newbigin, Lesslie
    1969   *The Finality of Christ*. Richmond, VA: John Knox.
    1978   *The Open Secret: Sketches for a Missionary Theology*. G rand Rapids, MI: Eerdmans.
    1981   "The Gospel Among the Religions." In *Mission Trends No. 5: Faith Meets Faith*. Gerald Anderson and Thomas Stransky, eds. Pp. 3-19. Grand Rapids, MI: Eerdmans; New York: Paulist.
    1986   *Foolishness to the Greeks: The Gospel and Western Culture*. Grand Rapids, MI: Eerdmans.
    1989   *The Gospel in a Pluralist Society*. Grand Rapids, MI: Eerdmans.

1989 "Religious Pluralism and the Uniqueness of Jesus Christ." *International Bulletin of Mission Research* 13(2):50-54.
1990 "Religous Pluralism and the Uniqueness of Jesus Christ." *The Best in Theology.* J. I. Packer, ed. Vol. 4. Pp. 267-274. Carol Stream, IL: Christianity Today, Inc.
1991 *Truth to Tell: The Gospel as Public Truth.* Grand Rapids, MI: Eerdmans.
1992 "The Legacy of W.A. Visser 't Hooft." *International Bulletin of Mission Research* 16(2):78-82.
1994 "Ecumenical Amnesia." *International Bulletin of Mission Research* 18(1):2-5.

Nicholls, Bruce
1979 "The Exclusiveness and Inclusiveness of the Gospel." *Themelios* 4(2):62-69.
1984 "A Living Theology for Asian Churches." In *The Bible and Theology in Again Contexts: An Evangelical Perspective on Asian Theology.* Bong Rin Ro and Ruth Eshenaur, eds. Pp. 119-138. Taichung: Asia Theological Association.
1990 "The Church and Authentic Dialogue." In *Practucak Theology and the Ministry of the Church 1952-01984: Essays in Honor of Edmund P. Clowney.* Harvie Conn, ed. Pp. 255-272. Phillipsburg, NJ: Presbyterian & Reformed.

Packer, J.I.
1986 "'Good Pagans' and God's Kingdom." *Christianity Today* 30(1): 22-25.

Padilla, Rene
1986 "Toward a Contextual Christology from Latin America." In *Conflict and Context: Hermeneutics in the Americas.* Mark Lau Branson and C. René Padilla, eds. Pp. 81-92. Grand Rapids, MI: Eerdmans.

Pannikar, Raimundo
1978 *Intra-Religious Dialogue.* N ew York: Paulist.

Phillips, James M., and Robert T. Coote
1993 *Toward the 21rst Century in Christian Mission.* Grand Rapids, MI: Eerdmans.

Pickard, William M.
    1991   "A Universal Theology of Religion?" *Missiology* 19(2):143-151.

Pinnock, Clark H.
    1991   "Acts 4:12—No Other Name under Heaven." In *Through No Fault of Their Own? The Fate of Those Who Have Never Heard.* William V. Crockett and James G. Sigountos, eds. Pp. 107-116. Grand Rapids, MI: Baker.
    1992   *A Wideness in God's Mercy: The Finality of Jesus Christ in a World of Religions.* Grand Rapids, MI: Zondervan.

Rahner, Karl
    1980   "Christianity and the Non-Christian Religions." In *Christianity and Other Religions: Selected Readings.* John Hick and Brian Hebblethwaite, eds. Pp. 52-79. Glasgow: Fount Paperbacks.

Rhem, Richard A.
    1988   "The Habit of God's Heart." *Perspectives* 3(7):8-11.

Rin Ro, Bong and Ruth Eshenaur, eds.
    1984   *The Bible & Theology in Asain Contexts: An Evangelical Perspective on Asian Theology.* Taichung: Asia Theological Association.

Rouner, Leroy S., ed.
    1983   *Foundations of Ethics.* Notre Dame, IN: University of Notre Dame.

Roukanen, Miikka
    1990   "Catholic Teaching on Non-Christian Religions at the Second Vatican Council." *International Bulletin of Mission Research* 14(2):56-61.

Runia, Klaas
    1984   *The Present-Day Christological Debate.* Downers Grove, IL: InterVarsity.

Sanders, John
    1992   *No Other Name: An Investigation into the Destiny of the Unevangelized.* Grand Rapids, MI: Eerdmans.

Sanneh, Lamin
    1989   *Translating the Message: the Missionary Impact on Culture.* Maryknoll, NY: Orbis.

Samartha, Stanley, ed.
    1977   *Faith in the Midst of Faiths: Reflections on Dialogue in Community*. Geneva: World Council of Churches.

Samartha, Stanley
    1981   "The Lordship of Jesus Christ and Religious Pluralism." In *Christ's Lordship and Religious Pluralism*. G. H. Anderson and T. F. Stransky, eds. Pp. 19-36. Maryknoll, NY: Orbis.

Schreiter, Robert
    1990   "Jesus Christ and Mission: The Cruciality of Christology." *Missiology* 18(4):429-438.

Scott, Waldron
    1981   "'No Other Name'—An Evangelical Conviction." In *Christ's Lordship and Religious Pluralism*. G. H. Anderson and T. F. Stransky, ed. Pp. 58-74. Maryknoll, NY: Orbis.

Song, C.S.
    1975   *Christian Mission in Reconstruction—An Asian Analysis*. Maryknoll, NY: Orbis.
    1987   "God's Grace in the World of Religions." *Perspectives* 2(1):4-7.

Stadler, Anton P.
    1977   "Dialogue: Does it Complement, Modify or Replace Mission?" *Occasional Bulletin of Missionary Research* 1(3):2ff.

Stott, John
    1970   *Christ the Controversialist*. Downers Grove, IL: InterVarsity.
    1975   *Christian Mission in the Modern World*. Downers Grove, IL: InterVarsity.
    1981   "Dialogue, Encounter, Even Confrontation." In *Mission Treandss No. %: Faith Meets Faith*. G. H. Anderson and T. F. Stransky, eds. Pp. 156-172. Grand Rapids, MI: Eerdmans; New York: Paulist.
    1989   "Taking a Closer Look at Eternal Torture." *World Christian* 8(5):31-37.

Taber, Charles R., and Betty J. Taber
    1992   "A Christian Understanding of 'Religion' and 'Religions'." *Missiology* 20(1):69-78.

Taylor, John V.
    1963   *Primal Vision*. London: Student Christian Movement.
    1981   "The Theological Basis of Interfaith Dialogue." In *Mission Trends No. 5: Faith Meets Faith.* Gerald Anderson and Thomas Stransky, eds. Pp. 93-110. Grand Rapids, MI: Eerdmans; New York: Paulist.
Thomsen, Mark
    1990   "Confessing Jesus Christ Within the World Of Religious Pluralism." *International Bulletin of Mission Research* 14(3):115-118.
Tillich, Paul
    1980   "Christianity Judging Itself in the Light of its Encounter with the World of Religions." In *Christianity and Other Religions: Selected Readings.* John Hick and Brian Hebblethwaite, eds. Pp. 108-121. Glasgow: Fount Paperbacks.
Troeltsch, Ernst
    1971   *The Absoluteness of Christianity*. Richmond, VA: John Knox.
    1980   "The Place of Christianity Among the World Religions." In *Christianity and Other Religions: Selected Readings.* John Hick and Brian Hebblethwaite, eds. Pp. 11-31. Glasgow: Fount Paperbacks.
Van Engen, Charles
    1981   *The Growth of the True Church*. Amsterdam: Rodopi.
    1989   "The New Covenant: Knowing God in Context." In *The Word Among Us: Contextualizing Theology for Mission Today.* Dean Gilliland, ed. Pp. 74-100. Waco, TX: Word.
    1991   "The Effect of Universalism on Mission Effort." In *Through No Fault of Their Own? The Fate of Those Who Have Never Heard.* William V. Crockett and James G. Sigountos, eds. Pp. 183-194. Grand Rapids, MI: Baker.
    1991   *God's Missionary People: Rethinking the Purpose of the Local Church*. Grand Rapids, MI: Baker.
Van Engen, Charles, Dean S. Gilliland, and Paul Pierson, eds.
    1993   *The Good News of the Kingdom: Mission Theology for the Third Millenium*. Maryknoll, NY: Orbis.

Verkuyl, Johannes
    1978   *Contemporary Missiology: An Introduction.* Grand Rapids, MI: Eerdmans.
    1986   "Contra de twee kernthesen van Knitter's theologia religionum." *Wereld en Zending* 2:113-120.
    1989   "Mission in the 1990s. *International Bulletin of Mission Research* 13(2):55-58.
    1993   "The Biblical Notion of Kingdom: Test of Validity for Theology of Religion." In *The Good News of the Kingdom: Mission Theology for the Third Millennium.* Charles Van Engen, Dean Gilliland, and Paul Pierson, eds. Pp. 71-81. Maryknoll, NY: Orbis.

Visser 't Hooft, W.A.
    1963   *No Other Name: The Choice Between Syncretism and Christian Universalism.* Philadelphia: Westminster.

Vroom, Hendrik M.
    1989   *Religions and the Truth: Philosophical Reflections and Perspectives.* Grand Rapids, MI: Eerdmans.

Watson, David Lowes
    1990   *God Does Not Foreclose: The Universal Promise of Salvation.* Nashville: Abingdon.

Wessels, Anton
    1992   "The Experience of the Prophet Mohammed." In *On Sharing Religious Experience: Possibilities of Interfaith Mutuality.* Jerald D. Gort, Hendrik M. Vroom, Rein Fernhout and Anton Wessels, eds. Pp. 228-244. Grand Rapids, MI: Eerdmans.

Wright, N.T.
    1975   "Universalism and the World-Wide Community." *The Churchman* 89(3):197-212.
    1979   "Towards a Biblical View of Universalism." *Themelios* 4(2):54-58.

Yoder, John Howard
    1983   "'But We Do See Jesus': The Particularity of Incarnation and the Universality of Truth." In *Foundations of Ethics.* Leroy Rouner, ed. Pp. 57-75. Notre Dame, IN: University of Notre Dame.

11

CHRISTIANITY AS A MINORITY RELIGION

Larry Poston

Majoritarianism versus Minoritarianism

In a recent article appearing in a missiological journal, Robertson McQuilkin listed as the first of "Six Inflammatory Questions" the query "Are we winning or losing?" (McQuilkin 1994:130). It is doubtless true that most have wondered at times just how well the church is doing with regard to the Christian world mission. It is not an easy matter to decide. One is confronted with the question again in reading George Otis, Jr.'s book *The Last of the Giants: Lifting the Veil on Islam and the End Times*. In the introductory chapter the author relates several demoralizing experiences that he underwent in Moscow, Beirut, and Mongolia, and in summary writes, "A decade of observations had convinced me that these experiences were not unusual, and that in fact very little of the world showed any tangible evidence of belonging to the Lord" (Otis 1992:25). But one hundred pages or so later, in a chapter entitled "Closing on Eden," he gives an entirely different evaluation of world conditions:

> Much to the dismay of the enemy, the borders of the unevangelized world have been heaved backward so forcefully that 75% of the world's population now have a reasonable opportunity to hear the Gospel ... at the end of the First Century, the

ratio of non-believers to Christians was 360 to 1. Today the ratio is 7 to 1 (Otis 1992:144-145).

Understood correctly, these are not necessarily contradictory statements. Communicating the Gospel and seeing "tangible evidence of belonging to the Lord" are two entirely different things. But it is a comparison of the *tone* of each statement that becomes problematic; the one is somber with despair, the other soars with optimism. Where does the church stand, really? Are the triumphalists correct, those who say that the possibility of actually fulfilling the Great Commission has never been greater? That, proportionally speaking, Christians have never had better odds when it comes to "preaching the Gospel to every creature," and that the church is on the verge of an immense harvest to be reaped before A.D. 2000? Or are those who fail to find convincing evidence that "the earth is truly the Lord's" the more realistic of the observers?

Consider these facts: the religion of Islam is growing so swiftly that the number of Muslims in the world could surpass the number of Christians within the next fifty years. Hinduism and Buddhism are growing rapidly as well, even in the Western world. A Shinto revival continues to expand in Japan, and Chinese religions have been so revitalized that some world leaders today speak of "Confucian capitalism" as an alternative to the Judeo-Christian model of the West. Meanwhile, the verdict concerning the Christian faith is mixed. Asia—with the possible exceptions of some of the northern and western republics of the former Soviet Union along with South Korea—continues to report abysmal statistics for Christian percentages throughout the entire continent. In Africa a four-way battle between Christianity, Islam, tribalism, and syncretism proceeds without a clear-cut victor in sight. And in the West, the decline of Christianity continues apace, both numerically and—especially—influentially, as secularism and New Age spirituality vie—or unite—on the television screens and in the movie theaters of American and European societies. Such observations appear to confirm Otis's negative evaluation of the world as a place exhibiting "little tangible evidence of belonging to the Lord." Those who view the current global situation from this perspective foresee a mushrooming of non-Christian religions that will gradually choke out Christianity in many parts of the world.

But statistics also indicate that between 1.5 and 1.7 billion people on the planet consider themselves to be Christian in some sense of the word, making Christianity—for the time being—the largest of the world religions, half again as big as its nearest competitor. The figures cited in Patrick Johnstone's *Operation World* reveal that Christians are a numerical majority in 143 nations or people groups, two-thirds of the total number listed in the book. The Christian world mission has been so successful that the ratio of non-Christians to evangelical Christians has dropped to a mere seven to one, and the church has established at least a beachhead in all but a handful of countries. The heady excitement arising from the opportunities created by the dissolution of the Soviet Union and the fervor of advocates of such concepts as the A.D. 2000 Movement have created in some circles an apocalyptic atmosphere similar to that which reigned during the closing years of the nineteenth century.

So what position should evangelical believers take? Should they be advocates of a "majoritarian" optimism regarding the expansion of the Kingdom of God, believing that Christians will maintain their majority status where they currently enjoy it and will develop such a status where they do not? Or should they be "minoritarians" in their thinking, maintaining that Christianity is indeed only a minority faith at the present time and that it will continue in a state of decline until the second coming of Christ? It is the intent of this essay to show that Christianity is currently no more than a minority faith in nearly every geo-graphic location on earth. Furthermore, Christians have every reason—from a biblical point of view—to expect that Christianity will remain so for the foreseeable future.

This assessment will admittedly not play well in missions publications or at missionary conferences. While skirting the triumphalist expectations and interpretations of current events that are characteristic of postmillennial eschatology, evangelicals nevertheless often give the impression that unless they can report victories won and progress toward an ultimate goal, the credibility of their entire enterprise may be suspect. But this is erroneous thinking. What evangelicalism actually needs in order to prepare its adherents for the next century is a mentality that acknowledges that Christianity is indeed only a minority faith.

Before proceeding, it should first be noted that the concept of "minority" can take at least three different forms. The most obvious is that of a *numerical minority*, in which the number of a specific group's adherents is proportionally smaller than the number of adherents of other groups in the same society. In most societies there is one group which, due to its size, is perceived as comprising a majority, automatically consigning other groups of a similar genre to the status of minorities. A second form could be termed that of *peripheral minority*, a title applied to a group which might be numerically large—even technically a majority— but which exercises little or no influence upon the society in which it resides. This lack of influence may be due to an advanced state of secularism and/or pluralism, or it might be attributable to a totalitarian political system that effectively neutralizes any potential influence such a group might seek to exercise. Finally, there is the concept of an *attitudinal minority*, which would characterize a group that is both sizeable and influential but which, due to a particular internal value system, refuses to assume the maximum power and influence that it could conceivably wield. Institutionalized groups and/or movements of advanced age, for instance, may lack the motivation and drive necessary to accomplish goals that an outside observer would judge the group to be easily capable of accomplishing. Or, from the standpoint of religion, a mass of believers might become so demoralized regarding their political, economic, social, or spiritual condition that they simply cease all efforts to expand their number and instead turn inward in an attempt at self-preservation.

Depending upon the geographic location considered, Christianity is a minority faith in each of these senses. For instance, of the 212 nations and people groups listed in *Operation World*, Christians are a numerical minority in sixty-nine, about one-third of the total. This would appear to indicate that the religion has majoritarian status in two-thirds of the world's nations, but when the actual *influence* of the religion upon society is factored in, the percentage drops precipitously. The country of Sweden, for instance, is a perfect case in point. Johnstone remarks that "94% of the population was, by default, born 'Christian'" (Johnstone 1993:518). The official Christian percentage, however, is listed at 64.1%, with a negative growth rate, and Christian churches are attended by no more than five percent of the Swedish population. Christianity thus stands at the periphery of Swedish society, since ninety-five percent of the people are not touched in any consistent or significant way by the Christian faith.

It is much more difficult to determine attitudinal minority, since this is essentially an internal concept and is closely intertwined with the first two types of minorities. A situation must be located in which Christians may be a numerical majority and, because of their influence upon society in the past, have at least the potential for societal influence today as well, but where, nevertheless, the overall attitude of believers is one of such extreme negativism, hopelessness, or separatism that they remain in virtual seclusion from each other and from society as a whole. Christians who lived under the former Soviet Union are a case in point, particularly those in such republics as Russia, Estonia, Latvia, and Lithuania. Numerically, Christians have formed a substantial majority of the populations of these countries for centuries. Even after seventy years of Communist repression, it is estimated that fifty-six percent of the Russian people are Christian, and the figures given for Estonia, Latvia, and Lithuania are sixty percent, fifty-five percent, and eighty-six percent respectively (Johnstone 1993:467, 211, 345, 357). The potential for influence certainly existed throughout the period of Soviet dominance; one could cite the case of Poland as an example. But since the time of the Communist conquests, the Christians of Russia and the Baltic nations have considered themselves to be hopelessly repressed populations.

As indicated previously, an attitude of minoritarianism is considered by some to be an altogether undesirable perspective with regard to the fulfillment of the Great Commission. But in actuality, is minority status—be it numerical, peripheral, or attitudinal—as negative as the focus of today's media tends to portray it? Are there not actually distinct *advantages* to seeing the Christian religion as a minority faith?

Now some may argue that it was the desire of evangelicals to make Christianity a *majority* faith, coupled with a conviction of the need to Christianize (read "civilize") the peoples of the earth by imposing upon them biblically-based cultural practices, that fueled the modern missionary movement of the eighteenth and nineteenth centuries. If this was indeed the case, then loss of such a motivation would clearly lead to a decline in missionary activity. But this interpretation is inaccurate. The *real* impetus for the tremendous rise in missionary activity seen at the end of the nineteenth century actually came during the last two decades and was mainly attributable to a change in eschatological expectations regarding the future of humankind. Premillennialist doctrine lent an urgency to the missionary enterprise, positing the necessity of world evangelization before Christ could return.

George Muller, A. T. Pierson, A. B. Simpson, D. L. Moody and A.J. Gordon called upon thousands of students to evangelize the world in their own generation. This "single-minded emphasis on evangelization" produced a situation in which "proclamation of the gospel took precedence over such traditional missionary activity as education and medicine" (Robert 1990:32). The new paradigm was thus the *opposite* of a majoritarian idea; the goal was now to *evangelize*, not to *Christianize*. A. T. Pierson in particular (as a convert from postmillennialism) defined evangelization as "the preaching of the Word to the world, regardless of whether people become believers" (Robert 1990:37). Premillennialism is essentially a minoritarian eschatology, advocating belief in an inevitable decline in the influence of Christianity as the return of Christ approaches.

The "majoritarian" optimism of postmillennialism died an early death, caused in part by biblical evidence submitted by premillennialists against it, and in part by the historical events of the early twentieth century. The majoritarian "superiority complex" suffered terribly as a result of the two World Wars, fought for the most part between "Christian" opponents, and also as a result of the resurgence of non-Christian religions, sparked to a large extent by the nineteenth-century missionary movement itself. As postmillennial optimism waned, ecumenicism followed in its wake, only to suffer in its turn a long and gradual decline in the face of the two warring giants of recent decades: an all-encroaching secularism and a rabid fundamentalism. The majoritarian ideals of both postmillennialism and ecumenicism failed to withstand the tests of time and historical events. Minoritarian premillennialism, on the other hand, with its emphasis on *obedience* to a specific interpretation of the Great Commission of Matthew 28:18-20 was and continues to be the engine of the modern missionary movement.

There is another type of minority mentality that is currently extant in Western Christianity, but there is a question as to whether or not this is a truly biblical mindset. Os Guinness has pointed out how unconscionable the actions of evangelicals have been during the last two decades in their transformation from a powerful influence in the late 1970s and early 1980s to the put-upon victims of a secularized society in the 1990s. "In ten short years," he states, "the public self-portrait presented by evangelicals has changed from the sleeping giant of American public life to the poor little whipping boy at the mercy of liberal forces"

(Guinness 1994:193). Guinness decries this surrender to the political and social trends spawned by secularists and accuses Christians of utilizing essentially the same tactics the oppressed minorities of the West have adopted in order to promote their own agendas. He asks pointedly, "Are evangelicals and fundamentalists prepared to participate enterprisingly in public life or are they determined to play the victim and portray themselves as a persecuted minority in need of special understanding?" (Guinness 1994:193).

Guinness is correct in this evaluation, but only up to a point. It is certainly wrong to whine, to portray oneself as oppressed as a strategy to gain the sympathy (or pity) of mainstream society. This is not the way that Jesus or the apostles interacted with the societies of their day. At the same time, it is futile to expect that evangelicals with their exclusivistic emphasis upon an internal and personal approach to matters of salvation and redemption will ever enjoy truly democratic prerogatives in societies where their agenda is widely known. Opposition to such perceived intolerance is inevitable, whether it arises out of the human sinfulness of the secular, humanistic realm or out of the demonic evil of the spiritual realm. Christians may insist that even exclusivists should be tolerated by those who advocate a consistent pluralism, but this insistence represents a logical con-tradiction that is essentially insuperable. Given the irresolv-ability of the conflict, who can blame secularists for taking a hard line and squelching for the sake of tolerance the one group that is perceived as being intolerant of all religious and ideological beliefs other than its own? Evangelicals can—and should—agitate for consistency, but given the spiritual struggle in which humankind has been embroiled since Eden, they should not expect to win. They will never be a "politically correct" minority. They should instead be thankful that they are tolerated as much as they are.

At the same time, minoritarianism need not result in an enervating pessimism or despair. Take, for example, the Jews and Muslims of America. According to many estimates these groups comprise roughly the same percentage of the American population: approximately six million each out of a total of 260 million persons. But even as a numerically negligible minority, Judaism has wielded an influence out of all proportion to its size. In education, the media, the arts, politics, science, literature—there is virtually no field in which the Jewish people have not excelled and made their presence felt. Indeed, so influential has their presence been in the Western world that they have brought upon themselves jealousy and envy which have at times led to persecution. But their experiences as a minority have allowed them to forge a way of life that is in many respects exemplary for Christians. The minority mentality has forced them to construct and maintain a unique identity which has imbued them with a sense of mission and calling that is not found among the greater part of the Christian population. There is an aspect of separatism, and even of elitism, that has protected the Orthodox Jews and the Hasidim in particular from the perils of assimilationism. But Jewish separatism—with only rare exceptions—has been attitudinal, not physical; a mirror image of their minority status, which is physical, not attitudinal. Such is the polarity that evangelical Christians in all societies should seek to emulate.

Muslims living in the West are beginning to benefit from their minority status as well. Their adaptation is occurring more slowly than it did for the Jewish people, to be sure, for Muslims have not been scattered *en masse* as the result of an involuntary diaspora. Though many have indeed entered the West as political refugees, there does not exist a centuries-long tradition of Muslim persecution as is the case with the adherents of the Jewish faith. On the contrary, the Muslim mindset is generally characterized by a pronounced *majoritarianism*. This has been problematic for Muslims living as a physical minority in non-Muslim lands, for as Abdur Rehman Doi states,—there is no clear-cut guidance or direction available in the Fiqh as to how [Muslim minorities] should survive as Muslims in non-Muslim states" (Doi 1987:43). But in most cases this problem does not result in an attitude of withdrawal and isolationism, for Muslims have understood that rather than maintaining and preserving one's identity, recourse to separatism in a physical sense will often produce a situation exactly the opposite of what is intended. As Doi notes:

> Muslims living in such conditions cannot and must not remain aloof. They must participate constructively in building up the traditions of the nation state. [Otherwise] their oversensitivity, suspicion, hesitation, and passivity may result in delivering the state into the hands of a narrow-minded coterie, full of hatred against Muslims, and who are in fact the enemies of equality and justice (Doi 1987:57).

Given time, Muslims will most likely infiltrate the same societal structures that the Jewish people have so successfully entered. Indeed, the late Temple University professor Ismail al-Faruqi's plan entitled *The Islamization of Knowledge: General Principles and Workplan* reveals a keen sophistication with regard to how the systems of higher education in the United States could be used as entry points for a Muslim transformation of American society. Al-Faruqi called his Muslim colleagues to an intellectual *jihad* when he stated that

> As disciplines, the humanities, the social sciences and the natural sciences must be reconceived and rebuilt, given a new Islamic base and assigned new purposes consistent with Islam. Every discipline must be recast so as to embody the principles of Islam in its methodology, in its strategy, in what it regards as its data, its problems, its objectives, its aspirations. Every discipline must be remolded so as to incorporate the relevance of Islam ... Never in Islamic history has the war-cry *Allahu akbar!* been more needed on the intellectual level as it is today (al-Faruqi 1982:Preface).

Applications

What does all of this mean for the missionary strategy and candidate training of evangelical Christians? Essentially there are three separate but related applications of the concepts discussed above. First, a biblically-informed minority mentality must be cultivated in missionary trainees, a knowledge of who evangelical Christians really are and where they stand vis-a-vis the other world religions. Secondly, evangelicals must have a clear idea as to what their missionary activity should involve at the socio-political level of human existence. And thirdly, evangelicals must understand what forms their missionary activity should take at the local and individual levels of society.

Adoption of a Minority Mentality

There are undeniable advantages involved in the adoption of a biblical minoritarianism by missionaries and missionary candidates. First, *the cultivation of a biblically-informed minority mentality ensures a more realistic attitude in dealing with missionary situations.* Nowhere is this more apparent than in discussions of eschatology. With regard to the final outcome of human history, Christians have been divided for centuries. A majority has opted for the amillennialist position, which is essentially an optimistic orientation with regard to the potential for expansion of Christianity throughout the world. Some have moved beyond this to postmillennialism—without question a truly majoritarian concept. Until quite recently, history seems to have supported these stances, as the officially Christian civilization of the West advanced both quantitatively and qualitatively around the globe. During the last half-century, however, the threads binding Christianity and the West have unravelled, and while Western influence continues to advance, this can no longer be said of Christianity. While their raw numbers continue to increase, the number of Christians as a percentage of the total population of the world has been slowly declining for many years now. Some are reluctant to admit these facts, and others are too extreme in their interpretation of them, but the middle path between optimism and pessimism would be a minority mentality, which lauds the advances that the church has made through the centuries but which soberly acknowledges both that other religions have been gaining ground since the late nineteenth century and that cultural overlays have created among many so-called "Christian" populations nominalism and syncretism, both of which have compromised the integrity of Christianity in the eyes of the world. With a minority mentality, however, one assumes neither the worst nor the best, but rather continues doggedly in obedience to the Great Commission without assigning significance to numbers or percentages. McQuilkin's question regarding "winning or losing" ceases to be "inflammatory" in the face of a minority mentality, and *obedience* assumes its proper place as the supreme expression of love for God (Jn 14:21), and the primary motivation for missions (2Co 5:14).

Secondly, *a biblically-informed minority mentality is a cutting-edge mentality, one that is awake and vibrant with life.*

Throughout history, minorities have proved to be the most creative, the most dynamic, the most efficient, and the most enduring of social groupings. The proverbial "cornered animal" is capable of actions far beyond the scope of its ordinary range of behavior. Poor odds for survival can challenge and motivate human beings as little else can do. A biblical minoritarianism can produce the same qualities in the Christian, enhancing energy output and efficiency as "the wisdom of the serpent" (Mt 10:16) is brought into play. A minority position strips away the unnecessary accretions of modern civilization and forces one to focus on fundamentals and essentialities. This focusing serves to narrow the parameters of one's identity, preventing or at least inhibiting the nearly universal affliction of Western individuals: the dispersal of one's energies in the multitude of directions dictated by modern multiplex cultures. With a minority mentality one is instead imbued with a focused sense of *mission*.

Thirdly, *a biblically-informed minoritarianism increases a sense of community and camaraderie which seldom—if ever—exists in majoritarian situations*. A heightened sense of identity results in an increased sense of community, since only individuals who are secure in their understanding of who they are can function together as true communities. This is especially true when minority status confers a sense of elitism. When members of a minority view themselves as having a special calling or mission and perceive themselves as having been endowed with special abilities and skills that set them apart from the rest of humanity, a sense of camaraderie is formed that expresses itself in several ways. Ritual ceremonies and other specially coordinated activities are developed that both confirm and increase the bond of unity. The Christianity of the New Testament was characterized by just such an elitist thinking. Not, of course, in the "snobby" way that the idea of elitism has unfortunately come to connote in modern speech. But certainly a sense of specialness pervaded the early church. As a tiny minority within the Roman Empire, the early Christians survived and thrived due to a profound sense of calling and mission. They were adherents not of *a* way but of ***The*** Way. They participated in a ceremony which commemorated the death of their movement's founder and which served at the same time as a reminder of their election to the service of that founder in accordance with the obligations his sacrificial death had placed all of them under (1Co 6:19-20). In societies where a sense of minoritarianism is lacking among Christians, however, these aspects of the communion service have been lost, and no amount of reactionary solemnizing can restore to the ceremony what it originally connoted. Only a sense of shared goals and objectives within the dynamic of a minority status can make this ritual a truly meaningful one.

Fourthly, *a biblically-informed minoritarianism results in increased creativity as ways must be discovered first to survive and then to continue the Great Commission without arousing unnecessary opposition.* To borrow from a familiar cliche, the exigencies of a minority status can become the mother of invention. History repeatedly attests to the heights to which human genius can be driven under adverse circumstances, whereas the comfort and security of majoritarian status appears to lead inevitably to decline and, eventually, decadence. This has certainly been true of institutional Christianity, as chroniclers of the Constantinian conquest consistently take pains to point out. Upon its official legalization and eventual attainment of a majoritarian status in the fourth century, Christianity lost the inventiveness and creativity that had allowed it to attract members of a diversity of cultures and races to itself. It eventually became necessary to expand "the Kingdom" further by means of forceful imposition through military power.

In the same way, Christians in societies where the faith enjoys majority status have rarely been characterized by creativity and inventiveness. On the contrary, charges of "traditionalism" and "irrelevance to contemporary cultural traits" are heard with regularity. Contextualization of the gospel message, careful reworking of the form and content of Christian discipleship and adaptation of the structure of church institutions are usually attempted only by those who are convinced that true Christians are no more than a minority within the societies in which they reside. Tragically, realists such as these are often severely castigated by proponents of majoritarian traditionalism, most of whom are mired in frustration due to declining church memberships and Christian commitment but who are at the same time reluctant to adopt a realistic view of the church as a minor-ity institution.

Finally, and perhaps most importantly, *a biblically-informed minority mentality increases one's dependence upon God.* Agur, the author of the thirtieth chapter of the book of Proverbs, prayed that he would be given "neither poverty nor riches" (v. 8). His reasoning is stated in the verse that follows: "otherwise I may have too much and disown You and say, 'Who is the Lord?' Or I may become poor and steal, and so dishonor the name of my Lord." While this passage finds its primary application within an economic context, it certainly contains implications for other Christian contexts as well. The comfort and ease of majoritarianism can all too easily lead to laziness, even forgetfulness, regarding one's relationship with God. The constant pressures of minoritarian living, on the other hand, serve to maintain and enhance the relationship between the disciple and his Master.

Macro-level Secularization

So far the discussion has centered around a *mentality*, which has to do with how a person should *think*. It remains to consider what one should *do* as a result of this thinking. Christians who are advocates of a minority mentality will need to be able to function at two distinct levels of human society which may be called the *macro-level* and the *micro-level*. By "macro-level" is meant a social stratum that includes, generally speaking, entire nations, cultures, and races. The key word for Christian activity at this level would be *secularization*, by which is meant the process through which a disjunction is made between the political, economic, judicial, and social systems of a nation state and any form of religious faith or practice. What is being advocated here is that Christians pray for and work to produce a complete secularization of the above-mentioned systems of all nation states, in particular those where non-Christian religions are adhered to by a majority of the population.

Those who hold to a majoritarian philosophy of Christian expansionism will likely put forth the claim that the only legitimate goal of missionary activity at this level would be the establishment of a *Christian* society. While this admittedly sounds more noble than an advocacy of secularization, it is difficult to maintain that the idea of a "Christian society" has any quantifiable meaning in the modern world. What would such a "Christian society" look like? One must have a model in mind—a definable goal or end result—if he or she wishes to transform a culture from one set of conditions to another. But what, for instance, would a truly *Christian* political system consist of? A *Christian* economic system? A *Christian* judicial system? A *Christian* social system? Would such a Christian society be founded on a Roman Catholic, Eastern Orthodox, Coptic, or Protestant model? If the

Christianity as a Minority Religion 231

latter were chosen, would it be Presbyterian, Anglican, Congregational, Baptist, or Anabaptist in form? Is there even the slightest hope of reaching even a nationwide—let alone a worldwide—consensus regarding what a Christian society should look like? Simple honesty leads to the conclusion that Christians cannot realistically expect to accomplish such a task.

Even if by some means agreement were reached upon a single alternative, would not such a system by its very nature need to be imposed as an external and institutional solution to an existential problem that is ultimately internal and personal in nature? Evangelicals hold that the "new birth" spoken of by Jesus is essential to attaining membership in the Kingdom of Heaven and that this is a process vitally connected to a *voluntary* and *deliberate* commitment to the lordship of Christ (see Ro 10:9-10). In order to achieve the results that evangelicals wish to accomplish, is it not necessary that a situation be created in which freedom of choice clearly exists? And must not such a situation be essentially secular and pluralistic in nature, since only in secular and pluralistic societies are guarantees of religious freedom found?

What would be the alternatives to such a scenario? There are only two: first, to advocate the development of a purely *Christian* state. But it was concluded in the discussion above that such a goal is untenable. The second alternative would be to allow the development of a purely *Muslim, Hindu, Buddhist, Jewish, Confucianist or Shinto* state, where Christians (as well as the adherents of other minority religions) would be relegated to (at best) a second-class status. Surely this alternative is even less acceptable than the first, for Christians would more than likely be severely restricted in their ability to bear testimony for Christ. A truly secular society, then, is the only alternative that gives an "open playing field" to all contenders. Of course there are risks involved in pursuing such a strategy. Perhaps the chief of these is the possibility of creating a society that pursues secularization past the point of societal survival such as some believe to be the case with certain Western nations today. But this is neither a necessary nor an inevitable end. The adherents of world faiths working deliberately via means of educational curricula, media presentations, literature distribution, political action committees and the like can work to keep secularization and its concomitant pluralism within carefully defined parameters. Within such a system Muslims, Hindus, Buddhists, Jews and others would be allowed to carry out their missionary activity, but Christians would be guaranteed the right to continue their own evangelizing, disciple-making and church-planting efforts, a right that they might otherwise lose were a purely Islamic, Hindu, Buddhist, or Jewish state to become a reality.

A second risk is that by allowing world religions to compete with local religions, one or more syncretistic systems of belief may be produced. The African "nativistic movements" are considered by some to be a classic case of such a phenomenon. But Humphrey Fisher has observed that allowing a secular pluralism to breed a form of syncretism nearly always results in an eventual "snapping" to one extreme or the other (Fisher 1991). The tensions and contradictions involved in trying to hold the aspects of a world religion such as Christianity together with animistic beliefs eventually become unbearable, and the adherents of a syncretistic faith would in such a situation choose to become either fully Christian or fully animist. Obviously there is risk here—but a risk that could work in the favor of Christianity.

The chief problem one encounters in advocating secularization and pluralization is the fact that adherents of other world religions, who operate in terms of an external and institutional rather than an internal and personal missiological strategy, see no need for such an "open playing field." The idea of a secular society is incompatible with the teachings of most of these religions. But here it becomes the responsibility of Christians to distinguish between "secularization" (a social process) and "secularism" (a social philosophy) (see Guinness 1983:51-55), and to point out that other religious belief systems are plagued by the same problems that Christians have encountered in attempting to define a religious state. The world's Muslims, for instance, are extremely divided over what a purely *Muslim* political, economic, social, and even religious system would consist of, and they should be made to understand that it would be to their advantage to adopt the "open playing field" that a secular society affords in order to have the opportunity to resolve these differences.

It is also important that Christians make clear to all concerned that a secularized society does not necessarily exclude all religious influences. While a society devoted to *secularism* as a philosophy might seek to banish or annihilate such influences *in toto*, classical *secularization*—as seen in such concepts as the separation of church and state—actually seeks to preserve them. Thus the social and moral precepts that Christianity, Judaism,

Islam, Hinduism and Buddhism have in common could conceivably become the basis for parameters that would define the limits of pluralism. Within these boundaries a society could be constructed without an enforced commitment to a specific soteriology. Once such a society has been established, soteriological (as well as other) differences could be presented, examined, and discussed, and voluntary commitments could be elicited from interested citizens. To summarize then, the process of secularization could be used at the macro-level as a bulwark against the establishment of a religious state and could function as a guarantor of religious freedom.

Micro-level Ministry

The micro-level, which includes individuals, neighborhoods, villages, towns, and cities, is where evangelicals should concentrate the majority of their efforts. The key concept at this level would be *particularistic evangelism and discipleship*, concepts that espouse the communication of the "good news" regarding salvation available in Jesus the Christ to as many individuals and/or family units as possible and instruction of those who attain that salvation concerning all that Jesus taught. This strategy is obviously best accomplished when the macro-level goal has been or is in the process of being achieved, for without the religious freedom that logically and normally accompanies the pluralism of a secular society, communication of and instruction concerning religious beliefs is often either prohibited or severely restricted. But whether or not such freedom exists or is forthcoming, the goal of the missionary agent must be nothing less than the transmission of the gospel of Jesus to every individual or family in such a way that a valid decision can be made either to accept or to reject the offer of God's grace. Missionaries must aim at nothing less than a total *saturation* of whole populations. The use of expatriate personnel and national church members must be maximized in order to fulfill the primary objective of an exponential multiplication of disciples, using every available means (including mass media technologies) but especially emphasizing face-to-face encounter and dialogue.

Such a plan must be developed with the knowledge that Muslims, Hindus, Buddhists and others will with increasing momentum be developing their own strategies and that the missionary activities of Christians will be occurring in a context of competition. Evangelicals may well find themselves in the midst of encounters such as the one recorded in 1 Kings 18 in which Elijah the Prophet challenges the priests of Baal. The outcome is that the religious constructs of Elijah are demonstrated to have clear superiority over those of the priests of Baal as Yahweh puts forth his power in a highly visible display of his sovereignty. In today's world Christians increasingly may need to exercise their faith and trust in God to work just as spectacularly. Adherents of non-Christian religions will be out there, functioning both offensively and defensively, from house to house and from street to street. At whatever cost, Christians must be out on the playing field as well.

Education and Training

The above three concepts—a minority mentality, macro-level secularization, and micro-level ministry—will need to be incorporated into missionary preparatory programs. A biblically-informed minority mentality will need to be cultivated in missionary candidates. It will also be necessary to inculcate a sophisticated awareness with regard to social and political issues in order to begin or sustain a movement toward secularization and pluralization on the part of nation states or people groups. And, finally, it will be necessary to formulate training in evangelism, discipling, and church-planting from a minority perspective. What pro-cedure should be used to accomplish these goals?

First and foremost, *the biblical parameters of minoritarianism must be studied in detail, understood correctly, contextualized appropriately, and incorporated into the lifestyle of each individual Christian.* Foundational passages for study, discussion, and application would include the following: Matthew 5:10-12, 13-16; 7:13-14, 15-23; 9:36-38; 10:16-23; 13:3-9, 18-23; 19:23-26; 22:8-14; 24:4-14; Luke 13:22-30; 17:20-21; 18:8; John 6:60-66; 15:16-25; 16:1-3; 17:6-9, 14-17; 18:36; Romans 13:1-7; Ephesians 1:4; 2:10; 2 Thessalonians 2:13; 2 Timothy 1:15; 3:12-14; 4:3-5, 9-16; 1 Peter 2:4-12; 3:13-17. Both the content and the practical implications of these (as well as other) passages will need to be mastered.

Secondly, at the macro-level, *a comprehensive education in social and political theory must be provided along with a thorough grounding in the history of democracy and pluralism.* Such an education will be necessary to enable these theories to become a part of the discipling process. While this recommendation is almost certain to arouse accusations that a paradigm is being espoused that is essentially neo-colonialist, such accusations may be met by observing that colonialism and imperialism are most often characterized as involving *imposition* of particular beliefs and practices upon others. What is being advocated here is a holistic discipling procedure that includes education and training in the areas of politics and sociology followed by the development on the part of the indigenous Christian population of a contextualized and biblically-informed version of both democracy and pluralism. Thus the parameters for pluralism established by, say, Koreans may differ from those established by Western Europeans or Americans, although it is to be hoped that the most fundamental principles will be retained in as many cases as possible. Paul's admonition in 1 Timothy 2 that "requests, prayers, intercession and thanksgiving be made for everyone—for kings and all those in authority" has as its motivation "that we may live peaceful and quiet lives in all godliness and holiness." The political ramifications of these verses should be apparent.

Thirdly, *training in evangelism, discipling, and church-planting must be accomplished from a minority perspective.* Strategies of evangelism and discipleship must regain the aspect of a calling of individuals or family units *out of* cultural patterns that involve active disobedience or passive non-conformity to the precepts of the Bible. More positively, they must include a calling *to* membership in a unique community of people and participation in a divinely ordained mission. Discipleship must return to an emphasis upon *all* that Jesus commanded (Mt 28:20) rather than to only those aspects deemed "culturally relevant" for today. Discipleship must also be redefined so as to conform to the biblical prerequisites enumerated in Luke 14:25-33 and to the primary characteristics discussed in John 8:31, John 13:34-35, and John 15:8. Each of these carries with it an aspect of elitism that needs to be carefully but firmly inculcated in the followers of Christ. The concept of the church must assume and continually maintain the tension seen in the New Testament accounts, a tension formed by the intersection of the institution's cultural fluidity (as evidenced by the differences seen between the church of Acts 2 and that of 2 Timothy) with its revelatory parameters (epitomized by 1 Corinthians and 1 Timothy).

Conclusion

The eschatological teaching of Jesus leaves no room for doubt concerning the intended extent of world evangelization: "this gospel of the kingdom will be preached in the whole world as a testimony to all nations, and then the end will come" (Mt 24:14). But this statement does *not* presume that Christianity will ever acquire majoritarian status. While the parables of the mustard seed and the leaven (Lk 13:18-21) have been utilized as support for a postmillennial theology, the implications of these verses are perhaps better interpreted internally and personally rather than externally and institutionally. To be sure, an exterior form—the institutional church—will grow, but membership in this organization will not in and of itself be a guarantee of right standing with God, since Jesus states elsewhere that at least some of "the subjects of the kingdom will be thrown outside, into the darkness, where there will be weeping and gnashing of teeth" (Mt 8:12). A majoritarian interpretation of the above-mentioned passages is also dramatically undercut by the verses which Luke places immediately after his recording of the mustard seed and leaven illustrations: "Make every effort to enter through the narrow door, because many [i.e. the majority] will try to enter and will not be able to." Matthew amplifies this exhortation with his addition of Jesus's explanation that "the broad [read "majoritarian"] way leads to destruction, and many enter through it. But small is the gate and narrow is the road that leads to life, and only a few [i.e., a minority] find it."

We as evangelical Christians are a minority—a subversive, radical underground, carrying the Kingdom of Heaven "within and among us." We are distinguished from worldly analogues by the fact that we offer no specific external or institutional solution to the human condition, but instead deal mainly with its internal and personal dimensions. We are called to operate in the midst of any and all external circumstances, though naturally we prefer the benefits of the open playing field that normally accompanies a pluralistic democracy. Along with other minorities, we must work to produce these conditions, set-ting the stage for the only kind of environment for spiritual decision-making we find biblically acceptable: an environment of freedom in which all alternatives may be examined and in which the prerequisites for and characteristics of discipleship as enu-merated by Jesus may be voluntarily fulfilled. Given such an open playing field, we must conduct ourselves in the face of non-Christian religious persons in the same way that Elijah conducted himself in the face of the worshippers of Baal. We must exercise faith—publicly and spectacularly when we are able. We must function as salt and light, in the village market or in the supermarket. When the Jezebels and Ahabs of our world begin to resist the light, we may find it necessary to retreat to the wilderness for a time. Unlike Elijah, however, we must not let our minority status become cause for self-pity or complaint. We must return, time and again to the playing field, wise as serpents and harmless as doves, appearing in the "temple courts" to proclaim our message, scattering ourselves among the masses as grains of salt.

We are a minority, followers of the Way. Not "the broad way that leads to destruction," but rather "the narrow way—the minority way—that leads to life." And as we accept our role, using it to our advantage in the ways enumerated above, we will find ourselves toughened by the physical, mental, and spiritual disciplines we will find it necessary to cultivate. But in the midst of a warfare made grim by the fact of our minority status, we can experience joy and echo Paul's triumphant words to the Corinthians back in the days when Christians were outnumbered 360 to 1: "I will boast all the more gladly about my weaknesses, so that Christ's power may rest on me. That is why, for Christ's sake, I delight in weaknesses, in insults, in hardships, in persecutions, in difficulties. For when I am weak, then I am strong."

These can only be the words of a minority.

Reference List

Doi, Abdur Rehman
    1987   "Duties and Responsibilities of Muslims in Non-Muslim States: A Point of View." *Journal Institute of Muslim Minority Affairs* (January):43.

al-Faruqi, Ismail
    1982   *The Islamization of Knowledge: General Principles and Workplan.* Washington, D.C.: International Institute of Islamic Thought.

Fisher, Humphrey J.
    1991   "Islam and Indigenous Tradition in Africa: Is Conversion to Islam a Continuing Process within Muslim Communities?" Paper delivered at the International Symposium on Islam and Ethnicity in Africa and the Middle East at the State University of New York at Binghamton, April 25-27.

Guinness, Os
    1983   *The Gravedigger File*. Downers Grove, IL: InterVarsity.
    1994   *The American Hour*. New York: The Free Press.

Johnstone, Patrick
    1993   *Operation World*. Grand Rapids, MI: Zondervan.

McQuilkin, Robertson
    1994   "Six Inflammatory Questions." *Evangelical Missions Quarterly* (April):130.

Otis, George, Jr.
    1992   *The Last of the Giants: Lifting the Veil on Islam and the End Times*. Westchester, IL: Crossway.

Robert, Dana L.
    1990   "'The Crisis of Missions': Premillennial Mission Theory and the Origins of Independent Evangelical Missions." In *Earthen Vessels: American Evangelicals and Foreign Missions, 1880-1980*. Joel A. Carpenter and Wilbert R. Shenk, eds. Grand Rapids, MI: Eerdmans.

PART III

SYNTHESIS

12

SYNTHESIS

Edward Rommen

This chapter is an attempt to synthesize the information presented in Parts I and II into a systematic statement of an evangelical theology of non-Christian religions. Methodologically, this approach is based upon a particular understanding of the nature and task of theology, as well as a limited application of the concept of formal systems.

As defined here, theology is a human activity resulting in the formulation of summary statements that capture the essence of revelation and help guide our application of that teaching. The theological process is generally triggered by some question or issue that arises out of the human situation, e.g., the meaning of life. This is followed by an analysis of relevant biblical, historical, and theological data. Finally, the theologian seeks to craft a set of theological definitions, axioms, and propositions which reflect the analysis of available biblical, historical, and theological data. This provides a basic conceptual framework that can serve as a basis for further reflection (see Montgomery 1970 and Pannenberg 1991).

Formal systems are abstract languages originally developed by logicians as a means of analyzing the concept of deduction (for a detailed description see Henkin 1967). Most formal systems are specified by three components. First, there is a list of symbols, e.g. 1,2,<, >, and =. In the case of theology, we use ordinary human language. Second, one needs a set of rules governing the way in which the symbols can be used. In ordinary language this is provided by grammar and syntax. Third, there must be a set of definitions and logical axioms. These are actually first principles that do not need proof and are, therefore, simply assumed. They provide a point of departure. Geometry, with its definitions, axioms, and proofs, is a good example of how all of this works (compare Carnes 1982). In the case of theology defini-tions and axioms are provided by the Bible which, being God's own self-revelation, is authoritative in all matters of doctrine.

In order to use the idea of formal systems in theology we will obviously have to relax the concept (compare Spinoza 1927). What is being suggested here is not an entirely deductive, *a priori* approach that is divorced from the empirical realities of the religions. No reflection on a theology of non-Christian religions could take place without knowledge of the actual phenomena that define the other religions. It should also be pointed out that the proposed use of formal systems does not imply some kind of neat package that precludes further reflection and development of the issues. In fact, the whole idea is to provide an open-ended framework for ongoing reflection. Thus, in spite of its limited usefulness, the concept of a formal system does provide a tool that can help us establish a basic theological orientation from within which additional principles can be deduced and evaluated.

A formal system, then, is an attempt to certify the truth of certain propositions based on a knowledge of the truth of others. As applied to the theological task at hand, we will use what we know to be true (based on our examination of biblical and historical data) in order to construct a set of definitions and axioms that will facilitate the formulation of propositions used to guide our reflection on the subject.

Before entering the discussion of specific propositions we must state our definitions and axioms. These are assumed to be true, based on our understanding of Scripture. Since much of the biblical data has already been presented in the preceding chapters, there is no need to repeat it here. However, some references will be cited in order to illustrate the process and document its origin in the biblical material.

Definitions

1. God: a personal, spiritual (omnipresent), infinite (omniscient, all powerful, ultimately authoritative), immutable, holy and righteous being (Pss 139:1-12; 145:1-21; Lev 11:45; Ro 11:33-36; Jas 1:17; Rev 1:8).

2. *Creation:* everything which, having not existed, has been brought into existence by a deliberate act of God (Ge 1:1-2:4; Col 1:16).

3. *Spiritual Beings:* angels (being benevolent, obedient servants of God), Satan (being the evil instigator of rebellion against God's authority, and subversion of God's will), and demons (evil servants of Satan) are personal, non-corporal beings created by God (Ps 148:2-5; Eze 28:12-15; Mt 25:31,41; Eph 2:1-3; Col 1:16).

4. *Human Beings:* personal, corporal beings created in the image of God, and thus morally responsible, intelligent agents, able to perceive and interact with the spiritual realm, and capable of knowing God (entering into a relationship) and his will for creation (Ge 1:26-27; Ro 2:14-15).

5. *Sin:* the universal failure of humankind to conform to God's will and purposes. It leads to distortion of truth, perversion of behavior, relationships and communication, and it will elicit a retributive response from God (Ge 3:1-19; Ro 1:18ff; 3:10,23; 5:12).

6. *Salvation*: divinely initiated, unmerited forgiveness of sin based on the redemptive work of Christ (God's Son), and the resultant restoration of human beings to their intended state (Ro 5:8; 2Co 5:21; Eph 2:8-9).

7. *Religion:* life-ordering, ultimate commitment to (faith in) an object (person) greater than the individual (usually supernatural), which is expressed in specific belief structures and behavioral patterns (individual, corporate, cultic), for the purpose of expanding and maintaining a knowledge of and relationship to the object of commitment, as well as resolution of the fundamental questions of life (Ex 20:1-17; Jas 1:27; 1Ti 3:16).

Axioms

1. God exists (Ps 8:9).

2. God is distinct from creation.

Explanation: There is an absolute, essential distinction between God and that which he has created. This eliminates all forms of pantheism, monism, and dualism (Ps 90:2; Col 1:16-17).

3. God can be known.

Explanation. This is the case only because he has chosen to make himself known. This act is not necessary, is not contingent upon human beings' ability to know, and without this self-revelation there would be no true knowledge of God. Divine self-revelation takes three forms: nature/history, Christ, and scripture, the unconditioned veracity of which establishes it as a normative source of information (Ps 19:1; Ro 1:18ff; 2Ti 3:16-17; 2Pe 1:21).

4. There exists a spiritual realm.

Explanation: there exists an unseen, spiritual, meta-physical realm, including God, benevolent creatures (angels), and malevolent creatures (Satan and his demons), which can and does affect the creation (Heb 1:13-14).

5. Human religious experience is universal..

Explanation: Human beings, having been created in the image of God, are capable of knowing God and entering into a relationship with him, interacting with the unseen, spiritual world, and expressing that experience and/or commitment religiously. All such experiences, commitments, and expressions are distorted by the universality of human sin (Ro 1:28-2:15).

Note: This raises the question as to whether or not this exercise is itself distorted by the effects of its author's sinfulness. Surely it is. However, divinely revealed knowledge (axiom 3) and effective countermeasure (axiom 8), minimize those effects, making valid theological conclusions possible.

6. God is the only object worthy of ultimate commitment.

Explanation: any other object of commitment (individuals, institutions, doctrines, material objects, other spiritual beings), although potentially greater than the individual, is nevertheless a created and therefore finite entity (Eph 1:4-5; 1Ti 2:5; Heb 2:7-8, Rev 5:12-13).

7. God is the only possible author of salvation.

Explanation: Being the omnipotent creator, the panto-cratic giver of all law, and the ultimate object of human defiance, God is the only being with grounds, means, ability, and necessary magnanimity to counteract the rebellion and its effects (Eph 1:4-5; 2Ti 1:9; Rev 4-5).

8. Jesus Christ, God incarnate, accomplished salvation.

Explanation: As deity incarnate, the sacrificial death of Jesus Christ is God's unique and all-sufficient atonement for human sin. By faith in him alone is the restoration of human beings to their intended status before and relationship to God possible. He is the one Lord and Savior for all persons (2Co 5:21; Gal 4:4-5; Heb 9:11-15; 10:10-14, 28).

9. *There exists a correspondence* between the human situation and divine self-revelation.

Explanation: The human situation refers to that which is observable (experiential), including both the negative and the positive, the contemporary and historical aspects of human existence. As used here, the positive aspects are seen to issue from God's creative involvement in things human and are reflected in individually expressed rational, emotional, and social traits as well as their cumulative expressions, i.e., philosophy, science, art, community, and tradition. The negative aspects give evidence of sin and its effects and confront us with questions of evil, injustice, and death. This categorization is not intended to imply parity between the two sources of data, but rather some degree of correlation. While revelation remains the primary source of theological data, the effect of the human situation must be deliberately factored into the theological process (see axiom 3). On the one hand, the situation of a given theologian determines the pre-understandings which he or she brings to the task as well as antecedent insights. On the other hand, the fundamental questions to which the human situation gives rise, prompt and sometimes guide theological inquiry. Not in the sense that the questions in any way dictate the content of revelation, but rather in the sense that revelation is sufficient What we need to know is provided by revelation.

10. *Christianity can represent what religion was intended to be.*

Explanation: By definition (see definition 7), Christianity is a religion. It does, in fact, represent a life-ordering, ultimate commitment to God that is expressed in specific belief structures and behavioral patterns. It does expand and help maintain a knowledge of and relationship to God. It does provide answers to the fundamental questions of life.

Christianity, like any other religion, is subject to all the distorting effects of sin and vulnerable to the corrupting influence of Satan and his servants. Given that vulnerability, there is no reason to believe that Christians might not ignore divine revelation, shift the focus of their allegiance, abandon Christ's offer of salvation, and engage in evil practices, all of which would render it illegitimate.

However, as long as Christianity appropriates the from-sin-liberating countermeasure of Christ's sacrifice and is guided by the content of revelation, it can fulfill the proper function of a religion. Thus, the legitimacy of Christianity is not derived from the inherent capacities of its adherents, but rather from the work of Christ and divine self-revelation.

Proposition 1: Christianity must acknowledge the existence of the other religions.

This is evident from definitions 1, 4, and 7, and axioms 1, 3, 5, 8. If there is an infinite, omnipotent God who reveals himself as such, and if human beings have the ability to perceive that which is revealed, and if religion is an expression of a commitment (relationship) to an object greater than the individual, then the existence of, or at least the desire for, commitment to the greatest of knowable entities can be reasonably assumed to be universal. Of course, acknowledging the existence of the other religions is not simply a matter of logical deduction. This proposition reflects the empirical realities of our world. Throughout history peoples and cultures have been incurably religious.

Nowhere in Scripture are we given the impression that the world's religions are not to be taken as a fact of human existence. Whatever we might say about their origin and value, they represent a real and undeniable aspect of the created order. As such, they must be acknowledged, i.e., they must be actively and sincerely engaged. It will simply not do to relegate them to a conceptual or emotional place of non- or pseudo-existence, either through deliberate disregard or categorical vilification. The challenge for Christian theology is to view the other religions with the illuminating insight of the Word of God. If the existence of the religions is not to be (cannot be) contested, one ought to ask what insight Scripture provides with respect to their origin (source), function, and legitimacy.

Source/Origin

In one sense, all religion issues from God's desire to interact with humanity. In order to facilitate interaction the Creator makes himself known and equips human beings with the ability to receive and respond to that information. Religions, then, have their origin in human ability to transcend themselves, i.e., perceive the spiritual realm, know God and creatively develop and record life-ordering systems of belief (doctrines, ideologies), adopt, enforce, and refine pertinent behavioral patterns, and establish cultic practices, practitioners, and institutions. As such, religious expression is a divinely enabled and desired human response to the information provided. Human religious expression is positively affected by the correlate of that self-transcendence, namely God himself, i.e., God not only provides information, he also responds to or reciprocates human spirituality and religiosity. Divine response ranges from general providence to miracles.

Human religious expression is negatively affected by human sinfulness (Ro 1:18ff), as well as those malevolent spiritual beings bent on subverting divine-human interaction. If the truth of divine revelation is either not understood, misunderstood or deliberately distorted, then beliefs, behavior, and cult will devolve and ultimate commitment will be focused on some aspect of creation.

This devolution of religion tends to mask both the source and the determinants. With the passing of time human religious expression itself assumes a dominant position. On the one hand, this may lead to a neglect or even denial of divine initiative (even when god-talk is still present), reducing religion to an exclusively human activity. On the other hand, the distorting effects of human sinfulness and the subverting influence of evil spiritual beings are either denied, tolerated, or even courted.

Function

Religion provides a paradigm for a) interpreting, structuring, and contending with the human environment, b) answering the questions (of both immediate and ultimate import) which arise out of the human situation, and c) establishing a framework within which divine-human interaction is conducted. This remains generally true in spite of the negative effects of sin. However, because of sin human religious expression will fail to accurately interpret the unseen spiritual world as well as the human situation (see note to axiom 5). That being the case, its answers to humankind's fundamental questions will ultimately be inadequate.

Legitimacy

In light of the possible distortions of religions expression it is reasonable to ask under what conditions a particular religion might be considered legitimate. To the degree that a religion represents a) an attempt to respond to divine initiative, b) an attempt to answer questions and structure life within the framework of divine self-revelation and c) an ultimate commitment focused on the source of that revelation (the God of the Bible), it may be considered legitimate.

To the degree that a religion represents an attempt to answer questions and structure of life a) based on a distortion of divine revelation, b) within a framework which excludes divine revelation, and/or c) with ultimate commitment focused on something (someone) other than God, it must be considered illegitimate.

There are, of course, a number of ways to understand legitimacy. A religion might be regarded as functionally legitimate in that it meets, at least to some extent, the perceived needs of its adherents. It could also be considered legitimate in the sense that it has some positive effect on individuals or societies. But the crucial question for Christians is whether a religion can be considered legitimate in the sense that it provides appropriate access to and relationship with God. Owing to human sinfulness and the influence (potential or actual) of Satan and his servants, no religion can claim legitimacy in this sense—unless the aforementioned obstacles (sin and Satan) are effectively counteracted.

Proposition 2: Christianity's evaluation of the other religions will be primarily negative, but must be highly differentiated.

This follows from definitions 3 and 5, and axioms 4 and 5. If human sinfulness and evil spiritual beings can distort the truth and subvert the affairs of creation (including religion), and if God is the only entity capable and worthy of ultimate commitment, then all human religious expression is likely to be flawed, but for a variety of reasons and to varying degrees. Once again, it must be pointed out that this is not simply a matter of deduction, or even the witness of Scripture alone. A careful phenomenological analysis of the religions themselves leads to the same conclusion.

There will, of course, be varying degrees of distortion, falsehood, and morally unacceptable values and behaviors. For example, the monotheism of Islam would have to be considered closer to the truth than the ontology of Therevada Buddhism, which is diametrically opposed to that of Christianity.

In light of the disruptive impact of sin and Satan, all human religious expression will have to be viewed with skepticism. However, one would be ill advised to simply dismiss as evil, demonically inspired, or illegitimate every expression of human religiosity. In order to be helpful one's evaluation would have to be based on concrete elements of religious expression, such as the object, practices, and outcomes of a particular religion.

The Object of Faith

If religion is defined in terms of a relationship (ultimate commitment) to an entity larger than the self, then the nature of that entity will determine the character of the religion. One theme consistently sounded in the studies presented in Part I was that of the uniqueness and incomparability of the God of the Bible. He is distinct from and greater than all other gods. There is none that can be even compared with him. He is Creator and sustainer of the universe, all-powerful, all-knowing, and omnipresent. He is full of compassion and redemptive power, as effectively established, once and for all time, in the life and work of Christ his Son, God-with-us. So much greater is he than all other aspirants to divinity, that one must conclude that in reality there simply are no other gods. He alone is God. There is simply no other object worthy of humanity's allegiance.

What then of the other gods? The Bible is consistent in its evaluation of them. They are empty, impotent, ineffectual. But do they exist? Perhaps we should distinguish between several modes of existence, for surely the other gods are believed to exist. An entity can be said to exist a) cognitively, as a category or an idea, b) emotionally, as a feeling, commitment, c) phenomenologically, based on some real or supposed empirical evidence, and d) ontologically, i.e., actual existence independent of any accidence. But, are gods, who exist only in human imaginations and emotions, gods at all? What of a god, for whom there appears to be some phenomenological evidence? There is a hidden reality behind many religions (see definition 3 and axiom 5), namely that of

Satan and his servants. Scripture indicates that many of the phenomena associated with idols and gods are in fact animated by demonic force. In that case, the god is still no god, but merely a would-be god, a usurper. We are thus left with the biblical witness, that there is but one God and He alone can serve as the object of human religious expression.

The Practices of a Religion

With respect to the behavioral patterns established and enforced within the context of religion, one would be justified in evaluating them against the revealed standards of God. Any deviation would require a negative evaluation. Such things would include:

1. Grasping for Power: It has already been noted (see definition 3) that Satan precipitated creation's slide to defiance by grasping at the power, knowledge, honor, and authority that belonged to God alone. Thus, any religious practice which attempts to wrest from and use that which is God's alone must be rejected, since it indicates complicity in Satan's rebellion. Of course, the practices that might have to be rejected could come from almost any domain of human activity. On the one hand, it might be the political ambitions of religious leaders seeking power, wealth, authority, and even adoration that is rightfully God's. On the other hand, the questionable practice might grow out of unbridled curiosity and interest in things like the future or even the spiritual realm. One example of this would be religious practitioners who seek or claim knowledge that God has not revealed or does not intend for us to have access to.

2. Distortion of Truth: Religious practices (or teachings), which deliberately distort or openly violate the revealed truth of God, such as religiously sanctioned immorality, slavery, injustice, and oppression.

The Outcome of a Religion

Scripture never acknowledges salvific potential in other religions, i.e., none of the other religions is described as being able to lead an individual to a "from-sin-liberating" knowledge of the one true God. Sin, which will be punished, is not dealt with, leaving the individual under the wrath of God. Stated in terms of the function of religion (see definition 7), none of the other religions can achieve the desired outcome.

Proposition 3: Christianity's mode of engaging the other religions depends on the intentional context.

This is follows from definition 6 and axiom 7. If there existed a religion in which the negative effects of human sinfulness and evil spiritual beings are effectively counteracted, then the adherents of that religion would be justified in their efforts to sustain and share those benefits.

Scripture presents us with a wide range of responses to the other religions: *Destruction,* as when the Israelites entered the Promised Land; *Polemic,* as in the case of the prophets' warnings, condemnation, and ridicule; *Aggressive Confrontation*, as with Moses in Egypt, Elijah on Mt. Carmel, and Paul on Crete; *Missionary Accommodation*, as was the case with Paul in Athens, Philip with the eunuch, and Peter with Cornelius.

From these examples it becomes clear that the approach taken in a given situation depends on the primary intention of the confronting party: is the purity of the believing community the primary focus or is a witness to the only effective means whereby sin, death and Satan can be overcome the overarching concern?

Purity

The Christian community, having been given effective countermeasures in the work of Christ, has a responsibility to vigilantly apply those benefits and seek to preserve its own religious integrity and purity. This is a constant theme throughout Scripture. On the one hand, this is an internal matter. Without vigilance Christianity, like any other religion, can devolve into a sinful expression of human religiosity. On the other hand, the presence of other religions poses a real threat from without. Most of the harsh treatment meted out on the other religions by God and his followers was designed to prevent encroachment and contamination. There being but one God, worshipping any other entity would have to be considered not only patently foolish, but also ultimately perilous—especially for those claiming a formal relationship with this one and only God. Seeking salvation at the hands of a "savior" other than the only possible Redeemer would be the height of folly and or deception. So, in word and deed, by means of historical events and specific commands God requires and seeks to maintain the religious purity of his followers in the face of a world of religions.

Witness

The Christian community, having been given access to effective countermeasures by the work of Christ, also has a stewardship responsibility to proclaim divinely revealed truth to humanity. The missionary mandate is motivated by a desire to share the only available salvation with as many people as possible. For that reason, it must be carried out in a spirit that balances realism and tolerance.

Christianity must remain realistic in its assessment of the human situation, refusing to ignore or deny the devastating effects of sin. At the same time, that evaluation must be tempered by humility. In light of the universality of sin, there is simply no room for judgmental self-righteousness and arrogance.

Christianity's engagement of the other religions should also be based on a sober and realistic acceptance of the failure of all human religious expression to fulfill its intended purpose. Apart from Christ there is no freedom from sin. For that reason there can be no true knowledge of and interaction with God with-out Christ. At the same time acknowledging the historical existence and continuity of the various religions should prevent harsh pessimism. If the origins of human religious expression can be traced to God-given capacity, then, no matter how badly distorted by sin or corrupted by Satan it might be at any given moment, there remains something to which the messenger can and must appeal.

Finally, Christianity must remain realistic and tenacious in its presentation of the only countermeasure, i.e., personal faith in the substitutionary death of Christ. Christ's act, the quintessence of mercy shown, should generate in its recipients a sense of urgency as well as love-sustained-patience, as they seek to engage the other religions.

Reference List

Carnes, John
    1982   *Axiomatics and Dogmatics*. New York: Oxford.

Henkin, Leon
    1967   "Systems, Formal and Models of Formal Systems." In *Encyclopedia of Philiosophy*. Vol 8. Paul Edwards, ed. Pp. 61-74. New York: Macmillan.

Montgomery, John W.
    1970   "The Theologian's Craft: A Discussion of TheoryFormation and Theory Testing in Theology." In *The Suicide of Christian Theology*. John W. Montgomery, ed. Pp. 267-313. Minneapolis: Bethany.

Pannenberg, Wolfhart
    1991   *An Introduction to Systematic Theology*. Grand Rapids, MI: Eerdmans.

Spinoza, Benedict
    1927   *Ethics*. W. H. White and A. H. Striling, trans. Oxford.

13

APPLICATION
MISSION IN A PLURALISTIC WORLD

Harold A. Netland

Central to the mission of the church is the task of making disciples of Jesus Christ of all peoples in all cultures. As we move into the twenty-first century it is increasingly clear that the world in which we are to do this is one characterized by religious pluralism. "Pluralism" is a term which can be understood in two senses, and in each sense it denotes a particular challenge to Christian missions. In this chapter we will look briefly at some of the distinctives of the pluralistic world in which evangelism and disciple-making are to be carried out, after which some broad guidelines for effective ministry in such contexts will be suggested.

"Pluralism" can be understood as referring to the mere fact of religious diversity in the world. The world in which the church is to proclaim the Lordship of Jesus Christ is one marked by many different religious traditions. There was a time, during the high point of optimism in the nineteenth century, when missions observers confidently spoke of the Christianization of the world. It was fully expected that within in the near future the entire world would be won for Christ and the non-Christian religions would simply disappear.[1]

This, of course, has not happened. Euphoria over the tremendous growth of the church in certain segments of the world during the past century must be tempered by the sober realization that after centuries of concerted missionary activity many parts of the world show little if any significant growth in the numbers of Christians. Historically, Christian missions have met their greatest resistance from societies strongly impacted by

Islam, Hinduism, and Buddhism. And, with a few notable exceptions, this remains the pattern today. The major religions have not disappeared. To the contrary, there has been a remarkable resurgence among the major religions, so that Islam, Hinduism, and Buddhism remain attractive and viable options not only in the non-Western world but increasingly in the West as well. The biblical injunction to make disciples of all peoples must be understood within this context: the church is to make disciples of Jesus Christ from among those who currently follow other religious paths.

We might, however, think of religious pluralism in an ideological sense as well, not simply referring to the fact of religious diversity but rather indicating a particular way of thinking about such diversity. Ideologically, pluralism is the view that religious diversity is a good thing and something to be affirmed, and it often finds expression in the view that the various religions are simply different historically and culturally conditioned responses to the same divine reality. The world in which we are to proclaim the gospel of Jesus Christ is one increasingly characterized by the values and assumptions of ideological pluralism in this sense. The particularity of the gospel—the message of salvation only through Jesus Christ—sounds naive and implausible in such contexts.

Modernity and Pluralism

It is essential that those engaging in mission in the com-ing decades understand the contexts in which they are to minister. A significant aspect of such contexts is the set of values and assumptions associated with ideological pluralism. This is already evident in the West. Similar dynamics are in place in many non-Western cultures as well, particularly those in Asia.

Although religious diversity has always characterized our world, it is especially within the past century that ideological pluralism has become a pressing issue for Christian missions. It is arguable that it is the impact of modernity as an increasingly global culture which lies behind the rise and dominance of ideological pluralism. By *modernity* is meant the increasingly global culture which is rooted in (1) the process of modernization, and (2) the intellectual heritage of the West during the past 300 years which includes, but is not limited to, the eighteenth-century

Christianity and the Religions

Enlightenment and its legacy. In very simple terms we might think of modernity as the culture—the worldview, set of values, ways of thinking and acting—produced by the process of modernization.

Modernization emerged first in the West around the seventeenth century, with the transformations introduced by the Industrial Revolution, the rise of free market capitalism, the shift from an agrarian economy to a technological production-based economy, and the accompanying trend toward urbanization. Today modernization is a thoroughly global phenomenon spawning an increasingly global culture, with certain values and assumptions shared in places as diverse as Hong Kong, Los Angeles, Paris, Tokyo, Mexico City, or Nairobi.

The process of modernization encourages certain patterns of behavior, values, and assumptions which make ideological pluralism very attractive—and conversely, which make the exclusive claims of the gospel increasingly implausible. For example, it has become commonplace to associate *secularization* with the process of modernization. As societies become modernized they become increasingly secularized. But the impact of secularization can be understood in at least two distinct ways. In some contexts secularization results in the decline and displacement of religion in modern life. Secularization then leads to secularism. And certainly there is ample evidence to support the view that some modern societies—one thinks of Europe in particular—are much less religious today than they were a century ago.

But secularization can take various forms and need not always result in the elimination of religious belief and practice. Rather, as is the case in the United States, secularization can coexist with religion, but it does so by dramatically altering the ways in which people are religious. Secularization gives birth to new forms of religiosity. One sees this "secular religiosity" not only in the U.S. but also in highly modernized Asian societies such as Japan.

Modernization also results in *the pluralization of ideologies and worldviews*. Integral to the modernization process is the rapid multiplication of options available to one—options not only in fairly trivial matters such as what brand of toothpaste, cars and clothing to purchase, but far more significantly, options in basic values, beliefs, ideologies, and worldviews. In much of the world today, particularly in the great urban centers, an astonishing variety of religious and secular worldviews are live options, and people choose among them much as they would select a new car.

The fact of pluralization has some important consequences for how people think about religion. For example, the availability of many alternative options tends to trivialize and relativize the significance of any one tradition. Loss of confidence in one's own tradition is not unusual. Furthermore, pluralization also encourages a consumer mentality regarding religion, which is reflected in a highly pragmatic view of religion, emphasizing what religion does for individuals or society at large and minimizing questions of truth. Accordingly, one does not expect religion to provide "objectively true" answers to fundamental questions about human origin and destiny. Various religions are to be evaluated pragmatically on the basis of how well they meet the needs and desires of their adherents. Related to this is the trend toward the privatization of religious belief. Religious belief is reduced to a matter of personal taste or expression of personal preference. The question of objective or universal truth is no more appropriate in religion than it is in music or art.

Now it is crucial to see that this way of approaching religious issues, influenced as it is by modernization, is not strictly a Western phenomenon. The case of Japan is particularly instructive here and has significant implications for missions. The Christian church has been in Japan for centuries, yet evangelicals remain less than one percent of the total population. One of the major obstacles to acceptance of the gospel in Japan is the Christian insistence upon Jesus Christ as the only Lord and Savior for all peoples. An ancient Japanese saying gives expression to the modern ethos of pluralism very well—"Although the paths to the summit may vary, from the top one sees the same moon."

In contemporary Japan we find a fascinating blend of a highly advanced stage of modernization with spiritual and cultural values which have their roots in centuries of tradition. There are remarkable similarities between some of the themes of modernity just noted and contemporary Japanese culture—e.g., a strong tendency toward religious relativism, lack of emphasis upon the importance of belief and doctrine in favor of personal experience, suspicion of exclusivistic claims made on behalf of any tradition, a highly pragmatic "this worldly" approach to religion. And yet the presence of these characteristics cannot be entirely attributed to the effects of modernization since they have been present in Japanese culture for centuries—they were entrenched in "Japanese religiosity" long before the process of modernization began in Japan in the late nineteenth century.

Nevertheless, the cumulative effect of the influences of modernity combined with the legacy of centuries of earlier Japanese tradition reinforces a social and intellectual environment in which the exclusive claims of the gospel appear highly implausible. Influences from the past and the present join forces in their hostility to what is central to orthodox Christian faith—belief in one God who has revealed himself uniquely through the Incarnation and the written Scriptures, and in one Lord and Savior for all humankind. The ethos of pluralism has ancient roots in Japan. But it is being powerfully reinforced today by the culture of modernity. One of the great challenges to Christian mission in Asia in the years ahead will come from this peculiar form of "syncretism"—the combination of indigenous influences from centuries of tradition with the more recent impact of modernity.

Guidelines for Missions Praxis in Pluralistic Contexts

In making some practical applications for missionary praxis it might be helpful to think in terms of both what kind of person the missionary should be and what kind of activity the missionary should be engaged in. What we do should flow from what kind of persons we are.

We must have an adequate understanding of other religions.

In spite of the rise of secularism in this century, the fact remains that most people are religious. Given that the religious dimension is integral to the worldviews of most people and the dominant role played by religion in culture, clearly the effective missionary must have an adequate understanding of this aspect of human life. It is essential to understand religions phenomenologically, culturally, and theologically.

Phenomenological understanding. On the phenomenological level, one must understand the distinctives of a given religious tradition—its practices, values, beliefs, stories, sacred scriptures (if any), institutions, etc.[2] It is important to try to understand and appreciate the tradition as the insider understands it, to grasp the meaning and significance of the beliefs, rites, and institutions within that particular culture.[3] The objective here is to have as accurate an understanding of the phenom-ena as possible.

Cultural understanding. Closely related to the phenomenological dimension is the need for understanding a religious tradition culturally. That is, it is important to be able to see how a given religious tradition has shaped a particular culture. It would be difficult indeed to understand Indian culture without an appreciation of the impact of Hinduism upon the culture, or Thai culture without an understanding of Buddhism, and so on. Even those who do not regard themselves as especially religious are often influenced in significant ways by the dominant religious traditions within their culture.

Conversely, in some cases one can observe how indi-genous cultures have modified major religious traditions as well. The case of Buddhism, as it moved from the Indian subcontinent up into Tibet, China, Korea, and Japan is instructive. The East Asian cultures modified Buddhism almost as much as Buddhism influenced the indigenous cultures.

The close connection between religion and culture can be seen in the fact that the issues of religious pluralism are a natural extension of the kinds of questions missiology has been grappling with under the rubric "contextualization." Serious consideration of contextualization inevitably leads to questions about the relation of Christian faith to indigenous religious beliefs and practices. For example, in Japan it is notoriously difficult to separate the "religious" dimension from what is strictly "cultural." Is the tea ceremony, with its origins in Zen Buddhism, to be regarded today as religious or simply cultural? What about ancestor veneration practices? Is burning incense at a Buddhist funeral a strictly cultural act or is it religious? Zen meditation? Sumo tournaments? etc. Any serious engagement with Japanese culture will necessarily involve struggling with questions about traditional Japanese religious values and beliefs.

Furthermore, the close relation between religion and culture means that rejection of traditional religious beliefs and practices can be misunderstood as implicit rejection of the culture itself as somehow inappropriate. In Japan, for instance, evangelical insistence that salvation is available only through Jesus Christ, and not through Pure Land Buddhism, can be interpreted as not only rejection of Buddhist teaching but also as rejection of Japanese culture as somehow inadequate or inferior to Western culture.

Similarly in the case of India today. Because of the long history of British colonialism, Christianity is often identified with the West, and with British colonialism in particular. Indian nationalism, as a reaction against Western colonialism, has emphasized Hindu tradition and spirituality as essential to Indian identity. It is thus very difficult in India to separate strictly religious or theological issues from broader historical and cultural factors. For an evangelical Christian in India to insist that salvation is in Jesus alone, and not in Hindu teachings and practices, sounds very much like Western religious imperialism which simply refuses to recognize the value of Indian culture. Thus, in Asia the question of the relation of Christian faith to other religions is intimately linked to the broader question of the relation of Christian faith to indigenous Asian cultures. Mission in such contexts must be very careful to distinguish strictly theological issues from broader cultural and historical factors.

Theological understanding. But merely phenomenological and cultural understanding of religions is insufficient for the Christian missionary. The missionary must also have an adequate theological understanding of human religion in general, as well as of the particular religious tradition with which he or she comes into contact.

Here one must go beyond accurate phenomenological description to evaluation of a given tradition. One can of course evaluate a religion on various grounds, and a balanced perspective will not hesitate to recognize positive contributions from a given religion. For example, one might appreciate the positive role played within society by a particular tradition—perhaps it promotes social cohesion, stability, a sense of meaning and purpose, etc. Or one might appreciate the impact that a given religion has had upon the music, literature, and art of a culture.

But for the Christian the ultimate question about any religion must be whether the religion helps or hinders one in establishing a proper relationship with the one true God. Theological understanding and evaluation of a given tradition must be based upon the teachings, principles, values, and precedents of God's special revelation, the Bible. Careful theological reflection will indicate that, although there might indeed be elements of truth, value, and beauty in non-Christian religions, they cannot be understood as providing legitimate or effective means for sinful humanity being reconciled to a holy and righteous God.[4] Scripture nowhere suggests that non-Christian religious traditions are legitimate alternative paths to reconciliation with God. The consistent perspective of Scripture is expressed by the prophet Isaiah: "Turn to me and be saved, all you ends of the earth; for I am God, and there is no other" (Isa 45:22).

Proper understanding of the religions will also demand that we distinguish between the religion as a social, cultural, and religious system or institution and people who happen to be adherents of that religion. We approach Islam as a religion, for example, in one way; we approach Muslims as people in a quite different manner. Although we reject Islam as a religion on theological grounds, we must never allow this to be translated into a rejection of Muslims as people. One can reject a particular belief or practice as incompatible with biblical faith while simultaneously accepting individuals who embrace those beliefs and practices. Chris Wright reminds us that we must never forget that adherents of other religions are persons created in the image of God, and are objects of God's limitless love.

> Our fellow human being is first, foremost, and essentially one in the image of God, and only secondarily a Hindu, Muslim, or secular pagan. So, inasmuch as his religion is part of his humanity, whenever we meet one whom we call "an adherent of another religion", we meet someone who, in his religion as in all else, has some relationship to the Creator God, a relationship within which he is addressable and accountable (Wright 1990: 84-85).

We must maintain the priority of evangelism in Christian mission

Both obedience to the explicit command of our Lord and the implications of the Biblical teaching on human sin and salvation make it clear that central to Christian mission must be the proclamation of the gospel of Jesus Christ. We are commanded to make disciples of all nations (Mt 28:19-20), and one cannot make disciples without first engaging in evangelism. Furthermore, if as

Scripture affirms, it is true that human beings live in a condition of deliberate rebellion against a holy and righteous God; that all persons are guilty of sin and face eternal separation from God unless restored by God's grace to a saving relationship with him; and that such salvation is only possible through the person and atoning work of Jesus Christ—if indeed these propositions are true, then clearly the message of salvation in Jesus Christ is something that must be made available to all persons in all cultures. As believers we are under a moral obligation to do so.

The statement on evangelism in the Lausanne Covenant is most helpful on this point.

> To evangelize is to spread the good news that Jesus Christ died for our sins and was raised from the dead according to the Scriptures, and that as the reigning Lord he now offers the forgiveness of sins and the liberating gift of the Spirit to all who repent and believe. Our Christian presence in the world is indispensable to evangelism, and so is that kind of dialogue whose purpose is to listen sensitively and to understand. But evangelism itself is the proclamation of the historical biblical Christ as Savior and Lord, with a view to persuading people to come to him personally and so be reconciled to God (Douglas 1975:4).

There may be more to Christian mission than just evangelism, but clearly there cannot be less than this. The very heart of biblical mission is the call to repentance and faith in Jesus Christ—and this call must be extended to sincere adherents of other religions as well as to secularists.

Christian mission, which today suffers from what Newbigin has aptly called a "loss of nerve" in the face of the challenges of the contemporary world (Newbigin 1988), must recover its conviction of the full truth and authority of the Word of God, and of the indispensability of the gospel as "the power of God for the salvation of everyone who believes, first for the Jew, then for the Gentile" (Ro 1:16). This is not religious arrogance or imperialism. Christian mission must hold fast its conviction of the truth of the gospel, but it must clothe its proclamation in the humble and gracious recognition that each of us is at best a sinner saved by

God's grace, and that what God has graciously done for us he longs to do for others as well through us.

We must engage the plausibility structures of modernity and pluralism

The plausibility structures—the set of institutions, forces, values, and assumptions—which reinforce the perspective of ideological pluralism must be vigorously challenged and shown to be unacceptable. The effectiveness of evangelism and discipleship in contexts impacted by ideological pluralism will be directly related to the church's ability to challenge and transform some of the dominant assumptions of the culture of modernity.

The priority of the question of truth. The contrast between the highly pragmatic, relativistic, and agnostic approach to religion of many today and that of the apostle Paul—the greatest missionary of all time—could not be more striking. Unlike many today, Paul unequivocally affirms the centrality of truth. Speaking of the resurrection in 1 Corinthians 15, Paul insists that what matters is not simply how the "Jesus story" affects us but rather whether or not Jesus was indeed raised from the dead. "If Christ has not been raised, our preaching is useless and so is your faith... And if Christ has not been raised, your faith is futile; you are still in your sins" (1Co 15:14, 17). The most significant question to ask of any religion is not what it will do for society at large or for its adherents, but rather whether its fundamental claims are in fact true. In our witness to others we must graciously but firmly press the question of truth, and we must direct others to Jesus Christ, who himself is the Way, the Truth, and the Life (Jn 14:6).

The need for a sound apologetic in Christian mission. Underlying the common charge that Christian mission is theologically and morally untenable in today's pluralistic world is a pervasive epistemological skepticism that regards basic Christian beliefs as simply incredible. To those who take it for granted that we cannot have certainty about basic religious questions, the proclamation of Jesus Christ as the only Way cannot help but sound naive and arrogant.

In such contexts the church must not only proclaim the gospel with humility and sensitivity but also must demonstrate to a skeptical and relativistic culture why it is that we can have certainty concerning such ultimate issues. What is needed, in other words, is a Spirit-controlled apologetic which aggressively challenges the plausibility structures of modernity, which insists upon Christian belief as universally valid public truth, and which restores confidence in the normativity of the gospel of Jesus Christ. Men and women today must be brought to the realization that Christian faith is not merely one of many equally legitimate alternative options, but that there is a significant sense in which they *ought to* accept Jesus Christ instead of opposing alternatives.

Some clarification on the place of apologetics in Christian mission is in order. We must recognize first that apologetics in and of itself will not result in the salvation of anyone. Nobody is argued into the Kingdom. Apologetics—just as evangelism—is ineffective apart from the power and work of the Holy Spirit. For ultimately it is the Holy Spirit who brings about conviction of sin (Jn 16:8-11) and who liberates the spiritually blind from the grasp of the adversary and gives new birth in Christ (Jn 3:5; 1Co 2:14-16; Tit 3:5). But, of course, this does not make apologetics unnecessary any more than it renders evangelism optional. Both evangelism and apologetics must be carried out with much prayer and conscious dependence upon the power of God. In our witness to an unbelieving world, primacy must always be given the simple, direct, Spirit-anointed proclamation of the gospel (Ro 1:16; Heb 4:12). But where appropriate, such witness should also be supplemented by informed and sensitive response to criticism and questions, and demonstration of why one should accept the claims of Christian faith (1Pe 3:15). Properly construed, then, apologetics is ancillary to evangelism.

Furthermore, the focus of apologetics must always be upon leading the other person(s) into a direct encounter with the risen Lord Jesus Christ. Discussions of doctrine and ideology, while perhaps interesting, are not the central concern. The distinctive feature of Christian faith is its ineradicable grounding in the historical person of Jesus of Nazareth—his life, death, and resurrection. And Scripture is unambiguous on the uniqueness and normativity of Jesus as the one Savior and Lord for all humankind.

The emphasis in apologetics, then, must be upon the uniqueness and sufficiency of Jesus Christ. This will involve, among other things, demonstrating the historically reliable nature of the Bible and why we should accept it as God's unique, special revelation instead of other sacred texts. The uniqueness of Jesus' life and teachings, his death, and his bodily resurrection must be carefully demonstrated. There is no need here to ridicule other religions or to attack other religious figures. But, in a careful and sensitive manner, the Christian evangelist and apologist should contrast Jesus with, for example, Muhammad, or the Buddha, or Confucius, or Shinran, showing clearly how they are different.

We must adopt appropriate forms of dialogue in mission

Recent discussions of religious pluralism have been dominated by the subject of interreligious dialogue. Evangelicals have generally been suspicious of the calls for interreligious dialogue, largely because of the implicit (and sometimes explicit) agenda associated with dialogue (cf Netland 1991:283-301; and Muck 1993). For example, it is often assumed by proponents of dialogue associated with the World Council of Churches that genuine dialogue is incompatible with evangelism and thus that no attempt should be made to persuade the other party to accept the Christian perspective; that neither party can assume to have access to "the truth" but that somehow through mutual dialogue both parties will gain deeper insights into "Truth"; that the only legitimate goal of dialogue is mutual understanding and acceptance between traditions; and that judgment or criticism of other religious beliefs or practices is always inappropriate.[5] Clearly so long as interreligious dialogue is defined in terms of these assumptions evangelicals will reject it as incompatible with a biblical understanding of mission.

But we should not allow such distortions to prevent us from utilizing what is a legitimate and necessary aspect of mission in pluralistic contexts. Dialogue as such is not incompatible with evangelism. Dialogue—understood as a serious conversation with someone from another religious tradition, marked by a genuine willingness to listen to and learn from the other, and respect for him or her as a person—should be part of our missionary encounter with others.

Surely this is consistent with the models we find in our Lord and in the apostle Paul. Neither Jesus nor Paul simply lectured in monologue fashion. Both demonstrate evidence of understanding well the contexts of the target audiences, sensing their needs, establishing common ground, using questions to prompt interest and understanding, and proclaiming in a clear and sensitive manner the truth which needed to be shared. Furthermore, such dialogue can be an expression of our willingness to take the other person seriously as a fellow human being created in God's image. A genuine willingness to listen to others, and to learn from them, can be a mark of humility and common courtesy. If we expect a Muslim or Hindu, for example, to listen carefully to our proclamation of Jesus Christ as Savior and Lord, surely we owe them the same courtesy and respect we expect from them. How can we expect a Buddhist to take Christian claims seriously if there is no evidence of willingness on the Christian's part to carefully consider the claims of the Buddhist? And finally dialogue is essential for effective evangelism. Effective communication of the gospel requires that we understand the religious worldview of others, and the only way to grasp their worldview is to listen to them and to ask questions about it.

Informal dialogue, as indicated above, is essential to effective ministry in pluralistic contexts. But should evangelicals participate in formal dialogue, that is, organized gatherings of representatives from two or more religious traditions in which well-defined procedures are followed in pursuit of agreed upon objectives? Much will depend here upon the ground rules for the dialogue and the objectives to be attained. There does not seem to be anything in principle which would rule out evangelical participation in such dialogue although great care must be exercised so that evangelical commitments are not compromised. There must be no hidden agenda, and the objectives and ground rules must be clear and mutually agreeable to all parties.

We must live consistently as disciples of Jesus Christ

Christian mission in contexts dominated by other religions and the values of ideological pluralism must reinforce the proclamation of the gospel with a visible demonstration of what it means to be a new creation in Christ. To our shame, we must admit that the failure of the church to live consistently as a community of the redeemed undermines all other efforts to demonstrate the truth of Christian faith to a skeptical and relativistic world. The glaring gap between what we profess with our lips and how we actually live has made the radical biblical claims about new life in Christ sound hollow to those who observe us. Jesus stated the basic principle 2000 years ago: "By this all men will know that you are my disciples, if you love one another" (Jn 13:35). In a world that is torn apart by ethnic and religious tensions, the church should stand out as a model of reconciliation and of the transforming power of God. Proclamation of Jesus Christ as the unique and only Savior for all peoples must take place within the context of the church as a community of the redeemed living out consistently the qualities we find in the life of our Redeemer.

We must immerse the encounter with other religions in prayer

All aspects of Christian mission are to be immersed in prayer. Christian mission is not to be conducted merely by human ingenuity and skillful technique. Ultimately, missions involves spiritual warfare—it involves opening the eyes of those who are spiritually blind, turning them from darkness to light, and from the power of Satan to God (Ac 26:18). The adversary is a spiritual one, and we dare not fight a spiritual battle with other than spiritual weapons, central to which is prayer (Eph 6:10-18).

A genuinely biblical perspective on other religions should recognize that much religious activity and belief is influenced and manipulated by Satan. It would be too simplistic to hold that all non-Christian religious phenomena are satanic, but it would be equally simplistic to suggest that none of them are satanic. The apostle Paul reminded his readers that the pagan sacrifices in Corinthian religion, which might seem quite innocent, are in fact offered to demons (1Co 10:20). This is a sobering warning which should caution us against treating non-Christian religious practices lightly.

The multiple challenges to Christian mission posed by religious pluralism will demand the very best of Christian missionaries. We must be as wise as serpents and as harmless as doves (Mt 10:16). In an age characterized by relativism and undisciplined tolerance, it is important to remember that it is the proclamation of the gospel that is the God-appointed means for bringing about the salvation of those who believe: "I am not ashamed of the gospel, because it is the power of God for the salvation of every-one who believes: first for the Jew, then for the Gentile" (Ro 1:16).

Notes

[1] In 1818 Gordon Hall and Samuel Newell published a work entitled *The Conversion of the World*, in which they suggested that Western churches could convert the world within the next twenty years. See Bosch (1991: 335).

[2] Ninian Smart offers a helpful sixfold classification of dimensions of religious phenomena—the ritual, mythological, doctrinal, ethical, social, and experiential dimensions (Smart 1983, chapters 3-8).

[3] See Terry Muck (1993) for a helpful guide to the phenomenological study of religion from an evangelical perspective.

[4] See Edward Rommen's chapter on the theology of religions in this volume.

[5] For an incisive critique of these assumptions, and a vigorous defense of the place of apologetics within interreligious dialogue, see Paul Griffiths's excellent *An Apology for Apologetics* (1991).

Reference List

Anderson, Gerald H.
    1993   "Theology of Religions and Missiology: A Time of Testing." In *The Good News of the Kingdom: Mission Theology for the Third Millenium.* Charles Van Engen, Dean Gilliland, and Paul Pierson, eds. Pp. 200-208. Maryknoll, NY: Orbis.

Bosch, David
    1991   *Transforming Mission: Paradigm Shifts in Theology of Mission.* Maryknoll, NY: Orbis.

Douglas, J.D., ed.
    1975   *Let the Earth Hear His Voice.* Minneapolis: World Wide Publications.

Griffiths, Paul
    1991   *An Apology for Apologetics.* Maryknoll, NY: Orbis.

Knitter, Paul
    1985   *No Other Name? A Critical Survey of Christian Attitudes Toward the World Religions.* Maryknoll, NY: Orbis.

Muck, Terry
    1993   "Evangelicals and Interreligious Dialogue." *Journal of the Evangelical Theological Society.* 36(4):517-529.

Netland, Harold
    1991   *Dissonant Voices: Religious Pluralism and the Question of Truth.* Grand Rapids, MI: Eerdmans.

Marty, Martin E., and Frederick E. Greenspahn, eds.
    1988   *Pushing the Faith: Proselytism and Civility in a Pluralistic World.* New York: Crossroad.

Smart, Ninian
    1983   *Worldviews: Crosscultural Explorations of Human Beliefs.* New York: Charles Scribner's Sons.

Wright, Chris
    1990   *What's So Unique About Jesus?* Eastburne, E Sussex: Monarch.

CONCLUSION

David J. Hesselgrave

A careful reading of the essays that make up this important book has brought to mind a personal experience that seems pertinent as we bring our discussion to a conclusion. Some years ago, I was invited to address a conference of world ecumenical leaders at Cincinnati on the subject "The Theology of Evangelism —An Evangelical Perspective." Informed that the evangelical position would not be represented otherwise, I somewhat reluctantly acceded to the request.

My schedule brought me to the conference just after Paul Knitter had read a paper in which he presented the thesis of his then forthcoming book, *No Other Name?* The paper had elicited an enthusiastic response on the part of many. Unfortunately, to my way of thinking, my assignment was overly general and, in any case, dealt with propositions that most conferees had already rejected. My hearers responded politely but with predictable reserve.

In the discussion period that followed the reading of my paper, Dr. Knitter inquired as to my thinking relative to Krister Stendahl's proposal that the apostles' pronouncements concerning Jesus were analogous to an adoring husband's adulation of his wife. The husband proudly describes her as the "most beautiful woman in the world"—an assertion that all can appreciate but few would be tempted to accept at face value!

To be honest, at this late date I do not remember exactly how I responded to Dr. Knitter's question on that occasion other than to indicate that I did not think much of the proposal and was quite convinced that the apostles would not have thought much of it either!

There are a variety of ways of responding to what the Bible writers had to say about such subjects as the deity of Christ, the futility of false religion, the way of salvation and the certainty of judgment. There was a time when it was usual to examine the text and conclude that it is true or false, or that some of it is true and some of it is false. More recently, however, it has become common to view the Bible (and, in many cases, all "sacred books") differently and conclude that one and the same text is simultaneously true *and* false—true in a poetic sense but false in a scientific sense, true in a mythological sense but false in a literal sense, and so on.

Evangelicals, therefore, not only ask what Christ and the apostles said but also how they intended to be understood. Accordingly, in reference to Stendahl's proposal, we might think of Peter's astounding reply to the Lord Jesus' question, "Who do you say I am?" Peter said, "You are the Christ, the Son of the living God" (Mt 15:15-16 NIV). Obviously, the Lord Jesus did not understand this to be hyperbolic adulation. Neither did he take it to be simply a subjective opinion. He accepted Peter's confession as being objectively and literally true. He replied, "Blessed are you, Simon son of Jonah, for this was not revealed to you by man, but by my Father in heaven" (Mt 16:17).

Call it what you will, this kind of excusivism is unpalatable to our pluralistic world and hardly adds to the popularity of evangelicals and the acceptability of their message. Nevertheless, evangelicals do not hesitate for a moment to proclaim that Christ is the one Lord and only Savior. As can be detected from a reading of the essays in this book, however, they, with others, may feel a certain uneasiness at the severity of the denunciation of false gods by the prophets and, especially, the so-called "hard sayings" of Jesus. No one I know experiences great exhilaration upon reading:

> Enter through the narrow gate. For wide is the gate and broad is the road that leads to destruction, and many enter through it. But small is the gate and narrow the road that leads to life, and only a few find it (Mt 7:13 NIV).

But liking it or not liking it has nothing to do with the matter. The fact is that the loving Lord Jesus said it and, as Matthew says of those who first heard it, they were amazed because "he taught them as one who had authority, and not as their teachers of the law" (Mt 7:28b NIV).

And so we come to the perspective that pervades this volume. The various authors are members of the Evangelical Theological Society and as such they have committed themselves to the inspiration, authority and perspicuity of Scripture and to such pertinent (to the present topic) matters as the uniqueness and deity of Christ, the necessity of Holy Spirit regeneration, and the resurrection of both the saved and the lost—the former to life and the latter to damnation. They do not speak univocally on every issue but, since their motivation is to be faithful to Scripture and our Lord Jesus Christ, rather than pandering to the sensibilities of their contemporaries, they are both univocal and unequivocal when it comes to the major issues posed by certain types of pluralism, inclusivism, and universalism.

Now my mind goes back once again to that gathering in Cincinnati.

I recall the applause that attended reports of places and times where representatives of the several religions had dialogued and worshipped together.

I remember the open discussion in which a number expressed misgivings with aspects of the Christian faith bequeathed to them in Scripture and the great confessions of the Fathers; how one prominent theologian confessed that he had thought of "giving up on Christianity" except for the fact that he had "always been a Christian and therefore would not be comfortable with any other tradition."

I recall how several of us observed the ecumenical celebration of the Eucharist—reported at the time to be one of the first in which Roman Catholics and Protestants "partook of the bread and the cup together." The ritual of songs, readings and prayers included multitudinous references to our Lord Jesus' atoning death, bodily resurrection and triumphant return; to our sinfulness, waywardness and need of his mercy and grace; and even to the future blessedness of those whose trust is in Christ and the hopeless condition of all others. Ironically, these were the very tenets of the Christian faith that had proved to be so problematic previously.

My kindly hosts called a taxi for me and I prepared to leave, quite convinced that my presentation and presence had been of no account whatsoever. At the last moment, a fellow conferee asked if he could ride with me to the airport. En route, he introduced himself as a chaplain at a certain Midwestern university and proceeded to explain that he had accompanied me by design. He wanted to express a deep sense of gratitude in that upon hearing the evangelical perspective on evangelism once again he had been reassured of the truth of Christ and had recommitted himself to Christian witness on his campus. I had been wrong. The preparation, the writing, the presentation—all had not been in vain.

On behalf of all of these who will benefit from this volume—and that should include many readers and every reader—allow me to offer heartfelt thanks to Michael Pocock and the executive committee of the Evangelical Missiiological Society, to Paul Hiebert and the members of the publication committee, to David Shaver and Ralph Winter and the staff at William Carey Library, and especially to co-editors Edward Rommen and Harold Netland and all of the contributing authors. In making this volume on a biblical theology of non-Christian religions available, you have placed in our hands and on our bookshelves a resource that we will consult again and again as we progress toward and into a new millennium.